THE

SECRET SIX

Other books by Edward J. Renehan, Jr.

John Burroughs: An American Naturalist

THE
SECRET SIX

The True Tale of the Men Who Conspired
with John Brown

EDWARD J. RENEHAN, JR.

UNIVERSITY OF SOUTH CAROLINA PRESS

Published in Columbia, South Carolina, by the
University of South Carolina Press

Originally published by Crown Publishing, Inc., 1995

First paperback edition 1996 by the University of South Carolina Press

Manufactured in the United States of America

01 00 99 98 97   5 4 3 2 1

ISBN 1-57003-181-9(pbk)

Library of Congress Cataloging-in-Publication Data

Renehan, Edward, 1956–
    The secret six : the true tale of the men who conspired with John
    Brown / Edward J. Renehan, Jr.
            p.   cm.
        Includes bibliographical references (p.   ) .
        ISBN 1-57003-181-9   (pbk.)
        1. Brown, John,   1800–1859—Friends and associates. 2. Harpers
    Ferry (W. Va.)—History—John Brown's Raid, 1859.   I. Title.
    E451.R44 1997
    973.7'116' 092—dc21   96–47366

Dedicated to
my partner in all things,
Christa,
with much
gratitude
and
even more
love

Contents

BOOK II

Acknowledgments

My agent, Julian Bach, was the first person besides my wife and me to have faith in this project. My editor, Peter Ginna, was next in line.

As a casual survey of the endnotes will reveal, *The Secret Six* simply could not have been written without access to the unparalleled anti-slavery collection in the Rare Books and Manuscripts Room at the Boston Public Library. My thanks to Laura V. Monti for granting access to the collection, and to Giuseppe Bisaccia and R. Eugene Zepp for providing quick, informed, and cheerful responses to my innumerable requests. I would have been lost without them.

The staff of the Reading Room at the Houghton Library, Harvard University, were equally generous and helpful, as were Virginia Smith, Peter Drummey, and Chris Steele at the Massachusetts Historical Society, and Esme Bhan at Howard University's Moorland-Springarn Research Center. I am also indebted to the staffs of the Library of Congress, Columbia University Library, Syracuse University Library, Ohio Historical Society, Western Reserve Historical Society, New York Public Library, Trevor Arnett Library (Atlanta University), Cornell University Library, and the Kansas State Historical Society.

The late Richard O. Boyer's classic work *The Legend of John Brown* served as an excellent basic reference on Brown and his epoch. And Boyer's papers—comprising what was literally a lifetime of copious research—at the Massachusetts Historical Society proved a rich, invaluable resource. Boyer's biography of Brown remains the very best of the many generally good assayings of Brown's troubled, heroic life. Many scholars for many years to come shall owe a great debt to Mr. Boyer. Another work that helped me was that of my old teacher the late Robert Penn Warren, whose 1929 biography, *John Brown: The Making of a Martyr,* was among the first to portray the more complex Brown: the cunning, deviant yet somehow also guileless soldier of a wrathful God.

Several friends and family members, all of them historians, writers, editors, or critics of great talent, commented on the manuscript at various stages. My thanks to Deb Hiett Borgia, Cindy Morgan Dale, Christa Renehan, Christopher Bentley, Dorian Dale, James Fallows, Arthur Goldwag, James McPherson, Garry Wills, and C. Vann Woodward. Many things that are right with the book can be traced to suggestions from these readers. Anything that is wrong with the book has but one author: me. I am also indebted to Robin Winks, to my nephew Jameson Ruby, and of course to the always gracious and responsive Thomas Wentworth Higginson Barney. And I would like to thank Steven Boldt for an outstanding job of copy-editing.

When I was a little boy, my father took me one day from our summer cabin on the shore of Lake Champlain at Westport, New York, to the nearby, lonely spot where, in the 1850s, the black colony of Timbucto had been a ragged, quaintly misspelled settlement, and where John Brown's body lies moldering in an oft-sung-of, yet obscure, grave. Now, a generation later, I am the father—and my family has defined the word *forbearance* in putting up with me and my distracting friends, the Secret Six. I hope my wonderful wife, Christa, will find the dedication a worthwhile (albeit partial) payment on many debts. And I hope my now-small children, William James Renehan and Katherine Eleanor Renehan, will one day read this book and think it worthwhile. Someday I shall pack them into the car and take them to that forgotten corner of the Adirondack woods where a dedicated band of black freedmen tried, long ago, to carve a free and good life in the world—and where one brooding, iconoclastic white man once cherished a dream of mountains.

THE
SECRET SIX

PROLOGUE: REUNION

THE DATE WAS OCTOBER 17, 1909—the fiftieth anniversary of John Brown's famous (some said infamous) raid of the federal armory and arsenal at Harpers Ferry, Virginia, which ended with the deaths of most of Brown's small band of men and led to the execution of Brown, making him the most celebrated martyr to the cause of abolition.[1] Newspapers North and South retold the tale for their readers, few of whom were old enough to remember Brown's bid to organize and arm a bloody slave insurrection in the southern Appalachians. Half a century later, almost all the editorial writers painted the raid at Harpers Ferry and subsequent execution of Brown as critical, defining moments in the American saga, for good or for ill. Looking back five decades, journalists and historians were unanimous in their belief that John Brown's raid and martyrdom so polarized Northern and Southern opinion as to make civil war virtually inevitable. "Harpers Ferry was to the Civil War," wrote a New York reporter, "what the Boston Massacre was to the American Revolution. It was the first battle clang, the first flow of blood. It was the small skirmish which foretold and made unavoidable the momentous, devouring battle that was to follow."[2]

There were many ceremonies on that anniversary day. At Harpers Ferry, not far from the site of the engine house where John Brown's enterprise ended in defeat, a small group of aging abolitionists held a quiet prayer meeting—anxious not to be taken much notice of. John Brown was still widely despised throughout much of the South, especially in the neighborhood where his terror had been an immediate threat. There were speeches at Brown's Connecticut birthplace, a pageant in the small Ohio town where he'd been raised, and prayers at the Adirondack farm, near Lake Placid, where the old firebrand lay buried. But the most poignant exercise of memory occurred at Concord, Massachusetts. This was a reunion of the surviving remnants of the Secret Six, that small, enigmatic cabal of northeastern aristocrats who financed John Brown's strange adventure.

The place of meeting was a fine gambrel-roofed brick house on Elm Street, by a bend in the Concord River. The imposing building was home to Franklin Sanborn, seventy-eight years old, distinguished author, educator, and social scientist. A former headmaster and retired commissioner of charities for the State of Massachusetts, the courtly, diminutive Sanborn was Concord's resident expert on the many great lights now gone—Emerson, Thoreau, and Alcott, among them—whom he had known well as a young man. The humorless Sanborn presented a constantly furrowed brow. When concentrating—and he always concentrated when discussing so serious a subject as the one at hand today—he would rub an index finger several times back and forth above his left eyebrow before answering a question. He was not in the habit of making eye contact with whomever he was addressing. He rather stared off into empty walls and against blank curtains while slowly recalling events and framing his words. Only once his point was made would his eyes return to the listener with an unspoken "So, there you have it."

In this, as in so many other ways, Sanborn was different from the most cantankerous of his three guests: the eighty-six-year-old writer Thomas Wentworth Higginson. Higginson always looked one right in the eye; and if one did not do the same, he was apt to ask why. Once a spry weight-lifter and road-runner, the tall but stooped Higginson leaned heavily on his cane when entering Sanborn's sitting room, insisting that he needed no assistance in getting where he wanted to go, but at the same time seeming grateful and relieved when he finally made it to the chair awaiting him. He was, he sighed after achieving his seat, on the back end of the last of his several lives. "And what lives were those?"

asked Katherine Mayo, the eager and attractive young reporter at whose behest Higginson had appeared. "I've been a minister," answered Higginson. "I've been a revolutionary and a fugitive from what some called justice. I've been a coward and an ambiguity. I've been a battlefield officer. I've been a writer. All of these titles and conditions carry lives within them. And now in my final life I am an anachronism distinguished from my fellow anachronisms"—glancing at Sanborn—"only in that I comprehend my destiny."

Already sitting when Higginson entered was the ninety-year-old poetess Julia Ward Howe. Remembered today as the woman who penned the lyric "Battle Hymn of the Republic" to the slowed tune of "John Brown's Body," the marching song that commemorated Brown's bloody heroics, Julia Howe was the widow of Sanborn's and Higginson's old partner in treason, the eminent Dr. Samuel Gridley Howe. Fifty years before, Julia had briefly entertained John Brown while he was in Boston consulting with her husband and his cohorts. Brown wrote to a friend that he liked Mrs. Howe, whom he described as "a defiant little woman" with a personality that was "all flash and fire."[3] Now, five decades later, she used an ear trumpet and sat with a shawl wrapped over her shoulders. When Higginson sat down, she reached over and rested her hand on his.

Katherine Mayo, the woman who had brought Sanborn, Howe, and Higginson together, was editorial assistant to the publisher, journalist, and historian Oswald Garrison Villard.[4] Villard, a grandson of the abolitionist William Lloyd Garrison, was working on a massive biography of Brown to be published the following year.[5] Mayo's intent was to get down for posterity, as accurately as possible, the tale of the five wealthy Boston Brahmins and the one moneyed New Yorker who, despairing of a political system that it seemed would tolerate slavery indefinitely, chose, via Brown, a drastic route toward annihilation of the peculiar institution. Thus the smart, smiling Mayo primly sat, pen in hand, anxious to jot down every word from the surviving members of that group who had purchased John Brown's guns, clothed and fed his men, and plotted with Brown for the nearly two years leading up to the bloody denouement at Harpers Ferry. Her extremely detailed notes provide a vivid picture of the gathering.

Just two of the Secret Six—Sanborn and Higginson—survived. The four other members of the clandestine committee had long since died. Sanborn—who Higginson once told a friend had "far too much a flair for the dramatic"—set out a chair for each of these vanished spirits from the past. For his part, Higginson pointed from one empty chair to another and described each invisible occupant for the entertainment of a delighted Mayo.

"Here," said Higginson, "sits the miracle-working Dr. Samuel Gridley Howe beside his beloved Julia." As he had so many times before when speaking of the man who he believed had been the least forthright of Brown's supporters, Higginson chose his words carefully. He did not want to offend the widow Julia. Dr. Howe, he said, "was a friend of Dickens, and as well the father of modern therapies for the blind and deaf, an honored son of Boston, and an often loyal supporter of John Brown." Next Higginson pointed to the specter of the Reverend Theodore Parker, "God's fanatic" who was "pompous, annoying, and eminently good. He died not long after Brown did, and was dying already at the time of the raid. Of all who betrayed Brown, he was the only one with an excuse. He also happened to be the greatest, most eloquent defender of the ideal of individual liberty in the modern era—a man whose words will be remembered for as long as the urge for natural religion endures."

Higginson's "darting finger," as Mayo described it, now moved to the next chair in the row. "There is Gerrit Smith, the only one of us not from Boston, a wealthy New York landowner. He was very nervous—a coward who was yet tempted by the romantic urge to do good in very dramatic ways. But he preferred the romance to the reality. He loved the idea of armed revolt until armed revolt drew near." The finger moved again, and Higginson introduced George Luther Stearns, "a wealthy Boston merchant who suffered from the same affliction as Smith. He was willing to buy all the guns in the world but unwilling to allow anyone to use them."[6]

Higginson had not wanted to meet with Mayo. "Why do you want to know of *us*?" he wrote in response to Mayo's initial request for an interview more than six months before. "Did any historian ever bother to write down the name of the man who bought the donkey on which Christ rode into Jerusalem? We of the Six were as unimportant and incidental to the real story of John Brown as that ancient Judean is to the story of our Lord. We were often unreliable—and often all-too-cynical—aiders and supporters of a truly great man who deserved better than what he got from us. (I am ashamed that we were not more true to our task—as true at least as he was to his.) We of the Six were not—are not—great men. We do not deserve remembering. Although there was no Judas among us, there were six Peters, all who denied John Brown at least once through some word or act before the cock crowed."[7]

Higginson went on to tell Mayo that it had been largely as an act of contrition—"partial expiation"—for the "abandonment" of Brown by himself and others of the Six that he raised and led a black regiment to fight for the Union cause in 1862. (Higginson was the first of Boston's elite to organize black freedmen into ranks of Union infantry. His model was soon followed by Charles Francis Adams, Jr., and the ill-fated Robert Gould Shaw.) The black regiment was Higginson's method for continuing the work begun at Harpers Ferry. "Never in history was there an oppressed people who were set free by others," wrote Higginson in 1858.[8] It was with this in mind that he chose to support John Brown's dream for a revolution by which blacks might stand up and seize both their freedom and their proud humanity.[9] The same principle lay behind Higginson's black regiment.

After Higginson refused to meet with Mayo, Sanborn urged him to reconsider. "My book about Brown was the biography for our generation," he wrote Higginson. "We need a biography for the new generation, a biography for the next thirty years. Young Villard is both a writer first class and certainly sympathetic to the subject—his Garrison blood will see to that."[10] Sanborn would regret his words. He was either overestimating the power of the Garrison blood or forgetting that William Lloyd Garrison, a pacifist, was himself at best lukewarm on the subject of the

Thomas Wentworth Higginson—aristocratic scion of one of New England's oldest families and unapologetic supporter of John Brown— photographed in old age. Photo courtesy Boston Public Library

violent insurrectionist John Brown. In the evenhanded and carefully researched biography that was shortly published, Villard portrayed Brown as inadequate in everything but the capacity to commit murder and inspire others to do the same. Villard's Brown was a confused, quarrelsome, gun-toting misanthrope who was at once a religious fanatic and a killer, with the habit of looking to the Bible for omens and a propensity for nurturing his own brand of Armageddon. Sanborn, who had long served as Brown's chief public apologist and mythmaker, would prove unwilling to accept Villard's portrayal of Brown as a bumbling yet bloodthirsty madman who stumbled into greatness through his last and most dramatic failure: Harpers Ferry. But for better or worse, not long after receiving Sanborn's letter, Higginson wrote once again to Mayo, this time agreeing to an interview. His ambition, as he recorded it in a private journal entry, was to see that the Six "do not garner credit from posterity that is *not* our due."[11]

It is possible that Sanborn unwittingly touched a nerve in Higginson by referring to Sanborn's own 1885 biography of Brown. Higginson was generally unimpressed with virtually everything his friend Sanborn ever wrote. In truth, he considered Sanborn something of a hack. "Sanborn has turned every great man he's ever met into a book," complained Higginson in a 1907 letter to Richard Watson Gilder, editor of the *Century*

Magazine. "What he wouldn't do to have known another Thoreau, another Emerson, another John Brown. My poor friend has run out of genuine heroes with which he has been personally acquainted. But still his rent must be paid. Now he is reduced to writing of himself. Soon he may even sink so low as to take me for a subject."[12]

Through the preceding five decades, Higginson had steadfastly avoided writing or lecture projects that would cause him to profit from his association with Brown. He published hardly anything on the topic and became annoyed when Sanborn brought out his account. Higginson wrote many books—novels, literary criticism, and an account of his Civil War exploits. He served several years as editor-at-large for the *Atlantic Monthly.* And he was the first to edit and bring to press the poems of his friend Emily Dickinson. But only on one or two occasions did he write of Brown, and never at length.

Higginson was proud to have been associated with Brown; but he was not proud of his membership in the Six. "Sanborn, is there no such thing as *honor* among confederates?" Higginson fumed when the skittish schoolteacher and other members of the Six, who had forced Brown into the postponement that Higginson believed killed both the project and Brown, absconded to Canada in the wake of the failure at Harpers Ferry. "Can your clear moral sense . . . justify holding one's tongue . . . to save ourselves from all share in even the reprobation of society when the nobler man whom we have provoked on into danger is the scapegoat of that reprobation—& the gallows too?"[13] Fifty years later, Higginson's rage was still evident as he spoke to Mayo of the "contemptible" way that Brown was abandoned "by those, including myself, who had for so long posed as his friends."

Higginson told Mayo that Gerrit Smith, Franklin Sanborn, George Luther Stearns, Samuel Gridley Howe, and Theodore Parker "had at least been honest enough with themselves" before Harpers Ferry. They "allowed themselves to understand" that Brown's plan for inciting a slave rebellion in Virginia invited defeat. Yet they persevered, believing correctly that the failure of Brown's enterprise would hasten civil war and thereby be worthwhile. Higginson said he had "refused to accept the fact" that Brown's wild mission was doomed. "I will be damned if I will let you . . . laconically tell me there is little chance for the great old man to return from this with breath in his lungs," Higginson wrote Gerrit Smith a few months before the raid. "I could not live with myself if I thought I were knowingly sending Brown in the way of certain death."[14] In a 1911 speech, after naming each member of the Six, Franklin Sanborn commented that "all these persons aided Brown's plans with money and active support, although none of them perhaps, except Higginson, had entire confidence in their earthly wisdom or success."[15]

Higginson wrote in a letter to Villard that his "great, personal crime" was one against friendship. He should have "been brave enough to understand," as others of the Six had, what in retrospect was the absolute inevitability of failure. Higginson had not been "wise enough to see" that Brown, who insisted on choosing his own mission and making his own plans, may not in the end have actually possessed "the wit, the capacity, or the penchant for sane, shrewd, pragmatic planning" such as was required to "make for successes, at Harpers Ferry or elsewhere." In his heart, Higginson despised the others, whom he believed realized the truth yet did not act to avert Brown's disaster. He also despised himself for refusing to comprehend the obvious. "I should have been the one," wrote Higginson, "to make my brave, mad, noble friend step back from martyrdom. I should have acted to force the sane decision toward reasonableness and safety he had not the ability to make for himself."[16]

History was all well and good, Higginson told Mayo. The long lens that enabled one to look back on an event in context, and see that it had been of importance in the epoch of a nation, was sometimes useful. Thus in retrospect the decision of the Secret Six to abandon futile political attempts to eradicate the "great crime" of slavery by legal means, and to pursue more direct action of the John Brown variety, seemed logical and good. But retrospection did nothing to make personal betrayal look more appealing. Higginson told Mayo that a drawing of "one friend using another as bait on a hook" would forever be the lingering pentimento on any canvas upon which a picture of John Brown at Harpers Ferry was painted. Beneath the heroic image, said Higginson, lay sad and disappointing human truth.

❋ BOOK ONE ❋

1

THE SECRET UNSPOKEN

ON A SWELTERING summer's morning in 1867, the portly, bald Gerrit Smith sat silently with his lawyer in the vestibule of a Chicago courtroom. Not a few passersby paused to notice the distracted, sixty-eight-year-old Smith. Bored, Smith effortlessly and probably unconsciously avoided the gaze of the curious, for he was by now quite used to being a celebrity. In 1860, he had run for president on the ticket of the Radical Abolitionists—that tiny residue of the old abolitionist Liberty Party that had not yet been absorbed by the Free Soil and Republican movements. In this capacity he took some votes away from the moderate antislavery Republican, Abraham Lincoln, but not enough to influence the outcome of the election. More recently, the millionaire Smith—who was one of the richest men in the country—made the newspapers again when he joined Horace Greeley and Cornelius Vanderbilt in offering to underwrite a $1-million bail bond for former Confederate president Jefferson Davis. With Greeley and Vanderbilt, Smith demanded freedom for Davis, who had been held without any charge for nearly two years. The gesture by the abolitionist Smith was even more remarkable than it appeared on its face. After all, Davis had tried his best to see Smith swing from the same gallows with John Brown only seven years earlier.

John Brown. Smith did not like to hear the name mentioned. He only uttered it himself when pressed to defend and explain his relations with Brown, as he would be forced to do in court today. As Smith's first and best biographer, Octavius Brooks Frothingham, has written, after Brown's disaster at Harpers Ferry "cool reflection came in" and the "ill-judged" nature of Brown's scheme "made [Smith] wish he had never been privy to it. His old horror of . . . violence as a means of redressing wrong, resumed its sway." That part of Smith that was a calculating, pragmatic man of business and politics in retrospect saw Brown ultimately as a noble fool, and his enterprise a fool's errand. "He set himself to . . . reducing his alliance with the audacious conspirator to sentiments of personal sympathy and admiration. . . . [He had a] desire to persuade all others as well as himself of his innocence of all complicity."

Thus he was trying to convince himself, as well as the court, when he took the stand in his libel suit against the Chicago *Tribune,* denying the *Tribune's* allegations of his deep complicity in Brown's fiasco. "John Brown talked to me—but never counselled with me—respecting his plans for freeing slaves," read Smith in a high, nervous voice from his prepared statement. "[I did not know the details of his plans, but] I learned enough of them to believe that, in addition to his former ways of helping off slaves, he meant to go into a mountain or mountains of a slave state, and invite slaves to flee to him, and give them arms to resist attempts at their recapture. . . . That Brown intended a general insurrection, or the taking of any life except his who was foolish and wicked enough to attempt to drag back into the pit of slavery those who had escaped from it, there is not the slightest reason to believe."[1]

In its defense, the *Tribune* produced evidence in the form of an affidavit from John Brown, Jr. Under oath before a United States commissioner, John Brown's eldest son and close confidante swore that Smith knew Brown intended to use the arms he'd helped buy "in making forays upon individual slaveholders [to liberate slaves], carrying away such slaves to such strongholds as could be made available; seizing slaveholders and their families as hostages, taking such property belonging to them as could be made available, either as subsistence, or in attack or defense; and to thus render slave property insecure and therefore unprofitable." The son of the guerrilla leader added that as early as 1858 "the whole plan, as far as then matured, was fully made known to Mr. Smith." When asked whether any efforts had been made to conceal any "essential parts" of the scheme from Smith, John Brown, Jr., answered categorically: "No attempt at concealment in any degree was had in the interviews with Mr. Smith."[2]

Nor was any attempt at concealment had with Smith's good friend Frederick Douglass. Apprised of John Brown's plan for a slave uprising just a week before it was revealed to Smith, Douglass wrote that "the horrors" Brown intended to visit upon the Southern slaveholders made him shudder, "but it was the shudder one feels at the execution of a murderer."[3] The levelheaded Douglass ultimately demurred from backing Brown's wild and bloody plot; Smith, however, was not so wise.

Always anxious to popularize Brown and chronicle his misadventure in a positive light, Franklin Sanborn was fast to grow weary of Gerrit Smith's denials and was happy when Smith lost his suit against the *Tribune*. Sanborn was ashamed of neither John Brown nor the event at Harpers Ferry and saw no reason for others to be. "From 1867 until his death in December 1874," wrote Sanborn, "I resolved to persuade my old friend [Smith], if possible, to publish [an account] in keeping with the facts, and with his own magnanimity. I therefore took some pains to preserve my own recollections and those of two other persons, who, like myself, had known Brown's plans and Smith's connection with them, and in the *Atlantic Monthly* for July, 1872, printed the narrative thus obtained, with many omissions of name and some circumstance, in deference to what seemed Mr. Smith's sensitiveness."

Shortly after this, deciding to assay a full biography of Brown, Sanborn wrote Smith to request his cooperation. "Before all the witnesses are dead," asked Sanborn, "would it not be wise to put upon record the authentic facts, in time to have any errors in the statement pointed out and corrected?"[4] Smith refused to participate. "When the Harpers Ferry

affair occurred, I was sick, and my brain somewhat diseased," he wrote
Sanborn. "That affair excited and shocked me, and a few weeks after I
was taken to a lunatic asylum. From that day to this I have had but a
hazy view of dear John Brown's great work. Indeed, some of my
impressions of it have, as others have told me, been quite erroneous and
even wild. I would not therefore, presume to pass any judgement in the
case. Let me however say that my brain has continued to the present
time to be sensitive on this John Brown matter, and every now and then
I get little or no sleep in consequence of it. It was so when I read the
articles in the *Atlantic* you refer to, and now your bare proposition to
write of this matter has given me another sleepless turn. In every fresh
turn I fear a recurrence of my insanity."[5] The note went on to request
that the full history of the transaction at Harpers Ferry be withheld
from the public until after Smith's death. Smith's wife wrote Sanborn
three days later, beseeching him to use Smith's name sparingly in any
account he should write.

Through all the obfuscation, Sanborn maintained a high opinion of
Smith. "I have never been able to satisfy myself, and cannot, therefore,
hope to explain to others the reason why Mr. Smith shrank from a full
disclosure, and preferred to pass away with the secret unspoken," wrote
Sanborn. "It was not for lack of courage or of magnanimity, —certainly
not for lack of admiration of Brown and his deed; nor through any dis-
loyalty to those, living or dead, associated with Gerrit Smith in that and
other enterprises undertaken for Liberty. Nor was it, I venture to say,
with any futile hope of averting the course of History, or mitigating the
verdict of mankind. Gerrit Smith was not of that quality or temper of
soul. . . . I prefer to maintain that opinion I early formed of my venerable friend; his errors of judgement were but the slight accidents of
human frailty, not to be cited as of a character that, in all essential traits,
was lofty [and] generous."[6]

☆

Gerrit Smith maintained a splendid study in his large mansion outside of Syracuse, New York. In the middle of the room was an ornate

Gerrit Smith in the mid-1850s. Photo courtesy Boston Public Library.

mahogany desk rumored to have once belonged to Napoleon. Floor-to-ceiling bookcases held over a thousand volumes. And large windows facing the desk overlooked the sweeping front lawn of Smith's sprawling estate. Behind the desk, a handsome framed map of the eastern seaboard showed vast sections—whole counties in some instances—colored in red. If a visitor asked the meaning of the red, he or she would learn that Smith was the closest thing to a landed lord that the United States had ever produced. Born near Syracuse in 1799, Smith was the fabulously wealthy inheritor of immense real estate holdings—more than 1 million acres in Virginia, Pennsylvania, and New York.

Several daguerreotypes sat in small frames on Smith's desk. One was a frowning portrait of his older brother, Peter Smith, Jr., a problem drinker and psychotic who died young. Another was a smiling, benign picture of his younger brother, Adolph—clinically insane and confined to a nearby institution. On the wall opposite the map hung a pencil sketch of Smith's father, Peter Smith, Sr., an early partner of John Jacob Astor's who made a fortune in the fur business and then married into the aristocratic, landed Livingston family. (Peter Smith eventually came to be worth approximately $400,000, most of which he invested in acreage throughout the Alleghenies, Mohawk Valley, and Adirondacks. Gerrit's subsequent annual income from the properties was never less than $60,000, the equivalent of more than a million dollars in today's currency.) It was Peter Smith who built the beautiful, columned manor-house that was home to Gerrit. There was no town on the spot at the time Peter Smith settled there, so he founded one and named it after himself: Peterboro.

The top drawer of Gerrit Smith's desk was filled not with pencils and envelopes, but with bottles of pills, potions, and elixirs. Like so many of his brooding relatives, Gerrit was a hypochondriac. He routinely suffered from some malady or another that he was sure foretold his certain and soon extinction. He was prone to remark on special holidays: "I shall not be here next Christmas" or "I shall not be with you next Easter." Every ache, every cough, every headache, was to be pondered and considered as the first symptom of some larger and far more dreadful thing. He dwelled so much on his physical well-being that this in turn prompted bouts of prolonged depression. There were days when he was charming, gregarious, full of optimism. There were others when he was plagued with deep bitterness, melancholy, and remorse. For all his fear of sickness and death, he once tried to commit suicide.

The fatalistic Smith was religious in a dark, almost medieval way. In this he resembled his father, who, after devoting his life to building a fortune, spent his last years immersed in a religious fanaticism that caused him to give up all his worldly goods. He signed them over to Gerrit, his most stable son, who, like the father, firmly believed the biblical admonition that it is as easy for a rich man to enter the kingdom of heaven as for a camel to pass through the eye of a needle. With this in mind, Gerrit wrote five-figure checks to help support Polish and Greek refugees, Irish famine victims, and industrial training schools for the deaf. He gave the Oswego Free Library a gift of $30,000. When Frederick Douglass moved to Rochester and founded his antislavery newspaper, the *North Star,* Smith was a strong and vital supporter. (Douglass dedicated the second of his several autobiographies, *My Bondage and My Freedom,* to Smith in 1855.)[7]

Another daguerreotype on Smith's desk was a framed, autographed picture of Douglass. "To Mr. Gerrit Smith," read the inscription, "a true friend of abolition and of freedom-loving men everywhere." Smith was one of the founders of the antislavery Liberty Party in 1840, and was elected to Congress on the party ticket in 1852 but resigned his office on a whim before his two-year term was completed. Always an abolitionist, Smith shifted with great frequency between a number of factions and ideologies within the movement. For a while he endorsed African repatriation and compensated emancipation. Then he abruptly rejected both ideas. His support for the Liberty Party meant that he believed in working nonviolently through political action within the system and under the Constitution to bring an end to slavery; yet he would defy the Liberty Party's fundamental governing principle by affiliating himself with the violent revolutionary John Brown.

Leaning back in the swivel chair behind his huge Napoleonic desk, the country squire brought an unconsciously aristocratic nonchalance to the art of making his vulgar wealth acceptable in the eyes of the Lord. In 1839, with the stroke of a pen, Smith donated 21,000 undeveloped acres in western Virginia (now northwestern West Virginia) to the strongly abolitionist Oberlin College. Owen Brown, a trustee of the college, used the gift as an occasion to give his ne'er-do-well, forty-year-old son a job. Thus the mercurial, bankrupt John Brown was contracted to survey Smith's land grant. It was during this surveying trip in early 1840 that Brown, who would not meet Gerrit Smith for another eight years, first came to know the rugged tangle of trans-Ohio backcountry where he would one day foment revolution.

Six years later, Smith set aside 120,000 acres of land in New York's Adirondack Mountains to be parceled into homesteads for black freedmen. (The exact spot was at North Elba, near Lake Placid in Essex. County.) Of a forecasted 3,000 families, 1,985 were given forty-acre plots. The properties were meant not only to give the blacks a new beginning, but also to qualify them to vote under New York State's property qualification of net assets representing at least $250 in value.

But the blacks at North Elba—on the settlement they came to call Timbucto—had a rough time of it. The Adirondack land and climate demanded completely different growing methods from what they'd learned in the South. Nor did they know the rudiments of house and barn construction. To compound their problems, the good people of

Smith's settlement were routinely harassed and sabotaged by their big-
oted white neighbors. Many families wound up destitute, hungry, and
nearly shelterless. But Smith, the easily distracted do-gooder, rapidly
moved on to other concerns. His lonesome, windswept colony of freedmen soon became little more to him than a yellow pin stuck into a vast
field of red on the map behind his desk.

2

A DREAM OF MOUNTAINS

GERRIT SMITH DID not quite know what to make of the blunt, impoverished, Bible-quoting John Brown when he showed up at Peterboro in April of 1848. "I am something of a pioneer," Brown explained in a letter of introduction that presaged his arrival on horseback by only two days. "I grew up among the woods and wild Indians of Ohio, and am used to the climate and the way of life that your colony [at North Elba] find so trying. I will take one of your farms myself, clear it up and plant it, and show my colored neighbors how much work should be done; will give them work as I have occasion, look after them in all needful ways, and be a kind of father to them."[1] When he read the letter, Smith had no idea who Brown was. Brown in turn knew Smith by reputation as an affluent friend of abolition—just the type of man he wanted to cultivate.

The forty-eight-year-old Brown, who was just one year younger than Smith, cut a strangely sad yet striking figure. Of medium height, but lanky, he was filthy from many days of travel by horse when he arrived at Smith's elegant house. His pants and shirt were homespun. One of his boots had worn through above the heel to show skin. Perhaps in a failed attempt to make himself more presentable for the

John Brown photographed in Boston in 1857.
Photo courtesy Massachusetts Historical Society.

finely dressed and carefully groomed Smith, he wore what had plainly once been a Sunday dress jacket. Now it was soiled with mud and, Smith thought, some blood as well. A cuff on one of the sleeves was loose and kept falling down below Brown's wrist. As Brown spoke, he nonchalantly rolled the cuff back up several times, then remedied the problem for a while by crossing his arms on his chest. Smith had some food brought out—a few muffins and a slice of bacon. Brown dove into the plate, famished. Before he did so, however, he recited out loud a prayer of thanksgiving. As he sat down on the little porch bench to eat, Brown's jacket opened to reveal a revolver.

We can rely on the eloquent description provided by Frederick Douglass, who met Brown one year before, to give us an accurate portrait of the man who now sat before Smith. "In person he was lean, strong and sinewy," wrote Douglass, "of the best New England mould, built for times of trouble, fitted to grapple with the flintiest hardships. Clad in plain American woolen, shod in boots of cowhide leather and wearing a cravat of the same substantial material, under six feet high, less than 150 pounds in weight . . . he presented a figure straight and symmetrical as a mountain pine. His bearing was singularly impressive. His head was not large, but compact and high. His hair was coarse, strong, slightly gray and closely trimmed, and grew low on his forehead. His face was smoothly shaved and revealed a strong square mouth, supported by a broad and prominent chin. His eyes were bluish gray, and in conversation they were full of light and fire. When on the street, he moved with a long, spring race [*sic*] horse step, absorbed by his own reflections, neither seeking or shunning observation."[2]

Questioning by Smith revealed fragments of Brown's checkered history. Brown described vaguely how his business endeavors—as a wool merchant based in Springfield, Massachusetts—had suffered of late because of his increasing preoccupation with abolition. Brown assured the deeply religious Smith that he was a God-fearing man, a strict Calvinist who believed in "the literal accuracy" of every word in the Bible. He had married twice and was the father of many children. Some of these were grown and gone, but a number were still with him. He had very little money, needed a place of his own, and sincerely wanted to help his black brothers. In short, he was desperate. And God had sent him here to Smith.

☆

There were many details of his troubled past that John Brown did not reveal to Smith. His father, Owen Brown, had emigrated from Torrington, Connecticut, to Hudson, Ohio, shortly after John's birth in 1800. Owen Brown owned a successful tannery; and John had been raised in the tannery business. But his temperament—independent, strong-willed, self-confident, and humorless—would not allow him to work for anyone (especially his own father) for very long. The desire to always be in charge, to be the director of anything he involved himself in, manifested itself early. Thus, at age seventeen, he and an adopted brother set up their own tannery to compete with that of their father. John Brown quickly became imperious, completely convinced of his infallibility in business matters. He gave orders about the tannery like "a king against whom there is no rising up," as one acquaintance recalled. Brown "doted on being the head of the heap, and he was."[3] (Years later, one of Brown's soldiers who was lucky enough to avoid the invasion of Harpers Ferry, and thus live to have recollections of him, would remember the commander as being "essentially vindictive in his nature" and possessed by an "imperial egotism.")[4] The tannery proved marginally successful: the

one business endeavor John Brown ever engaged in that did not come
crashing down around him.

His first wife was the nineteen-year-old Dianthe Lusk, whom he
married when he was twenty. Like him, she was solemn and puritanical.
She was also a manic-depressive: sensitive, scared, easily tearful. Dianthe
suffered at least one nervous breakdown and was afflicted with what a
friend called "an almost constant blueness and melancholy." Some neighbors called her a madwoman. She was capable of silences that lasted for
days, these interrupted by only the submissive "Yes, husband" that the
domineering John Brown expected and got whenever he asked anything
of her. Eight children arrived in rapid succession during the eleven years
between 1821 and 1832. The six who survived would remember their
mother as sad, their father as severe. Dianthe passed away in 1832 at
New Richmond Township, Pennsylvania, where the Browns had moved
in 1826. She died of an extreme fever after having given birth to yet
another son, who died even before she did. In the spring of 1833, less
than a year after Dianthe was buried, the thirty-three-year-old Brown
married sixteen-year-old Mary Day. Within ten months, Mary presented
Brown with his eighth child, Sarah, who herself was to be the first of a
second set of nine, five of whom would die in childhood.

Such adjectives as *stern, frugal, temperate,* and *domineering* crop up in
almost every contemporary description of Brown. Recalling a visit to one
in the long string of John Brown's many homes, Frederick Douglass
wrote that "plain as was the outside of this man's house, the inside was
plainer. Its furniture would have satisfied a Spartan. It would take
longer to tell what was not in this house than what was in it. There was
an air of plainness about it which almost suggested destitution. . . .
Innocent of paint, veneering, varnish, or table-cloth, the table announced
itself unmistakably of pine and of the plainest workmanship. . . . It is
said that a house in some measure reflects the character of its occupants;
this one certainly did. In it there were no disguises, no illusions, no make
believes. Everything implied stern truth, solid purpose, and rigid economy." Douglass added that he was not long in the company of the master
of the house before "I discovered that he was indeed the master of it, and

was likely to become mine too if I stayed long enough with him. He fulfilled St. Paul's idea of the head of the family. His wife believed in him, and his children observed him with reverence. Whenever he spoke his words commanded earnest attention. His arguments, which I ventured at some points to oppose, seemed to convince all; his appeals touched all, and his will impressed all. Certainly I never felt myself in the presence of a stronger religious influence than while in this man's house."[5]

After Dianthe died, Brown's fortunes subsided. His tannery at New Richmond failed. He was completely bankrupt by the spring of 1835, at which point he abandoned all his Pennsylvania property as partial payment on his many debts and brought his family back to the Western Reserve to begin again. In Ohio, he tried his hand at land speculation, focusing on the region of Franklin Mills, not far from Hudson. His only capital was $20,000 in the form of state bank notes and personal mortgages from friends and family. The land depreciated. By the end of 1837, Brown was being sued by most of his dissatisfied investors. Matters were complicated by the fact that Brown (whose business failures were almost always to be accompanied by accusations of fraud) had written three separate mortgages on one piece of land without informing lenders about the competing liens.

A succession of businesses came and went after his collapse in real estate. He tried raising and trading cattle, then sheep, and finally started another tannery that also failed. He was bankrupt again in 1846 when, with money from the wealthy Akron businessman Simon Perkins, he set up the firm of Perkins & Brown and opened an office/warehouse in Springfield, Massachusetts. The plan was for Perkins & Brown, in the person of John Brown, to take in wool from shepherds throughout the Midwest and East, then sort and sell the wool by grades, thus compelling New England buyers to pay the highest reasonable price. In giving Brown the several thousand dollars required to start the business, Perkins wrote that he should run the Springfield office according to his own "will" and "impulses."[6] It was after several years of doing just that, and seeing the business come to nothing as a result, that a weary John Brown first approached Gerrit Smith, petitioning for a retreat to North Elba.

Throughout his misadventures in business, Brown was always active in the antislavery movement. He subscribed to William Lloyd Garrison's *Liberator* and Frederick Douglass's *North Star,* opened his various homes to runaway slaves traveling on the Underground Railroad, flirted with the idea of starting an occupational school for fugitive slaves in Pennsylvania, and was expelled from an Ohio Congregational Society for allowing blacks to use his family pew. While entertaining Frederick Douglass at dinner in Springfield in 1847, he startled the abolitionist leader by remarking that only open warfare could ever free the black people. The slaves, Brown told Douglass, had a right to achieve their freedom "any way they could." Shortly after his visit, Douglass published a note in the *North Star* to the effect that he had enjoyed "a private interview [with John Brown, who,] though a white gentleman, is in sympathy, a black man, and as deeply interested in our cause, as though his own soul had been pierced with the iron of slavery."[7]

Douglass's friend Gerrit Smith decided he had nothing to lose in granting John Brown a stake at North Elba. He would not give Brown land as an outright gift, but he would sell him all he wanted at the very low price of $1 per acre. And most importantly to Brown, Smith was willing to wait indefinitely for payment.

"I was on some of the Gerrit Smith lands lying opposite Burlington Vt. last fall that he has given away to the blacks & found no objection to them but the high Northern latitude in which they lie," Brown wrote to his father. "They are indeed rather inviting on many accounts. There are a number of good colored families on the ground; most of whom I visited. I can think of no place where I think I would sooner go, *all things considered* than to live with those poor despised Africans to try, & encourage them; & show them a little so far as I am capable how to manage. You kneed [*sic*] not be surprised if at some future time I should do so."[8]

Brown selected 244 acres of Smith's land for himself. The spot was idyllic. Whiteface Mountain rose majestically to the north, and Mount Marcy, the tallest peak in the Adirondacks, sprang up high to the south.

Years later, while Brown lay in the jail at Charles Town, Virginia, waiting to die, Thomas Wentworth Higginson would visit this windswept outpost and write of the "little frame house, unpainted, set in a girdle of black stumps, and with all heaven about it for a wider girdle; on a high hillside, forest on north and west, —the glorious line of the Adirondacks on the east, and on the south one slender road leading off to Westport, —a road so straight that you could sight a United States marshal for five miles."[9]

One day in June 1849, three strangers emerged from the woods near the Adirondack farm of John Brown. One of them turned out to be Richard Henry Dana, Jr., of Boston, attorney and celebrated author of *Two Years Before the Mast.* Dana explained first to Brown's daughter Ruth and then to an amused Brown that he and his friends had wandered through the "barren mountains" all night (in fact, for eighteen hours) completely lost. "Three more worn, wearied, hungry, black-fly bitten travellers seldom came to his humble, hospitable door," recalled Dana. Brown brought them into his house and fed them a meal of venison and speckled brook trout. As they ate, Brown explained to Dana that he was only a part-time resident at North Elba. He often had to leave his family here for long periods while he returned to his business as a wool merchant in Springfield.

Dana wrote that Brown's family seemed to consist of an unlimited supply of children, "from a cheerful, nice healthy woman of twenty or so, and a full-sized red haired son, who seemed to be foreman of the farm, through every grade of boy and girl to a couple that could hardly speak plain." The farm itself was barely there. It was, wrote Dana, "a mere recent clearing. The stumps of trees stood out, blackened by burning, and crops were growing among them, and there was a plenty of felled timber. The dwelling was a small log-house of one story in height, and the outbuildings were slight. The whole had the air of a recent enterprise, on a moderate scale, although there were a good many neat cattle and horses. The position was a grand one for a lover of mountain effects; but how good for farming I could not tell."[10]

Dana found Brown to be "a strong abolitionist and a kind of king" among the blacks in the area. He noted with disapproval (for like many abolitionists he did not believe in social equality for blacks) that Brown referred to blacks as "Mister" and let them eat at the same table with his family. Dana believed two blacks at the table to be travelers on the Underground Railroad, headed for Canada, though Brown did not explicitly say this.

During the evening that Dana spent with Brown, it is likely that Brown fantasized aloud by the light of the cooking fire, as he was often known to do, about his long-cherished dream for the wholesale liberation of thousands of Southern blacks. His scheme was to found a heavily armed and fortified colony of runaways high up in the Allegheny wilderness. Staring almost hypnotically into the embers of the fire, Brown spoke of mountains as God's hand-made bastions of liberty, natural homes for the poor, the hated, the despised—all victims who fled injustice. "There was indeed," Thomas Wentworth Higginson would recall, "always a sort of thrill in John Brown's voice when he spoke of mountains. I shall never forget the quiet way in which he once told me that God had established the Allegheny Mountains from the foundation of the world that they might one day be a refuge for fugitive slaves."[11]

The Allegheny Mountains, Brown told Frederick Douglass as early as 1847, "are the basis of my plan. God has given the strength of the hills to freedom, they were placed there for the emancipation of the negro race; they are full of natural forts, where one man for defense will be equal to a hundred for attack; they are full also of good hiding places, where large numbers of brave men could be concealed, and baffle and elude pursuit for a long time. I know these mountains well, and could take a body of men into them and keep them there despite of all the efforts of Virginia to dislodge them."

Brown envisioned what he called a "Subterranean Pass Way" amid the Alleghenies, through which vast numbers of blacks could be smuggled to Northern freedom under the protection of their fellow fugitives, who would have de facto control over the mountainous countryside. His idea, he told Douglass, was to "take at first about twenty-five picked men, and begin on a small scale; supply them arms and ammunition, post them in squads of fives on a line of twenty-five miles, the most persuasive and judicious of whom shall go down into the fields from time to time, as opportunity offers, and induce the slaves to join them, seeking and selecting the most restless and daring." Slowly, Brown planned to build up his force to "one hundred hardy men, men who would be content to lead the free and adventurous life to which he proposed to train them," recalled Douglass. "When these were properly drilled, and each man had found the place for which he was best suited, they would begin work in earnest; they would run off slaves in large numbers, retain the brave and strong ones in the mountains, and send the weak and timid to the north by the underground railroad." As the numbers of men at his command grew, Brown told Douglass somewhat ominously, so too would his operations expand and "not be confined to one locality" nor "one mode of justice."[12]

Brown drew many a map of the Allegheny wilderness that August, talking up his scheme with abolitionists in London. He had ostensibly gone to Europe not to promote his antislavery initiative, but rather to salvage his wool business with a large export sale. But his plan to save Perkins & Brown via direct sales into the European market failed miserably. He came nowhere near getting the price per bale that he needed in order to save his business. One buyer after another—in London, Paris, Brussels, and Hamburg—rejected the American wool as being of poor grade.

And Brown had no better luck in finding people willing to buy into his slave rebellion. He garnered some sympathy, but no currency. And sympathy could not buy guns. When he boarded a boat at Liverpool in mid-October to return to the United States, Brown's business was as good as bust (although he would spend several years nursing it in its death throes and tidying up its loose ends). His hopes to do something major to liberate the slaves seemed to be equally vain.

During frequent visits to his North Elba farm through the next several years, Brown did a great deal of surveying. He became a fairly common sight, stoically dragging his equipment across the mountainsides, always dressed with shabby formality in his heavy frock coat. He worked "early and late," as he recalled, "tracing out old lost boundaries."[13] Sometimes he labored for the county; more often he was in the employ of Gerrit Smith. But most often he labored in Springfield, trying unsuccessfully to save his shirt in the wool business.

3

THE CHEVALIER

SPEAKING AT A memorial service for Samuel Gridley Howe in 1876, Thomas Wentworth Higginson refrained from mentioning John Brown, whose trust he believed Howe had betrayed on more than one occasion. Instead, Higginson focused on what he could truthfully say that was good about his old friend Howe, applauding his tireless efforts at the Perkins Institute for the Blind, where he had served as director since 1831. Gazing down at the white-bearded Howe in his casket, Higginson pushed the inconvenient memory of John Brown to the side. Higginson instead recounted a long string of triumphs that he instructed his listeners to take as the sum of Howe: his invention of the style of braille known as Boston Line Lettering and his use of it to print the first braille edition of the New Testament in 1836, his genius at founding the first industrial training shop for the blind, and his vision in starting the first braille circulating library. Above all else, said Higginson, Howe should be remembered for his greatest conquest when, in the 1830s, he became first in the world to teach language to a blind-deaf mute. (Howe's friend Charles Dickens wrote at length about Howe and his student, Laura Bridgman, in *American Notes*.) An aging Miss Bridgman—her vacant eyes red with tears—sat dark and silent in a pew as Higginson eulogized her teacher. One of Howe's apprentices sat beside her, using the finger-code language Howe had invented to tap Higginson's words of appreciation into her open palm.

Thirty-five years later, Higginson was still unwilling to dwell publicly on what he privately called Howe's "cowardly abandonment" of John Brown. During May of 1910, after reading proof sheets for Oswald Garrison Villard's biography of John Brown, Higginson wrote Villard to request a change. He asked that Villard understate the vehemence of the denunciation he'd leveled at Howe after Howe's desertion of Brown in the panic following Harpers Ferry. "This would save the feelings of the Howe family . . . , " wrote Higginson to Villard, "who have always been warm friends of mine, in successive generations."[1]

Like Higginson, Howe's family also tried to avoid the subject of the doctor's relationship with Brown. Always anxious to paint her father as a fearless, selfless champion of noble causes, Howe's biographer-daughter, Laura Richards, thought it wise to ignore Howe's betrayal of the man who in death became the patron saint of abolition. In 1911, Richards published a joint biography of her parents in which the name John Brown appeared not once. Two years earlier, in a full biography of her father entitled *Life and Letters of Samuel Gridley Howe,* Richards briefly brought up Howe's association with the abolitionist militiaman Brown just long enough to deny that Howe had prior knowledge of the Harpers Ferry invasion.

Before we can proceed with the narrative of John Brown and the Secret Six, we need to achieve an intimate understanding of the unique personality that was Samuel Gridley Howe—or at least to do so as well as we can from the few genuine shreds of recollection that survive more than three generations after the fact of the man. We need to dig deep into old diaries and letters to get a glimpse of the genuine, historical Howe not considered in the adoring memoirs penned by Franklin Sanborn, Laura Richards, and the circumspect Julia Ward Howe. We need to go also, however, to these published sources to examine those few places where the truth of the troubled and troubling Howe was occasionally and inadvertently mixed with the contrived adulation. Thus shall we come to shake hands with Howe, look him in the eye, and feel the curious mix of positive and negative forces that defined him and propelled him into John Brown's orbit.

☆

Samuel Gridley Howe had always been attracted to the romance of high-minded battle—a romance that many of his contemporaries felt he personified. His house in Boston was full of cherished mementos from great crusades. A glass case housed muskets and sabers used by his forebears in the American Revolution. A hat tree in the foyer held the gold-inlaid and azure-plumed helmet that Lord Byron took with him through the battles of the Greek War for Independence. This relic was the souvenir a young Howe brought back from his own several years of fighting for Greece.

A lover of the poetry of Byron, the dashing Howe lived a life that was itself quite literally the stuff of poetry. Oliver Wendell Holmes wrote a stirring lyric about him. So did John Greenleaf Whittier, who entitled his piece "The Hero" and used it to portray Howe as a "knight of a better era, without reproach or fear," akin to Bayard, who would go to fight "wherever rise the peoples, wherever sinks a throne." In one of her lesser-known poems entitled "The Rough Sketch," Julia Ward Howe— who shared a bed with Howe for more than thirty years—portrayed a less romantic side of the man whom other poets were not so well positioned to know. Julia characterized him as "a restless spur" with "small patience for the tasks of time." In looking back on her unhappy marriage, which included a host of insults, infidelities, and desertions on the part of Howe, Julia would write a confidential—and, for a long time, unpublished—poem that began: "Hope died as I was led,/Unto my marriage bed . . ."

Born in Boston on November 10, 1801, Sam Howe came from old Plymouth Bay Colony stock. His grandfather, Edward Compston Howe, participated in the Boston Tea Party. His mother's uncle, Richard Gridley, was a soldier, surveyor, and civil engineer who was in charge of fortifying

Bunker Hill the night before the famous battle and who, under the direct orders of George Washington, aided in preparing the siege works that were instrumental in driving the British from Boston. Both forebears were neighbors and friends of Paul Revere, with whom the teenaged Howe was acquainted. Howe's father—another friend of Revere's—was a once affluent Boston rope maker who lost most of his small fortune when the U.S. Navy failed to pay for large amounts of cordage that he supplied during the War of 1812.

Dr. Samuel Gridley Howe in the 1850s. Photo courtesy Boston Public Library.

Howe graduated from Brown University in 1821, and from the Harvard Medical School in 1824. Shortly after his medical school graduation, following a failed romance, Howe joined thousands of other idealistic young men from around the world—Philhellenes, "lovers of Greece," they called themselves—who went to join the Greek fight for independence from Turkey. Howe quickly rose in rank, becoming Surgeon General to the Greek Army and later to the fleet. "The only fault found with him," recalled one old comrade, "was that he always would be in the fight, and was only a surgeon when the battle was over."[2]

In 1830, his service to Greece having been rewarded by his being knighted by the king as a Chevalier of the Order of St. Savior, Sam Howe stopped in Paris to further his medical studies. During his stay, he enthusiastically participated in the 1830 uprising against the restored

Bourbon monarchy. "I knew it was none of my business," he wrote, "but I could not help joining in." During the same period, Howe became a friend of the aged Lafayette. At Lafayette's request, Howe traveled into Prussia to visit Polish insurgents and deliver funds sent for their aid from Lafayette's contacts in the United States. Arrested in the midst of his errand and thrown into a medieval Berlin dungeon, Howe was eventually released through the intervention of the American consul, but only after five weeks of what his wife would later call "a tedious imprisonment *au secret.*"[3] He spent the entire time in solitary confinement, allowed absolutely no contact with the outside world. He did not know when or if he would be released. For a good part of the time, he did not even know whether his family and friends knew what had happened to him.

The experience left him with a consuming fear of jails, chains, and confinement. Visiting the British prison at Bridewell in the mid-1840s with his friend Charles Dickens, Howe seemed to Dickens "strangely anxious" to get outside the prison walls. Dickens had "never seen a man so nervous." (In January of 1860, writing to Sen. Henry Wilson of Massachusetts regarding a request that he come to Washington to testify about John Brown, Howe would express his willingness but also explain that he was "a little wary, for I was once hurried into a prison under pretext that my testimony was wanted by legal authority about matters and things on the frontiers of rebelling Poland, and I did not find it easy to get out. I have since learned that no European despotism is more regardless of justice than is the one we have at home.")[4]

Howe was tall, lean, and athletically built. When he stood, he stood erect, like a soldier at attention. He wore a beard. Franklin Sanborn wrote that Howe was "an Arab in figure and in horsemanship" with "a manner that bespoke energy."[5] The forty-one-year-old doctor cut a fine figure when the poet Longfellow introduced him to the wealthy, young, New York poetess Julia Ward in 1842. Twenty-three-year-old Julia was a cousin of the Astors and a sister of the Wall Street financier Sam Ward. During their brief engagement, Howe demonstrated the impatience with which his Julia would become all too familiar. "The Chevalier is very presumptuous—says that he will not lose sight of me for one day, that I must stay here [Boston] till he can return with me to New York," she wrote to her brother in February 1843. "The Chevalier is very impertinent, speaks of two or three months, when I speak of two or three years, and seems determined to have his own way: but, dear Bunny, the Chevalier's way will be a very charming way, and is, henceforth, to be mine."[6]

Julia would soon join the long list of people who found Howe's impertinence, by and large, to be something less than charming. "He has terrible faults of character," she would write of him, "is often unjust in his likes and dislikes, arbitrary, cruel, with little mastery over his passions, incapable of enduring criticism or of profiting by it. He is much led by flattery and prizes above all a certain obsequiousness which always implies a want of character in those who show it. I know that there are rotten hearts that he will cherish to the grave and sincere ones whose affection will be little regarded by him."[7]

As Julia admitted in the privacy of her journal, Howe could be quite cynical, suspicious, and spiteful. He was in the habit of seeing plots against him lurking where they did not, and he was easily insulted. He read too much into almost every action and utterance of friend and enemy alike. ("You think me much more complicated in nature and method than I am," Theodore Parker wrote him in late 1854, after Howe took offense from a stray comment that Parker felt had no importance whatsoever.[8])

Strong-willed and domineering, Howe was brash and quickly bored. He was prone to speedy judgments that triggered immediate action. "I do not like caution," he wrote. "It betokens little faith in God's arrangements." Julia would recall that she did not enjoy journeying with him, for he was "too rapid and restless a traveler for pleasure." His daughter Laura Richards would write that "life with a Comet-Apostle was not always easy." Laura remembered that her father "was not a patient man. He did not suffer fools gladly; he rent them in pieces and went on over the trampled bodies. . . . *Impatient!* he springs into life at the word."[9]

One instantaneous, long-standing decision of Sam's was that his wife should not be a writer. He tried to stop Julia from publishing her verses.

He took manuscripts and tossed them into the fire; he took acceptance letters from magazine editors and did the same; he sat by her as she tried to compose and made rude remarks about her and her "silly little papers." Howe continued to be hostile to her writing until he started a small antislavery newspaper, the *Commonwealth,* and Julia became a conveniently located and attractively priced columnist. Howe paid her nothing. (Thomas Wentworth Higginson, not being married to the founder, was paid $2.50 per column for his contributions. Nevertheless he found publication in the *Commonwealth* to be a frustrating endeavor. He was unhappy about the many typographical errors that appeared in his articles. "This makes five articles of mine in your unhappy paper and there has been some diabolical erratum in each one," he wrote Howe. "I shall try no further."[10])

Launched in 1851, the *Commonwealth* was published for three and a half years. Most people—even friends of abolition—considered it a rag. As Howe's most astute biographer has pointed out, the tone of many of the articles in the *Commonwealth* could only be described as offensive. "There was," reports Harold Schwartz, "no depth of vulgarity and vituperation to which its writers would not descend to pillory the opposition." In one characteristic piece, the paper printed an article about how the conservative proslavery politician Caleb Cushing "hurried" his dying sister into her grave during the end of the senatorial campaign of 1851 and then rushed back to Boston to lead the fight against the antislavery candidate Charles Sumner, without observing a proper period of mourning. The paper also mocked Harvard's Edward Everett as being a weak figure, "abject before the bullies of the slave power," a mere rhetorician incapable of genuine action for liberty.[11] A friend of Howe's, Professor Felton of Harvard, was so infuriated by such attacks that he canceled his subscription to the paper, telling Howe bluntly that the *Commonwealth* was "unfit to be seen on the table of a gentleman."[12]

☆

The legendary impatience of the complex Dr. Howe did not extend to Laura Bridgman and the many other blind and deaf patients with whom he worked slowly and methodically, year upon year, over the course of a lifetime. He was most secure when he was with his invalid students. He was their guide to the world and the most important authority figure in their lives. And with them he was in complete control. "It will be long," wrote Julia Ward Howe, "before the world shall forget the courage and patience of the man who, in the very bloom of his manhood, sat down to besiege [Laura Bridgman's] almost impenetrable fortress of darkness and isolation and, after months of labor, carried within its walls the divine conquest of life and of thought."[13]

Julia was choosing her analogies carefully. She knew her husband well. Every good cause was, to Howe, quite literally a battle to be won. He did *lay siege* to the limitations imposed by blindness and deafness in the same way he laid siege to all other things and people with which he found himself at odds. "Chev's is one of those characters based upon opposition," wrote Julia. "While I always seem to work for an unseen friend, he always sees an armed adversary and arms himself accordingly." Commenting on an antislavery speech by Dr. Howe, Higginson would admiringly recall that "every sentence was a sword-thrust."

In abolition, as in everything with which he involved himself, Howe favored direct action. Soon after taking up the cause he told a friend that "some move of actual force" against slavery should be taken as soon as possible.[14] When a free black came to Howe showing references and asking for money with which to buy his slave daughter to prevent her being sold into the deep South, Howe refused to underwrite the purchase. He did not wish to legitimize the institution of slavery by actually engaging in the act of purchasing another human being. Instead, he offered to provide money—in the end, far more than the likely price of purchase—to support a team that would kidnap the girl and bring her to freedom.

Such was the temperament of the Chevalier, the short-fused and self-confident knight who, though himself the father of countless personal injustices, would not suffer the foolishness of any social injustice gladly, or for long, without doing his best to run it through.

4

One Bright, Clear Flash

S EQUESTERED IN A Canadian hideout a few days after the mid-October rout at Harpers Ferry, Franklin Sanborn posted a letter to an address in Rome where Boston's Rev. Theodore Parker—forty-nine years old—lay wasting away from tuberculosis. "Our old friend struck his blow in such a way, —either by his own folly or the direction of Providence, —that it has recoiled, and ruined him, and perhaps those who were his friends . . . , " wrote Sanborn. "The poor old man fought like a hero, and will die like one, —by the rope, it is most likely. Two of his sons were shot by his side, and three-fourths of his men. There has been nothing so much in 'the high Roman fashion' seen in this country for many a year. Now he lies in a Virginia jail, tormented with questions, wounded, and waiting his trial for murder and treason. . . . What course the government will pursue remains to be seen; but most likely they will follow up the matter as closely as possible; and we shall have plenty of treason-trials, and bloody threats, and some bloodshed. All this will weaken the Slave Power; and the good of the tragedy will outweigh the evil, no doubt."[1]

The dying Parker's response was nothing short of gleeful. "The Northern sky is full of lightning long treasured up: Brown was one bright, clear flash into the southern ground." The flash, said Parker, was bound now to detonate civil war during which "The Fire of Vengeance" would run "from man to man, from town to town" across a South that would be saturated with the "white man's blood."[2] Writing to Parker on November 14, Sanborn was equally enthusiastic as he analyzed the situation in a calculating, pragmatic way that would have enraged Higginson, with whom Sanborn was supposedly at work on a plan to rescue Brown. "The feeling of sympathy with Brown is spreading fast over all the North, and will grow stronger if he is hanged. . . . The *failure* is a success; it has done more for Freedom than years of talk could. . . . It grieves me sadly to think that Brown must die, but he is ready for it; and if we cannot avert it, we must think it best. It will undoubtedly add millions to the righteous side."[3]

In Rome, Theodore Parker visited the catacombs of St. Calixtus regularly, fascinated by the underground city of the dead. After John Brown's sentencing, Parker took special interest in the burial places of martyrs in the combs, these being distinguished by the outline of a hand rudely impressed on the tufa out of which the graves had been hollowed. As Parker, weak and coughing, walked the old, cold Roman streets, his greatcoat protecting him from the early winter chill, he must have reminisced about how it had been in this ancient city fifteen years before, in a suite of fine rooms on Via San Nicola da Tolentino, that he'd first gotten to know his fellow coconspirator in Brown's enterprise, Samuel Gridley Howe.

That was back in 1844. Sam and Julia were on their honeymoon; Julia was already pregnant with their first child. Parker, then aged thirty-four, and his wife, Lydia, were on a European tour. And both couples had chosen to winter in Rome. "As Dr. Howe had some slight acquaintance with [Parker]," recalled Julia Ward Howe, "we soon invited him to dine with us. He was already quite bald, and this untimely blemish appeared in strange contrast with the youthful energy of his facial expression. He was accompanied by his wife, whose mild countenance, compared with his, suggested even more than the usual contrast between husband and wife."[4]

Julia was at first put off by the prospect of receiving Parker, whose reputation for being dogmatic and egotistical—and, it was whispered, an *atheist*—preceded him. Acquaintances told Julia that Parker was boorish: a high-handed intellectual bully who went at all theological and political debates in a routinely condescending, brusque manner. Margaret Fuller wrote that she disliked his "polemical" style. Parker himself was fully and unapologetically aware of what he called his "blunt modes of

The Reverend Theodore Parker in the 1850s. Photo courtesy Boston Public Library.

mental operation."⁵ He prided himself on valuing "truth over friendship, candor over decorum," and, as he told a friend, "war over any peace that compromises liberty." (Speaking at a memorial service for Parker in June of 1860, Ralph Waldo Emerson said that Parker "never kept back the truth for fear to make an enemy."⁶ In the 1890s, after visiting Parker's grave in a picturesque Florentine cemetery, Franklin Sanborn commented that the peaceful scene of the minister's repose seemed ill-fitting after his "life of warfare.")⁷

Despite all this, Julia Howe was relieved to find the incessant warrior quite charming at dinner as he rehearsed the story of his early life for the entertainment of her and Sam. Lounging in the dining room of the Howes' spacious apartment, Parker noted that he and the doctor were both of fine Revolutionary ancestry. While Howe was the great-nephew of Bunker Hill's Captain Gridley and the grandson of a Boston Tea Party "Indian," Parker was the grandson of the famed Captain Parker who commanded the Minutemen on Lexington Green. It was Parker's grandfather who uttered the much quoted words, "Don't fire unless fired upon, but if they want to have a war, let it begin here."

The ghost of Parker's Revolutionary grandfather traveled with him always. "You know I do not like fighting," he said once during a talk about his defiance of the fugitive-slave law. "But what could I do? I was born in the little town where the fight and the bloodshed of the Revolution began. . . . My grandfather drew the first sword in the Revolution; my fathers fired the first shot; the blood which flowed there was kindred to this which courses in my veins today. Besides that, when I write in my library at home, on the one side of me is the Bible which my fathers prayed over, their morning and evening prayer, for nearly a hundred years. On the other side hangs the firelock my grandfather fought with in the old French war, which he carried at the taking of Quebec, which he zealously used at the battle of Lexington. And beside it is another, a trophy of that war, the first gun taken in the Revolution, taken also by my grandfather. With these things before me, these symbols; with these memories in me, when a parishioner, a fugitive from slavery, a woman, pursued by the kidnappers, came to my house, what could I do less than take her in and defend her to the last?"[8]

Just as Parker could not forget his ties to those who were the first defenders of American liberty, so would he not let his friends forget their links to the fighters of '76, or their duty to those ghosts. In urging Howe to help an abolitionist initiative in December of 1851, Parker would write: "Now nobody is so fit as you to move in this matter. You must do it. If you do not I shall expect to see a great commotion in one of the churchyards of Boston, & then the bones of Captain Gridley will come out of the ground & attack you—&—I will not say what they will do to you."[9] (In 1860, testifying before the Select Committee of the Senate appointed to inquire into the events at Harpers Ferry, Howe was asked a question the answer to which said volumes about the genesis of his and Parker's instinct to aid John Brown. "What ends are to be attained by promoting . . . antislavery sentiment?" asked the committee chairman, Virginia's James Mason. "What is the object in view?" The object, Howe responded dryly as the committee's chief inquisitor, Jefferson Davis of Mississippi, glared at him, was "the promotion of freedom among men; the same object as the fathers in the Revolution."[10])

☆

While his grandfather had helped spark a political rebellion, Parker believed his own chief calling was to spark a different kind of revolution: a revolution in theological thought. His mission, he wrote a British acquaintance, was nothing less than to redefine man's perception of and relation to God. In his dogma-smashing 1841 sermon entitled "The Transient and the Permanent in Christianity," the Harvard-educated Parker shocked conservative congregants by endorsing and extending the ideas his friend Emerson had put forth three years previously in his famous address to the graduating class of the Harvard Divinity School. Parker joined Emerson in assaulting the remnants of "historical Christianity," especially the notion of the partial divinity of Christ as espoused by formalist (Parker called them "spectral") Unitarians. Parker argued that Jesus was most real and most valuable as a transcendentalist inspiration— *an ideal to be aspired to*—rather than as an enduring, conscious, supernatural force.

Parker's personality rose to the occasion when, as a result of his radical notions, he was denied access to most pulpits. He took the rejection as a sign of affirmation. Parker saw little use in debating fine points of theology with what he considered to be lesser minds. There were sheep and there were shepherds, he told a friend. And no good shepherd ever allowed the flock to dictate its own path through the hills. The church that Parker founded when he was banned from all others—a Unitarian establishment that for some reason was called the Congregational Society of Boston—met first at the Melodeon Theater and then later at the Boston Music Hall, where he preached every Sunday to a large and enthusiastic band of followers.

"I cannot remember that the interest of his sermons ever varied for me," wrote the adoring Julia Ward Howe, who joined Parker's society as soon as she returned to Boston. "It was all one intense delight. The luminous clearness of his mind, his admirable talent for popularizing the procedures and conclusions of philosophy, his keen wit and poetic sense of beauty, —all these combined to make him appear to me one of the oracles of God." She recalled "the sublime attitude of humility" with which Parker rose for prayer before his congregation, "his arms extended, his features lit up with the glory of his high office. Truly, he talked with God, and took us with him into the divine presence."[11] After hearing one of Parker's sermons in early 1857, the old-school, fire-and-brimstone Calvinist John Brown would say that while he and the liberal Parker were "worlds apart in theology," he respected Parker's "deep piety, popular eloquence, and devotion to liberty."

Parker's argument with slavery was that as an institution it flew in the face of what Parker considered one of the most sacred documents ever penned: the Declaration of Independence. In his orations on abolition, Parker never oversimplified the complex problem of slavery. He refused to label it a Southern crime. Instead he described slavery as "the great national sin." Parker criticized not only Southern planters, but also Northern individuals and institutions that profited from the system of Southern impressed labor. (As "the snake" of slavery came crawling northward in the guise of the fugitive slave law, said Parker in one famous sermon, so at the same time did avarice—"the foulest worm which Northern cities gender in their heat"—go crawling south. "With many a wiggling curl it wound along its way. At length they met and twisting up in their obscene embrace, the twain became one monster . . . there was no North, no South, they were one poison."[12])

Exercising what Julia Ward Howe called his fierce "power of denunciation," Parker made many enemies by publicly naming and attacking individual members of the North's conservative elite who assisted in perpetuating the institution of slavery.[13] In widely published speeches, he indicted those—such as Northern shippers, textile-mill owners, and bankers—who, through commercial connections to the South, profited as much if not more from slavery than did any plantation owner. He hoped, he said, to bring those he named to "a crucifixion of reputation" after which they might be resurrected and redeemed.

Like many other abolitionists, Parker was convinced that blacks, on the whole, were inferior to whites in "general intellectual power." He had black friends—among them Frederick Douglass—whom he recognized as possessing superior minds and whom he considered exceptions to the rule of black inferiority. But in general Parker had what Garry Wills calls a "constricted" view of the black race's place in the social hierarchy.[14] "What a pity," he wrote Howe from Rome in anticipation of the civil war Brown was meant to spark, "that the map of our magnificent country should be destined to be so soon torn in two on account of the negro, that poorest of human creatures, satisfied, even in slavery, with sugar cane and a banjo."[15]

As one of Parker's biographers has pointed out: "Parker's estimate of the negro, intellectually and morally, was low. He exaggerated the sensuality of the negro. . . . Moreover the negro had for him a certain physical repulsion."[16] Parker's friends, the Howes, while being as strongly antislavery in their views as Parker, shared his low estimate of the black race. Julia Ward Howe wrote of how the "ideal negro" would be one "refined by white culture, elevated by white blood." The "negro among negroes," she wrote, "is a coarse, grinning, flat-footed, thick-skulled creature, ugly as Caliban, lazy as the laziest brutes, chiefly ambitious to be of no use to any in the world. . . . He must go to school to the white race and his discipline must be long and laborious." While opposed to slavery as a concept, Julia wondered in print whether compulsory labor for blacks was not "better than none."[17] Higginson also believed that the black, on average, came up short vis-à-vis intellectual prowess. At the turn of the century, he would recollect the black troops he helped muster during the Civil War as ". . . a thousand half-childish minds, gathered beneath the solemn moss-hung forests of South Carolina."[18]

☆

Often terse and sarcastic in public, Parker was by most accounts mild-mannered in his private life: a loving husband, a generous friend, a charitable stranger. "I have rarely met any one whose conversation had such a ready and varied charm," remembered Julia Howe. "His idea of culture was encyclopedic, and his reading, as might have been inferred from the size of his library, was enormous. The purchase of books was his single extravagance. One whole floor [of his house] was given up to them, and in spite of this they overflowed into hall and drawing room."[19]

Parker owned more than twelve thousand volumes; yet he led a far more energetic life than most bibliophiles. "I did not answer before for I had no time—and a hundred letters now lie before me not replied to," he wrote in April of 1856 to his friend William Herndon, the law partner of the up-and-coming Illinois politician Abraham Lincoln. "When I tell you that I have lectured 84 times since Nov. 1, and preached at home every Sunday but 2 when I was in Ohio—and never an old sermon, and have had 6 meetings a month at my own house—and have written more than 1000 letters—besides doing a variety of other work belonging to a Minister and a Scholar—you may judge that I must economize minutes and often neglect a much valued friend."[20]

The person Parker valued most in the world was his wife—the former Lydia Cabot. Julia Ward Howe, who was enamored of Parker in a chaste and controlled way, wrote cattily that Lydia Parker "came near being very handsome. . . . A certain want of physical maturity seemed to have prevented her from blossoming into full beauty." Parker himself seems to have been considerably less aware of Lydia's physical drawbacks than Julia. He often called Lydia by the nickname he'd bestowed: Bear. He told friends that the pet term for his gentle, delicate wife sprang from his love of paradox. He decorated his home with miniature wood-carved and porcelain bears. The same image was painted on all the household's cups and plates. Parker's gold shirt stud bore the impress of a bear. One Christmas he gave his wife a fine silver candlestick in the shape of a bear and staff.

The only unhappy part of the marriage was the couple's childlessness. "What are you?" Parker would ask his wife. "A bear," she would answer. "And what must a bear do to be saved?" he'd ask. "Have pups," she would answer. Parker eventually became so desperate for a child that he asked his friend Howe, who had four children by 1853, permission to adopt the next. For reasons known only to himself, Howe neither said yea or nay to Parker, nor did he inform his wife of the request. Through most of 1854 Parker waited eagerly while Julia Ward Howe proceeded through her fifth pregnancy. Parker told Howe that he planned to name the child Theodore if a boy, Theodora if a girl. Julia Howe, who would have none of the scheme once she finally heard of it, named her daughter Maude.

☆

Not long after Theodore Parker's death in 1860, Thomas Wentworth Higginson summed up his old friend in an obituary published in the *Atlantic*. "In the midst of his greatest cares there never was a moment when he was not all too generous of his time, his wisdom, and his money," wrote Higginson. "Borne down by the accumulation of labors, grudging, as a student grudges, the precious hour that once lost can never be won back, he yet was always holding himself at the call of some poor criminal at the Police Office, or some sick girl in a suburban town, not of his recognized parish perhaps, but longing for the ministry of the only preacher who had touched her soul. Not a mere wholesale reformer, he wore out his life by retailing its great influences to the poorest comer. Not generous in money only, —though the readiness of his beneficence in that direction had few equals, —he always hastened past that minor bestowal to ask if there were not some other added gift possible, some personal service or correspondence, some life-blood, in short, to be lavished in some other form, to eke out the already liberal donation of dollars.

"There is an impression that he was unforgiving," Higginson reminded the readers of the *Atlantic*. "Unforgetting he certainly was; for he had no power of forgetfulness, whether for good or evil. He had none of that convenient oblivion which in softer natures covers sin and saintliness with one common, careless pall. So long as a man persisted in a wrong attitude before God or man, there was no day so laborious or exhausting, no night so long or drowsy, but Theodore Parker's unsleeping memory stood on guard full-armed, ready to do battle at a moment's warning. This is generally known; but what may not be known so widely is, that, the moment the adversary lowered his spear, were it for only an inch or an instant, that moment Theodore Parker's weapons were down and his arms open. Make the slightest concession, give him but the least excuse to love you, and never was there such promptness in forgiving. His friends found it sometimes harder to justify his mildness than his severity. I confess that I, with others, have often felt inclined to criticize a certain caustic tone of his, in private talk, when the name of an offender was alluded to; but I have also felt almost indignant at his lenient good-nature to that very person, let him once show the smallest symptom of contrition, or seek, even in the clumsiest way, or for the most selfish purpose, to disarm his generous antagonist. His forgiveness in such cases was more exuberant than his wrath had ever been."[21]

5

FUGITIVES

ONE PARTICULARLY FAIR autumn Sunday in 1850, a larger than normal crowd poured into Boston's Melodeon Theater to hear Theodore Parker's sermon. It had been announced that Parker's topics would be the new federal fugitive slave law and Daniel Webster, the previously revered Whig senator from Massachusetts who in his last great effort to preserve the Union voted for passage of the despised measure. "I was helped to hate slavery by the lips of that great intellect," shouted Parker, pounding his fist down on his lectern as he attacked Webster. "And now that he takes back his words, and comes himself to be slavery's slave, I hate it tenfold harder, because it made a bondman out of that proud, powerful nature." Two years later, upon the death of Webster in the late autumn of 1852, people would once again crowd the Melodeon to hear Parker eulogize Webster and revisit the crime of the fugitive slave measure. "Do men now mourn for him, the great man eloquent?" asked Parker. "I put on sackcloth long ago. . . . I mourned when the fugitive slave bill passed Congress, and the same cannons which have just fired minute-guns for him fired also one hundred rounds of joy at the forging of a new fetter for the fugitive's foot . . . . O Webster!

Webster! would God that I had died for thee!"[1] Returning home late for dinner after listening to Parker's final speech on Webster, Julia Ward Howe announced: "Let no one find fault. I have just heard the greatest thing I ever shall hear!"[2]

Parker was not alone in condemning Webster. William Henry Seward, senator from New York, who had opposed the fugitive slave law, dryly remarked that the "moral sense" and "conscience of the age" had outgrown Webster. The normally reserved Emerson wrote in his journal: "The word *liberty* in the mouth of a Webster sounds like the word *love* in the mouth of a courtesan." Elsewhere he asked, "Could Mr. Webster obtain now a vote in Massachusetts for the poorest municipal office? Well, is not this a loss inevitable to a bad law—a law no man can countenance or abet the execution of, without loss of all self-respect, and forfeiting forever the name of gentleman? . . . Union is a delectable thing, and so is wealth, and so is life, but they may all cost too much if they cost honor."[3] Longfellow wrote that Webster was "fallen, fallen from his high esteem." Horace Mann gave a speech announcing, "Webster is a fallen star! Lucifer descended from Heaven." And John Greenleaf Whittier eulogized the pre-Compromise Webster: "When faith is lost, when honor dies, the man is dead!"

The fact that the fugitive slave law was the fulcrum of a series of compromise measures—Henry Clay's Compromise of 1850—that included the admittance of California into the Union as a free state and the banishment of the slave trade (though not slavery itself) from the District of Columbia did little to make it easier for the antislavery community to accept. To many, the fugitive slave law was the ultimate insult: the final proof of the futility of political abolitionism. For radical disunion abolitionists such as William Lloyd Garrison, it provided bitter satisfaction in proving the fundamental flaw in the Constitutional Union: the fact that it enabled the Slave Power majority in the Senate to impose upon free states a law meant to buttress and extend what Parker called "the thousand mile chain" of the peculiar institution.

The fugitive slave law entitled bounty hunters to take custody of and return to the South any runaway found in any free state. It went so far as to say that children of female runaways (even if born in a free state of a free father) could be claimed by slaveholders and returned to bondage. Under the statute, there were to be no trials for fugitive slaves—not even a hearing on a habeas corpus writ. Affidavits taken in slave states were admitted as evidence without cross-examination or rebuttal testimony by those facing rendition. U.S. commissioners specially appointed by the federal courts decided upon claimants' rights to fugitive "property." And there was no appeal of any commissioner's opinion. Commissioners were paid $10 for every instance where the seized individual was returned to slavery, but only $5 for cases where the remanded person was set free. (The rationale was that more paperwork was involved in the former instance.) The penalty for inhibiting the rendition of fugitive slaves could be up to six months in prison and a $1,000 fine.

Four years before what Parker called "the formal federal endorsement of kidnapping as an enterprise in the fugitive slave law," both Parker and Howe were appointed members of a committee of vigilance formed with no particular sense of urgency to give general aid to fugitive slaves in and around Boston.[4] "You are the chairman I think of the 'committee of vigilance' & therefore I will [send] you a word by way of suggestion," Parker wrote Howe at the end of September in 1846. "I suppose we are to be a committee of *vigilance* & not of *dormitance* & therefore it becomes us to be up & doing. It seems to me that we must (or should) have a full meeting of the committee as soon as possible to determine on the course to be pursued. . . . Then it seems to me that we ought 1. *to propose & publish a Proclamation,* setting forth our intention . . . to aid all fugitive slaves as fast as they may arrive at Boston . . . to find them places of employment. . . . 2. to write a letter to governor Briggs, asking him if he will remember the national sin of slavery in his future Proclamations (for Thanksgiving and Fast-days), if he will strive to promote the abolition of slavery in the District of Columbia & in Territories, if he will endeavor (also by means of the Legislature) to help forward a change of the Constitution of the U.S. so that the free states which choose may be free from all part & lot in the sin of slavery. . . . It seems to me that we want *action* to make the 'Revolution' keep."[5]

Everything Parker outlined for the vigilance committee of 1846 was essentially peaceful. Up until the passage of the fugitive slave law, Parker tacitly supported Garrisonian pacificism, asking people to rescue slaves "with only the arms their mother gave them." In a sermon delivered shortly after the enactment of the law, however, Parker gave his first pub-, lic endorsement to violent resistance. "The man who attacks me to reduce me to slavery," said Parker, "in that moment of attack alienates his right to life, and if I were the fugitive, and could escape in no other way, I would kill him with as little compunction as I would drive a mosquito from my face." In this same sermon he said that it was the "natural duty" of all Americans to rescue fugitives being returned to slavery by federal officials, "peaceably if they can, forcibly if they must, but by all means to do it."[6]

A few weeks later, when Parker officiated at the wedding of the fugitive slaves Ellen and William Craft in a ceremony conducted at his home, he gave a blatant demonstration of his new radicalism. Ellen and William were in hiding from three slave-catchers who'd come to Boston intent on returning them to a Georgia plantation. In the midst of the service, Parker laid a Bible and a sword on the table. After testing the sword and "finding the blade had a good temper, stiff enough and yet springy withal; the point was sharp," he gave it to the groom and charged him to kill any "United States officer or slaveowner" who tried to return either Ellen or himself to slavery. "'With this sword, I thee wed,'" Parker wrote, "suited the circumstances of that bridal." Subsequent to the wedding, when William was moved to another secret location and Ellen was left with the Parkers for several days, Parker wrote his sermons with yet another sword—the sword handed down from his Minuteman grandfather—ready in the open drawer under his inkstand. There was a loaded pistol in the flap of the desk, a cap on the nipple.[7]

While taking the first precaution of hiding William Craft and his new wife, the rejuvenated vigilance committee did not let its activities stop there. The committee went on to systematically harass and intimidate the slave-catchers. With some sense of irony, Parker and Howe engaged a black attorney to obtain warrants against the slavers, charging them with the malicious slander of William Craft. As a consequence, several

Boston politicos with Hunker ties and lucrative posts as U.S. commissioners were obliged to furnish bail in the amount of $10,000 to keep the would-be slave-captors themselves out of the Boston City Jail. Next, Parker led a crowd of some sixty armed abolitionists to accost the slave-catchers as they sat eating dinner at the United States Hotel. While the ominous delegation lounged in the lobby, Parker told the slave-catchers "that they were not safe another night. I had stood between them and violence once, I would not promise to do it again. They were considerably frightened." And they left town that same evening.[8]

Parker was soon joined by more leading citizens in suggesting the possibility of armed resistance to the fugitive slave law. Even the moderate Charles Francis Adams, Sr.—the son and grandson of presidents, a "Conscience" Whig soon to be appointed ambassador to the Court of St. James—said that though he did not favor "irregular action" against the law, he was sure it could never be enforced in Massachusetts. If the Congress and president of the United States insisted on bringing "the sense of right in every man's bosom in direct conflict with the law," wrote Adams, they must not be surprised to see the law disregarded. The system did nothing but knock itself off a pedestal when it demanded that its citizens assist in capturing and enslaving their fellow men.[9]

Charles Francis Adams was correct in foretelling the black magic the fugitive slave law would work on Parker and other abolitionists. The harassment of the slave-catchers at the United States Hotel was to be just the first instance of what Adams refererred to as "irregular action" against slavery and the statutes that promoted it. Through the next nine years, the operations supported by Parker, Howe, and their brethren would become more and more "irregular," moving subtly and slowly from defense to offense, and leading (almost inevitably, it seems in retrospect) to John Brown's armed attack on the federal armory and arsenal at Harpers Ferry.

For the moment, late-night meetings of the vigilance committee—which now included no less than three future members of the Secret Six, in the persons of Theodore Parker, Samuel Gridley Howe, and Thomas Wentworth Higginson—were held in Parker's home at 1 Exeter Street. There, with two guards watching the front and back doors and several others keeping the street outside under surveillance, the group made plans for sudden and secret escapes by train, boat, and coach. They also mapped strategies to challenge the fugitive slave law on a case-by-case basis in court. And they made long, secret lists of men, white and black—nineteenth-century Minutemen—who might be quickly armed and activated to do whatever was necessary to stop slave-catchers from accomplishing their ends. With such an agenda as this, the committee was already committing a federal crime simply by meeting.

In February of 1851, the committee became involved when one Frederic Wilkins (or Jenkins), a runaway slave who lived in Boston under the name of Shadrach, was seized by the United States marshal. With the approval of the committee, Lewis Hayden—a runaway slave from Kentucky whose house on Southac (now Phillips) Street was a station of the Underground Railroad—mounted a rescue. Hayden led twenty black men into Shadrach's rendition hearing. The outnumbered guards did nothing when Hayden's contingent seized Shadrach and rushed him outside "like a black squall" into a waiting carriage. Weeks later, when Shadrach was safely in Canada, Hayden and several of his confederates were put on trial for riot. The case ended in a mistrial when one juror (secretly a confederate himself) held out for acquittal.[10]

☆

One of the younger members of the vigilance committee was the minister Thomas Wentworth Higginson. Still in his late twenties when the fugitive slave law was passed, Higginson (who went by the name Wentworth) was articulate and athletic. He came from one of the most distinguished families on the eastern seaboard. Higginson was descended on his mother's side from John Wentworth, the first royal governor of New Hampshire. Through his mother, Higginson was also connected to Boston's influential Storrow family. On his father's side he claimed descent from Francis Higginson, the English nonconformist clergyman who emigrated to Salem in 1629 and whose book *New-England's Plantation* enjoyed something of a vogue in Britain during the 1630s.

Born in 1823, Higginson was raised quite literally within the shadow of Harvard University, on Kirkland Street (also known as Professors' Row) in Cambridge. His father, Stephen Higginson, Jr., was an affluent federalist merchant ruined by the Jefferson embargo who was subsequently appointed bursar of Harvard College.[11] Higginson's childhood playmates included Margaret Fuller and James Russell Lowell. He was only thirteen years old—the youngest in his class—when he entered Harvard just a few weeks after the graduation of Henry Thoreau in 1837.

Thomas Wentworth Higginson in 1857. Photo courtesy Massachusetts Historical Society.

Edward Everett Hale—a nephew of Edward Everett, great-nephew of Nathan Hale, and future author of *The Man Without a Country*—was a fellow undergraduate and a lifelong friend. Like Hale, Higginson went on to attend the Harvard Divinity School. He then married into the influential Channing family of ministers, physicians, and poets. At his ordination as a Unitarian minister in September of 1847, William Henry Channing, a cousin by marriage, preached the sermon. The eminent James Freeman Clarke gave the charge, exhorting his young brother to reform by construction, not destruction.[12]

Higginson was an activist minister, as a journal note attests. "A pure earnest aim is not enough," he wrote. "Intellectual as well as moral armor must be bright for I know I shall have to sustain a warfare. I feel that if I do justice to my own powers (i.e., if I do my duty) I cannot remain in the background. . . . Preaching alone I should love, but I feel inwardly that something more will be sought of me—An aesthetic life—

how beautiful—but the life of a Reformer, a People's Guide 'battling for the right'—glorious, but Oh how hard!" The list of things the earnest young Higginson wanted to eradicate, change, or improve was a long one. Writing to his fiancé, Higginson, then twenty-one years old, gave a ringing endorsement to the cause of women's suffrage. "I do go for the rights of women as far as an equal education and an equal share in government goes . . . ," he wrote. "I think it a monstrous absurdity to talk of a democratic government and universal suffrage and yet exclude one-half the inhabitants without any ground of incapacity to plead. . . . I think there is no possible argument on the other side excepting prejudice." He was also an advocate of trade unions, free public education, and temperance. "I have read the articles on the organization of labor," he wrote, "and were I a rich man would have 30,000 printed and distributed."

Then, of course, there was the antislavery movement, within which Higginson quickly migrated to the radical fringe. "I might have recorded on my birthday or New Year's Day, my final self-enrollment in the ranks of the American Non-Jurors or Disunion Abolitionists," Higginson wrote in his journal in early 1846, "and my determination not only not to vote for any officer who must take an oath to support the U.S. Constitution, but also to use whatever means may lie in my power to promote the Dissolution of the Union. . . . To Disunion I now subscribe in the full expectation that a time is coming which may expose to obloquy and danger even the most insignificant of the adherents to such a cause."[13] Higginson's friend Henry David Thoreau also dreamed of dismantling the country and the Constitution that sanctioned slavery. "My thoughts are murder to the State," wrote Thoreau in his journal. "I endeavor in vain to observe nature; my thoughts involuntarily go plotting against the State. I trust that all just men will so conspire."[14] While political abolitionists sought to work within the system to eradicate slavery through legal means, disunion abolitionists had given up on the system and condemned the Constitution as a tool of the slave power majority in congress. By renouncing the Constitution, disunion abolitionists sought to hold true to the ideals of the Declaration of Independence.

It was a time when the word *treason* was employed with great subver-

William Lloyd Garrison in the 1850s. Photo courtesy Massachusetts Historical Society.

sive relish. Writing of John Brown to the Boston financier and abolitionist John Murray Forbes just a few months before Harpers Ferry, Samuel Gridley Howe would say with happy confidence that Brown was formulating "what might perhaps seem at first to be treason."[15] In a note to Higginson more than a year before the raid, Sanborn said, "The Union is evidently on its last legs. . . . Treason will not be treason that much longer, but patriotism."[16] William Lloyd Garrison believed the term *traitor* to be a mark of high honor. "The fanaticism and infidelity and treason which are hateful to traffickers in slaves and the souls of men must be well pleasing to God and are indications of true loyalty to the cause of liberty," said Garrison when introducing Theodore Parker before a New York antislavery meeting in 1856. "I have the pleasure of introducing to you a very excellent fanatic, a very good infidel, and a first rate traitor, in the person of Theodore Parker of Boston." All the Founding Fathers had once been branded traitors by an unjust establishment power structure. So too, before them, had the Plymouth and Salem Puritans to whom so many of the Boston abolitionists traced their roots. For Higginson, Parker, Howe, and those like them, there was no small amount of honor attached to the word *traitor* when applied in the right context.

Garrison proudly called himself a traitor for decades. But for all his condemnation of the Constitution as a tool of the Congress's slave-power majority, and all his rhetoric of disunion, Garrison's pacifist (he called it "non-combatant") approach to treason had little appeal for some, among them the always impatient Higginson. Writing of the early fugitive-slave period in Boston in the late 1840s, Higginson would look back and remember how frustrated he felt. "While the air was full of revolution, almost all the revolutionists were hampered by reverence for law, or else by non-resistance. Most of the Garrisonian disunion abolitionists were non-combatants on principle; while, on the other hand, the voting [Liberty Party] abolitionists had a controlling desire to keep within the law."[17]

Handsome and well-spoken, Higginson was viewed by some as having great potential as a politician. Therefore Higginson broke his disunion pledge in the fall of 1848 and briefly joined with the dwindling number of political abolitionists who still believed it possible to eliminate slavery by working within the system. At the urging of Charles Sumner and others, he accepted the nomination of the newly formed Free Soil Party to run for Congress from Newburyport, where he was minister of the Unitarian church. Spearheaded by Salmon P. Chase of Ohio, the Free Soil Party was a spirited coalition of rebellious, anti-Webster Whigs and Democrats united less to abolish slavery in the South than to keep it out of the western territories. "Free Soil doesn't prosper much in this town," Higginson wrote from Newburyport to one of his brothers.[18] Not only did Higginson lose the election, but his frequent sermons against slavery undermined his position with his congregation, including as it did many ship owners and sea captains whose fortunes were tied to the export of plantation cotton. Higginson was forced to resign his pulpit in the autumn of 1849, after just two years as minister.

He continued to preach to that small segment of his congregation that followed him to a rented hall. ("I was amused yesterday," he wrote his mother, "by reading in a note of Dr. Young's *Chronicles* that when Francis Higginson, the ancient, became a non-conformist 'he was accordingly excluded from his pulpit; but a lectureship was established for him, in which he was maintained by the voluntary contributions of the inhabitants'; so I have good precedents."[19]) With extra time on his hands, he began to pay more attention to his writing than before, publishing essays and poems in a range of magazines.

6

RIOT

ONE CURMUDGEONLY yet extremely self-confident man sat relatively quiet at the meetings of the vigilance committee. The sober, methodical George Luther Stearns was capable of spending hours without comment while others hotly debated strategies and procedures at Parker's dining table. When he finally (and succinctly) stated his point of view, he always did so in the terse, reasoned, sensible manner that was his hallmark. All the agitated and often loud voices in the room stopped at the sound of his restrained, soft one; all quieted to catch his valuable words. His peers recognized him as unique: a man possessed by the same fierce rage and demand for justice as they, but with a point of view moderated by a useful pragmatism. Stearns, after all, had made a fortune through a lifetime of weighing and taking shrewd risks. After careful and due consideration, he had embarked upon radical, innovative steps in business that served him well. And now, in the face of the fugitive slave law, the thoughtful Stearns had decided to abandon political abolition in favor of more direct action. But even this he would do slowly, methodically, and at least with a veneer of reasonableness.

In his midforties, a bit wide about the waist, Stearns suffered from

chronic bronchitis so badly that
he always wore a long, full
beard—one that his friend John
Brown would later mimic—in
order to protect his chest from
the cold. He dressed in expensive
suits custom-made for him by his
London tailor, sported shoes
with fine leather uppers, and
hated exercise in all its forms.
(He often called his carriage to
take him the length of one short
block.) Stearns was in many
ways the epitome of conservative
affluence (and downright opu-
lence) and was a most unlikely
revolutionary. But the United
States in the mid-1850s was full
of unlikely revolutionaries.

*Newspaper portrait of George Luther
Stearns published shortly after the fiasco
at Harpers Ferry. Author's collection.*

"The fugitive slave law af-
fected Mr. Stearns like the blow of an assailant," recalled his son. "He
purchased a revolver and declared that no fugitive negro should be taken
from his premises while he lived."[1] Stearns's Medford mansion became a
much-frequented station of the Underground Railroad. He hid one
black man beneath the floorboards of his bathroom for a week before
being able to pass him on to Canada. And he later made headlines when
he defiantly brought the same man back again, setting him up as a barber in Harvard Square. The businessman Stearns wrote that he believed
entrepreneurship to be the first, best hope for all capable blacks just as it
was for all capable whites. The barber was to be neither the first nor the
last smart young fellow, black or white, whom Stearns would pick from
the crowd and declare too clever to work for the profit of others. And he
was neither the first nor the last that Stearns would underwrite and then
coach in the ways of fiscal success, in which he was an authority.

Stearns was born in Medford, Massachusetts, in 1809. His beginnings were modest. He clerked in the store of an uncle at age fifteen, then worked in a ship-chandlering warehouse on Boston's India Wharf. When still in his twenties, he invented a new, economical method to produce linseed oil. Stearns built a mill based on his vision using $20,000 in borrowed funds. Half the money came from a Medford deacon; $5,000 came from his mother's wealthy Boston cousins, the Lawrences. And another $5,000 came from his mother, who mortgaged her only principal asset, her house, to muster the investment. All the loans were cleared, and the operation declared profitable, within three years. Stearns then returned to chandlery, this time as an investor. And he acquired New England rights to a patent for flexible lead pipe. He was soon clearing from $15,000 to $20,000 per year on this investment alone.

In the late 1840s, Stearns somewhat rashly tried to corner the market on lead and failed disastrously. He wound up facing bankruptcy and pondering suicide. Yet he endured. Based on his reputation for making good on debts, his creditors gave him time to resolve his affairs. Soon his financial position was stronger than ever. He married, became a father, and acquired a fine house. His office at 129 Milk Street was ornately decorated with classic and contemporary sculpture, a particular passion for him and his wife. Stearns sat on the boards of numerous philanthropic institutions throughout Boston, including the Massachusetts General Hospital, the Boston Orphans' Asylum, and the Perkins Institute. He gave liberally to a host of charities, his name appearing on contributor lists for libraries, halfway houses, and public monuments.

Stearns claimed friendship with virtually all the leading northeastern abolitionists. His wife was a niece of Lydia Maria Child. Among the regular guests at his large oak dining table were Charles Sumner, Wendell Phillips, and Frederick Douglass. Lewis Hayden came to supper and dazzled Stearns's sons with tales of moonlit escapes through the woods and swamps of the South. "I would mortgage all I own," the inspired Stearns wrote Howe after Hayden's visit, "to see the end of slavery. I would give every farthing to support any venture that promised success. For such a thing was the money coined, and for nothing less."[2]

☆

The impetuous and impulsive Thomas Wentworth Higginson, who would come to dislike Stearns's voice of reason, got his first taste of it in April of 1851. It was then that a seventeen-year-old fugitive from Georgia by the name of Thomas Sims was arrested in Boston for rendition to the South. Stearns, Higginson, Parker, and Howe were among those who gathered in William Lloyd Garrison's seedy *Liberator* office to ponder—and, at Stearns's urging to abandon—a brazen plan proposed by Higginson for Sims's rescue. (Steadfastly noncombatant, Garrison sat nearby, refusing to discuss the armed attack of the courthouse that Higginson loudly urged. Garrison instead occupied himself at his type bench, painstakingly composing an editorial about Sims and his predicament.) A letter Higginson addressed to the editors of the *Newburyport Evening News* revealed the scrutiny he had given to Sims's security arrangements, seeking a hole in the armor.

"One would think your readers would come up to Boston to see for themselves what is going on," Higginson wrote home to peaceful Newburyport. "No panorama of rocks and rivers can equal the living panorama of our institutions, now on exhibition. The Courthouse in chains, under which chief justices bow their heads in passing. Police officers marshalled and drilled, with drawn cutlasses, every day at daybreak in Court Square. The third story of the building converted into a slave-jail, with irons at the windows. A trial proceeding, from which spectators are excluded without a permit from the U.S. Marshal, and to which even reporters sometimes find it hard to gain admission. . . . There are between one and two hundred armed police-men in and around the courthouse. The U.S. Court room is up two high and narrow flights of stairs, every turn of which is guarded. . . . Six men guard the door of the court room. The prisoner, a weak slender boy of 17, sits with two powerful men on either side and five more in the seat behind him, while none but his counsel can approach him in front."[3]

Stearns successfully argued that the vigilance committee was dramatically outgunned and outmanned. In the end, the only force the committee would bring to bear in the Sims case was free speech and active

Samuel May, Sr., leading northeastern abolitionist. Photo courtesy Massachusetts Historical Society.

protest. At three o'clock in the morning on April 13, a heavily guarded Sims was walked to the schooner in Boston harbor that would carry him back to slavery. Several committeemen, including Theodore Parker, Wendell Phillips, and Nathaniel Bowditch, marched behind the procession bearing an improvised coffin draped in black. Parker was to turn the anniversary of the surrender of Sims into an annual day of mourning. "Four citizens of Massachusetts have been sold into slavery in New Orleans lately," wrote Parker to Howe in February of 1852. "Don't you think we ought to take some public notice of it? Again, I think there ought to be a public meeting at Faneuil Hall on the Anniversary of the rendition of Sims."[4]

Across the North, abolitionists began taking more and more strident measures to oppose and undermine the fugitive slave law. In Syracuse, during the fall of 1852, Gerrit Smith became one of the first men to successfully take up arms against the law. In an uncharacteristic moment of self-confidence and inspired leadership, Smith headed an armed mob of preachers, freedmen, and abolitionist farmers in a successful move to rescue the fugitive slave Jerry McHenry. With Samuel May, Sr., Smith was at the forefront of the crowd as it attacked the Syracuse police station where McHenry sat, awaiting his rendition. Smith stood tall in the midst of the firefight as the windows of the police station were blown out. He calmly took control of the room where the police marshals were held captive, in chains, until McHenry was successfully spirited away.[5] Smith (who, it must be remembered, owned most of the town) was never charged in what came to be called "the Jerry rescue." In fact, shortly afterward he was elected to a term in Congress on the strength of his participation.

John Brown stopped briefly at North Elba during the early autumn of 1850 and was there on the day the fugitive slave measure became law. In early November, shortly after enactment of the measure, Brown once again left his family at the Adirondack farm and returned to Springfield to deal with a host of lawsuits against his floundering wool business. He wrote to his sons John, Jason, and Frederick—who were taking care of Perkins & Brown's large flock near Akron, Ohio—that he had different claims facing him, his share of which amounted to some $40,000, "& if [I] lose will leave me nice & flat."[6] Through the next four years, his life would revolve around the virtually constant, ritualized torture of giving and listening to testimony meant to chronicle the many large and irreversible failures that were the hallmark of his professional past. Suits were brought against him in the courts of New York, Massachusetts, and Pennsylvania. Every single one of the suits called into question Brown's veracity and trustworthiness.

An upstate New York wool farmer by the name of Henry Warren alleged that Brown had paid him several thousand dollars less than the worth of the wool he'd entrusted to Brown for sale. Conversely, the Burlington Mills Company of Vermont filed a $60,000 suit in Boston alleging that they had continually been billed by Brown for a higher grade of wool than that which he provided. In New York City, the Pickersgill Company charged that they had advanced Brown many thousands of dollars more for transporting their wool to England than what they received back after the European sale. And several Pennsylvania sheep farmers also filed a suit (this one in Pittsburgh) citing a breach of a promise for payment by Brown. Using Springfield as his base of operations, Brown commuted regularly between Troy, Boston, Manhattan, and Pittsburgh, where he attended court proceedings with the lawyers Perkins had retained in each district.

At Springfield, Brown organized a branch of the United States League of Gileadites, a society of black fugitives banded together to resist the fugitive slave measure. At secret meetings with dozens of black men and women, Brown set out specific strategies for threatening and killing any federal officers or slave-hunters who attempted to return Springfield fugitives to the South. One night Brown ominously discussed the necessity of executing traitors. As he spoke, remembered one participant in the meeting, his piercing eyes moved from one black face to another and seemed to be able to read what was written on the heart of each man and each woman.

There was no discussion, no debate, no election of officers. Brown was the sole commander, tactician, and ideologue. He no longer had any command of his business life due to his long string of blunders. His professional self was largely under the authority of any number of civil claims courts. And his senior partner Perkins had, of course, removed him from virtually all decision-making vis-à-vis the current business of the firm. But in fighting slavery Brown had one last chance to prove himself the consummate, albeit bloodthirsty, manager. Through the Gileadites, he would control the destinies of others though he realized he'd lost control of his own. He would exact God's justice and wield power over life and death. Something in him needed to do this; something in him told him God had chosen him to do this.

Brown wrote an explicit charter for the Springfield Gileadites that all forty-four members were made to sign. The document prescribed mercilessness. "Should one of your number be arrested," read the paper entitled "Words of Advice," "you must collect together as quickly as possible, so as to outnumber your adversaries who are taking an active part against you. Let no able-bodied man appear in the group unequipped, or with his weapons exposed to view: let that be understood beforehand. . . . *Let the first blow be the signal for all to engage; and when engaged do not do your work by halves, but make clean work with your enemies.* . . . A lasso might possibly be applied to a slave catcher for once with good effect. Hold on to your weapons, and never be persuaded to leave them, part with them, or have them far away from you."[7]

The black writer William Wells Brown visited Springfield in June of 1854 and found Brown's group at arms, ready to fight a group of slavers who were rumored to be in the area. Sentries were posted throughout all the black neighborhoods. Women were organized in "boiling water brigades," intent on scalding any slave-catchers who tried to accost them. "Returning to the depot," wrote William Brown, "to take the train for Boston, we found there some ten or fifteen blacks all armed to the teeth and swearing vengeance upon the heads of any who should attempt to take them. True, the slave-catchers had been there. But the authorities, foreseeing a serious outbreak, advised them to leave, and feeling alarmed for their personal safety, these disturbers of the peace had left in the evening train for New York. No fugitive slave was ever afterwards disturbed at Springfield."[8]

☆

Thomas Wentworth Higginson moved from Newburyport to take up duties as pastor for the Free Church of Worcester in 1854. Here, he told a friend, there were "radicals of all descriptions" who would support his angry denunciations of slavery. It was a congregation that understood completely when Higginson became what Henry Thoreau described as "the only Harvard Phi Beta Kappa, Unitarian minister, and master of seven languages who has led a storming party against a federal

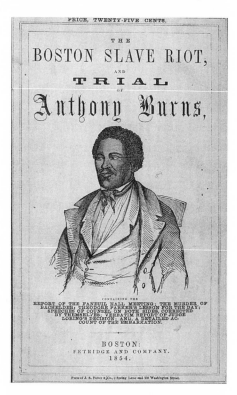

Anthony Burns pictured on the cover of a book about the Boston Slave Riot of 1854. Courtesy Massachusetts Historical Society.

bastion with a battering ram in his hands."[9] The event, known thereafter as the "Burns riot," occurred on Friday, May 26, 1854.

The United States commissioner in charge of the rendition of Anthony Burns—a fugitive slave who worked as a presser in a tailor shop on Brattle Street— knew enough to expect trouble from Boston's abolitionists. The vigilance committee had already promised to intercede in the case and win Burns's freedom "by every and any means necessary."[10] Anthony Burns, they declared, would not be another Thomas Sims. In response to the abolitionists' threat, the Boston city marshal's guard was beefed up. An unattractive collection of criminals, informers, pimps, jailbirds, and gamblers was deputized. Richard Henry Dana, Jr., who appeared in court as amicus curiae for Burns, remarked that since the marshal had recruited his deputies "people have not felt it necessary to lock their doors at night, the brothels are tenanted only by women, fighting dogs and racing horses have been unemployed."[11] A somewhat whimsical check by Theodore Parker revealed that more than a third of the new deputies had criminal records. When several deputies threatened Parker with murder, he responded with characteristic bravado. Parker sat in the middle of them during Burns's hearing. "I sat between men who had newly sworn to kill me, my garments touching theirs," he wrote. "The malaria of their rum and tobacco was an offense in my face. I saw their weapons and laughed as I looked at these drunken rowdies in their coward eye."[12]

A letter from Wendell Phillips notified Higginson of "another kidnapping case . . . you'll *come* of course." Phillips signed the missive "in no hope," but the infuriated Higginson was not so pessimistic. "The man must be taken from [his cell in] the Courthouse," wrote Higginson. The effort must have behind it "the momentum of a public meeting. . . . Let all be in readiness; let a picked body be distributed near the Courthouse and Square; then send some loud-voiced speaker, who would appear in the gallery of Faneuil Hall and announce that there was a mob of negroes attacking the Courthouse; let a speaker, previously warned, — Phillips, if possible—accept the opportunity promptly and send the whole meeting pell-mell to Court Square, ready to fall behind the leaders and bring out the slave." A placard headed "A Man Kidnapped" was posted outside Faneuil Hall, calling for a meeting the following Friday. "Shall he be plunged into the hell of Virginia slavery by a Massachusetts judge of probate?" asked the placard.

Faneuil Hall. Parker called it a sacred place. He said that if there ever was a spot haunted by the spirits of the Revolutionary fathers, Faneuil Hall was it. The large eighteenth-century building, with its straight-backed seats and rows of Doric columns, was to Parker a holy temple within which to seek communion with Hancock, Adams, and the other fiery orators who made their first, eloquent public appeals for independence within its walls. It was at Parker's suggestion that John Swift, abolitionist and attorney, summoned Faneuil Hall's meaning as part of his, the first speech of the Burns protest meeting. At the outset of a program carefully scripted to both inspire and rationalize a courthouse raid, the opportunity for which would shortly present itself, Swift incited the crowd to go from Faneuil Hall, the "Cradle of Liberty . . . to the tomb of Liberty—the courthouse" to demand Burns's freedom. Higginson, who was to lead the attack on the court building, attended the first portion of the Faneuil Hall meeting and heard Swift's speech. He told a friend later that the Burns protest was "the largest gathering I ever saw in the hall. The platform was covered with men; the galleries, the floor, even the outer stairways, were absolutely filled with a solid audience. . . . I never saw such enthusiasm. . . ."[13]

Speaking after Swift, Samuel Gridley Howe introduced a defiant resolution, unanimously approved: "That which is not just is not law, and that which is not law ought not to be obeyed. . . . No man's freedom is safe unless all men are free." Wendell Phillips declared that "there is no law in Massachusetts, and when law ceases the people may act in their own sovereignty." And Theodore Parker, addressing the audience as "fellow subjects of Virginia," said, "Gentlemen, I am a clergyman and a man of peace. But there is a means, and there is an end; liberty is an end, and sometimes peace is not the means towards it. . . . In this law the bulwarks of liberty are all broken, and it is a base libel to call it a constitutional law. We must trample it under our feet. It expects and provides for disobedience; God forbid that it should be disappointed. . . . We must interrupt the slaveholders and say that the fugitive who has breathed Massachusetts air shall never go back. Many have been here from twelve to twenty years, and we are not going to people southern plantations with men born in Massachusetts."[14]

A few blocks away, the mood was tense as Higginson and his small group of confederates—most of them from his Worcester congregation—lurked in the shadows by the courthouse. The wait for the Faneuil Hall crowd seemed to go on for-

Higginson's friend Lewis Hayden, a fugitive slave from Kentucky who was conspicuous in both the Shadrach and Burns episodes and was eventually elected to serve in the Massachusetts State Legislature. Photo courtesy Massachusetts Historical Society.

ever. Then, finally, there was "a rush of running figures, like the sweep of a wave." Higginson was relieved that his comrades had at last arrived. But a second glance "brought the conviction to disappointment. We had the froth and scum of the meeting, the fringe of idlers on its edge. The men on the platform, the real nucleus of the great gathering, were far in the rear, perhaps were still clogged in the hall."[15] Although Higginson did not care for the quality of his recruits, he had to either press on with the attack immediately or abandon it forever. The loud mob had alerted Burns's guards.

Higginson's raiders seized a heavy beam (the banister from the steps of a nearby museum) and used it as a battering ram against the court's west door, springing the hinges and making an opening. A burst of gunfire from within sent many in the Faneuil Hall crowd fleeing. "You cowards, will you desert us now?" screamed Higginson just before he and two companions pushed in beyond the door that hung askew. A black man went in before Higginson; then went Higginson and his Worcester friend Martin Stowell. Inside, in half darkness, shots were exchanged. One deputy fell dead; a dozen more attacked Higginson and the other two men with clubs.

He wrote later that he wondered at the time why the blows did not hurt. A deputy slashed Higginson's chin with a saber. Blood ran from his face, but there was no pain. Miraculously, Higginson and his comrades managed to retreat back out of the door and down the courthouse steps. Lewis Hayden (the fugitive from Kentucky who rescued Shadrach) fired from the street at the pursuing police in order to cover the escape of Higginson and his two confederates. (Later, hearing that Hayden fired at one of the despised deputies but missed, a frustrated Parker would demand loudly, "Why didn't he hit him? Why didn't he hit him?"[16]) In the midst of his dash out and away from the building, Higginson saw the normally restrained and quiet Concord philosopher Bronson Alcott (father of Louisa May Alcott) breaking out of character, attempting to rally the crowd for another assault. Alcott stood alone on the steps of the courthouse, a cane in his hand, turning to cry to the retreating raiders, "Why are we not within?"[17]

7

REBELLION AGAINST TYRANTS IS OBEDIENCE TO GOD

"THERE HAS BEEN an attempt at rescue, and failed," wrote Higginson in a hurried note to his wife, Mary, from the Boston home of a Channing cousin, where he found refuge from the police. "I am not hurt, except a scratch on the face which will probably prevent me from doing anything more about it, lest I be recognized."[1]

He was back home at Worcester within two days of the riot. "Of course, I was in Boston on Friday night and had something to do with the demonstration in court . . . ," he wrote his mother. "That attack was a great thing for freedom, and will echo all over the country. It came within an inch of success at any rate. Of course, I was unarmed, hurt nobody but a door, and was unhurt myself but for some knocks and a scratch. . . . I am sorry for the death of the man [but] it is my clear conviction that he was killed by one of his own blundering comrades. . . . At any rate, they are making arrests, and I think it more than probable that I may come in for a share. [If I am arrested] I shall

consider it the highest honor yet attained by a Higginson." He assured
her that he would serve no time in jail. "I don't believe that any jury will
convict in this affair."[2] In two days, after speaking with several attorneys,
he was not so confident; and he wrote his mother to tell her so. "I think it
altogether probable, now, that I shall be arrested soon, imprisoned till the
trial and perhaps again after."[3]

Higginson remained at home in Worcester a week later while half
of Boston watched Anthony Burns march from the courthouse to the
waterfront, where a revenue cutter waited to take him south. The New
England Women's Rights Convention, meeting at the Melodeon Theater, adjourned so that Higginson's Worcester neighbor Abby Kelley
Foster and other delegates could join fifty thousand protesters standing
along the line of march. Flags all over the city hung at half-mast.
Buildings were draped in mourning cloth. Portraits of Pres. Franklin
Pierce were hung upside down out of windows. Two thousand federal
troops patrolled the line of march. The Marine band that walked
behind Burns mocked both him and the crowd by playing "Carry Me
Back to Old Virginny." Once aboard the revenue cutter, Burns
remarked, "There was a lot of folks to see a colored man walk through
the streets." The entire affair (the troops, the revenue cutter, the
cleanup after the crowd of onlookers) cost an estimated $100,000,
which, said Higginson cheerfully in a letter, made Burns "the most
expensive slave in the history of mankind."[4]

Higginson gave a sermon in his Worcester church the Sunday after
the extradition of Burns. His talk was entitled "Massachusetts in Mourning," and his theme was revolution. "You have imagined my subject
beforehand, for there is but one subject on which I could preach, or you
could listen, today," Higginson told his congregation. "Yet, how hard it is
to say one word of that. You do not ask, at a funeral, that the bereaved
mourners themselves should speak, but you call in one a little farther
removed, to utter words of comfort, if comfort there be. But today is, or
should be, to every congregation in Massachusetts, a day of funeral
service—we are all mourners—and what is there for me to say?"

Higginson reveled in the fact that the actions of himself and others at the courthouse had forced the federal government to virtually occupy Boston in order to inflict its will: much in the same way that the British had been forced to occupy the town two generations earlier to enforce an unjust tax. ". . . That first faint throb of Liberty [the attack on the courthouse] was a proud thing for Boston; Boston which was a scene so funereal a week after," said Higginson. "Men say the act of one Friday helped prepare for the next; I am glad if it did. If the attack on the court house had no greater effect than to send that slave away under a guard of two thousand men, instead of two hundred, it was worth a dozen lives. If we are all slaves indeed—if there is no law in Massachusetts except the telegraphic orders from Washington—if our own military are to be made slave-catchers—if our Governor is a mere piece of State ceremony, permitted only to rise at a military dinner and thank his own soldiers for their readiness to shoot down his own constituents, without even the delay of a riot act—if Massachusetts is merely a conquered province and under martial law—*then I wish to know it,* and I am grateful for every additional gun and sabre that forces the truth deeper into our hearts. *Lower, Massachusetts, lower, kneel still lower. . . .*"

Disunion, he suggested, was an historical inevitability. " 'Do not despair of the Republic,' says someone, remembering the hopeful old Roman motto. But they had to despair of that one in the end,—and why not of this one also?," asked Higginson from his pulpit. "Why, when we were going on, step by step, as older Republics have done, should we expect to stop just as we reach the brink of Niagara? The love of Liberty grows stronger every year, some think, in some places. Thirty years ago, it cost only $25 to restore a Fugitive Slave from Boston, and now it costs $100,000; *—but still the slave is restored.* I know there are thousands of hearts which stand pledged to Liberty now, and these may save the State, in spite of her officials and her military; but can they save the Nation? . . . For myself, I do not expect to live to see that law repealed by the votes of politicians at Washington. It can only be repealed by ourselves, upon the soil of Massachusetts. For one, I am glad to be deceived no longer. I am glad of the discovery—(no hasty thing, but gradually dawning upon me for ten years)—that I live under a despotism. I have lost the dream that ours is a land of peace and order. I have looked thoroughly through our 'Fourth of July,' and seen its hollowness. . . . At any rate my word of counsel to you is to learn this lesson thoroughly—*a revolution is begun!* not a Reform, but a Revolution."[5]

Despite his public bravado, Higginson's grave fear was that he would be put on trial for murder of the deputy marshal killed during the riot. Still he put on a brave face in letters to his mother. "Nothing as yet," he wrote her on June 6. "We have nice times and plenty of laughter. Mary and Louisa [his wife and her sister] have gay times, and so do I. L's latest plan is to have Mary's dagerratype [*sic*] hang in the street, marked 'M.E.H., the Martyr's Wife'; and also one of the white kitten, labelled 'the Martyr's Kitten.' Stephen [his brother] has just come up. He finds us very bright and is tolerably so himself; hasn't scolded me yet but perhaps will; knows no more than I do as of yet. I told him I had found a way to attract him at last."[6]

It was just a few days later that Higginson was summoned to Boston. Higginson telegraphed his wife from there on June 10, after his indictment, saying that he was all right and that his trial would be in July.[7] (The trial wound up being delayed until January.) To his brother he reported, with some relief, that he was arrested "for riot only" and was "free on bail."[8] Six others were also charged. Two of them, Parker and Wendell Phillips, had spoken at the Faneuil Hall meeting, where they were on record as urging the convergence on the courthouse. The remaining four defendants were all of Higginson's core band of Worcester raiders.

Glad to have escaped the prospect of trial for murder, Higginson proceeded to spend a relaxed June in Worcester. He wrote to his mother that while waiting for his trial, he and Mary "go quietly on, play with the kittens, and do what we please." He was expecting to be convicted, but was not anticipating a stiff sentence. "We have agreed that should I be shut up a part of the summer, [Mary] may go to Rockport. . . . [Louisa] proposes that every jail should have a boarding house annexed, called 'A Home for AntiSlavery Wives' for such as Mary."[9] While under investigation, Higginson brazenly continued his extensive involvement as one of several Worcester conductors for the Underground Railroad. Many was the night when he personally conducted fugitive slaves to the home of Abby Kelley Foster for forwarding to the next stop on the railway, most often the home of Samuel May, Jr., in Leicester.

It was in October that a stocky U.S. marshal by the name of Asa O. Butman—one of the officers who originally arrested Anthony Burns, guarded him in Boston, and escorted him south—came to Worcester in search of evidence against those involved in the riot. Abby Kelley Foster's husband, Stephen, led a small group of about fifty Garrisonian noncombatants to the American House hotel to confront Butman. "Our plan," Foster wrote his wife, "was to present ourselves in as large numbers as possible and fastening upon him an indignant gaze to follow him wherever he went till he should leave town." The group stood vigil outside the hotel for several hours until a belligerent (and, some said later, drunken) Butman came out on the porch and threatened them with a gun. Foster had him arrested. By the time Butman was arraigned the next morning, the Worcester courthouse was surrounded by more than a thousand angry antislavery men chanting "Bring out the kidnapper" and "Kill the scoundrel!" At one point, during a break in the court proceedings, six black men broke into Butman's holding cell and beat him.

When it became clear that Butman's life was at risk, it was Higginson himself who rescued the terrified marshal from the mob that threatened to lynch him. After a conference with the mayor and the judge, Higginson and Foster personally escorted Butman out of the court building and down the steps directly into the hushed yet menacing crowd. Higginson linked arms with Butman. Foster walked slightly behind them with one hand on the marshal's shoulder and another ready to fend off anyone who might approach from behind. Pushing his way into the throng and never stopping for a moment, Higginson announced loudly that Butman had been promised safe passage out of the city in return for a promise never to return again. What this meant, shouted Higginson as he steadily continued cutting a path through the crowd, was that the abolitionists had won the day in Worcester. The fight was over, and there was no more to be done until the next battle. The best thing that could happen, said Higginson at the top of his lungs, would be for the terrified Butman to make it back to Boston safe and sound, there to fully inform his colleagues of the terror that awaited proslavery men in Worcester. Some of the mob laughed in agreement, disarmed by Higginson's comradely rhetoric. Others still silently weighed the possibility of hanging Butman. Rocks were thrown once Butman and his odd duet of protectors made it to the waiting carriage.

"I was not seriously damaged in the Butman trouble," wrote Higginson to a friend. "It was a time of peril, however, though it ended in nothing worse than frightening a bully into a coward. I wish the poor creature's face could have been daguerreotyped as he crouched into the bottom of the carriage when the stones came crashing in; I never saw such an image of abject fear. Our City Marshal had to drive him the whole way to Boston, too frightened to get into the [train] cars; when they changed horses half way, he hid himself in the woods and could hardly be found again; he would not enter Boston till after dark, nor go to his house even then, but spent the night at a hotel. They have arrested a few persons for riot, chiefly those who were most instrumental in saving him!—so that not much will come of it." A newspaper reported that Butman "awards praise to those who defended him after the storm had been roused, especially Mr. Higginson. . . . Some of the crowd did not distinguish in their attacks between Mr. Butman and Mr. Higginson. The latter gentleman received a considerable share of the missiles, and one large stone was thrown into the carriage, narrowly missing his head."[10]

On the Sunday after the Burns riot, Parker gave a sermon in which he condemned United States commissioner Edward Greeley Loring as the murderer of the federal deputy who'd been killed at the courthouse. A judge of probate in the Massachusetts courts and a teacher at Harvard College, Loring had issued the warrant for Burns's arrest and also signed the order for his return to slavery. "Judge of probate for the County of **Suffolk, in the State of Massachusetts, fugitive slave bill Commissioner**

of the United States, before these citizens of Boston, on Ascension Sunday, assembled to worship God, I charge you with the death of that man who was killed last Friday night," declared Parker. "He was your fellow-servant in kidnapping. He dies at your hand. You fired the shot which makes his wife a widow, his child an orphan. . . . I charge you with filling the courthouse with one-hundred and eighty-four hired ruffians of the United States, and alarming not only this city for her liberties that are in peril, but stirring up the whole Commonwealth of Massachusetts with indignation which no man knows how to stop—which no man can stop. You have done it all!"[11]After Parker's sermon, the women of Woburn, Massachusetts, sent Loring thirty pieces of silver.

Through November and December of 1854, Parker labored long on a speech that he intended to deliver in court. Parker's defense strategy was quite simply to refuse to acknowledge the need for a defense. Parker contended that any actions meant to bring down slavery were inherently correct, while, conversely, all actions that enforced and continued slavery were indefensible. (It was the same logic that would enable him, several years later, to support John Brown. Rebellion against tyrants, he wrote a friend, was "obedience to God.")

In the 125,000-word speech that he would eventually publish as *The Trial of Theodore Parker for the "Misdemeanor" of a Speech in Faneuil Hall against Kidnapping, Before the Circuit Court of the United States, at Boston, with the Defence,* Parker attacked the trial judge, Benjamin R. Curtis, using the judge and members of his family as case studies of the corruption embodied in New England Hunkerism. (Curtis had prosecuted Lewis Hayden and others involved in the Shadrach rescue. Edward Greeley Loring was Judge Curtis's first cousin. The judge's brother George was the United States commissioner who, wrote Parker, "had the glory of kidnapping Mr. Sims.") In his *Defence,* Parker chronicled the Loring/Curtis family's "private personal malice [and] deep, long cherished rancorous" emotion toward him. Parker confidently made plain his moral superiority over them, as well as what he took for their recognition of it. He recalled, for example, when he was summoned to court on November 29, 1854, for his arraignment. "Curtis sat on the bench and determined the amount of my bail," wrote Parker, "and the same eye which had frowned with such baleful aspect on the rescuers of Shadrach, quailed down underneath my look and sought the ground."[12]

☆

Parker intended his speech as an utterance of conscience, not as a pragmatic, serviceable defense. He fully expected to be convicted. And he was ready for it. "What shall I do if I am sent to gaol?" he asked himself in his journal.

1. Write one sermon a week and have it read at Music Hall, and printed the next morning. Who can read it [aloud to the congregation]? Write also a prayer, and correspondence. (Prayer, Saturday night)
2. Prepare a volume of sermons from old MSS.
3. Write Memoirs of Life and correspondence.
4. Vol 1 of "Historical Development of Religion," i.e. The Metaphysics of Religion.
5. Pursue the Russian studies.[13]

While Parker was concluding the writing of his defense in late December and making plans for his time in prison, his combustible friend Howe did him the favor of distracting him. Howe suggested that Parker use Horace Mann as his attorney in the upcoming trial. Parker wrote Howe to say he would rather use Charles M. Ellis, a Boston attorney who, unlike Mann, had often set aside lucrative commercial cases in order to assist in a score of antislavery cases free of charge. In writing Howe, Parker suggested that the wily, political Mann was too conventional, too correct, and too concerned with his image in the community to bring a strong defense to bear in so notorious a case as this. "If Mann undertakes the defence of one so unpopular as I am, will it not be thought a little eccentric: —and so harm and damage the reputation of said Mann?" Parker assured Howe that should he need "more aid than Mr. Ellis has at his command," he would engage his friend Sen. John P.

Hale of New Hampshire, who, "when he goes into battle, is not afraid of splitting his flint while he pulls the trigger, and like good Capt. Gridley at Bunker Hill when he lets fly at a red coat [does not] inquire if the shot may not hurt his reputation."[14]

Howe was offended by Parker's implied criticism of Mann and decided to show it by absenting himself from a New Year's party at Parker's house. He sent Julia to Parker's festivity by herself, while he stayed home to sulk. "Your absence cast a cloud over our little company tonight when I had Sunday nice little things to say to you," wrote Parker to Howe on New Year's Eve, "and when J. told me *why,* the cloud settled in to a rain, sad and cold. I am surprised that you should be offended (as I *hear*), or feel wounded, (as it is plain you do), at what I wrote in the note. . . . The note was partly for you, partly also for Mann. I still think it will not be worth while for him to come [to defend] one so *widely odious as I am,* and shall do nothing toward asking him to lift an arm in my defense."[15]

In fact, there was to be little need for Mann or anyone to lift an arm in the defense of Parker or others charged in the Burns case. Parker never got to deliver his speech. Brief arguments were made by Parker's attorneys (Ellis and Hale) and by the attorneys for Higginson, Phillips, and the other defendants.[16] The scowling Parker, sitting at the defendants' table, took notes furiously. Years later, Higginson would remember that Parker, "busy with his terrible notebook . . . seemed as important a figure in the scene as the presiding judge himself."[17] After several days of legal maneuvering, all the indictments were dismissed. It was determined that United States commissioner Loring was not correctly described in the indictments. Therefore the indictments were void. In truth, what had probably happened was that the trial judge decided he would rather let Parker and his cohorts off on a technicality than allow Parker the forum of a trial in which to unleash his scathing eloquence on the fugitive slave law and those who served it.

Benjamin F. Hallet, the United States attorney in charge of the prosecution, was the same man who had once threatened to hang for treason all violators of the fugitive slave act. For him, the abandoned prosecution of the Burns rioters was a particularly bitter pill. As Parker left the court, Mr. Hallet—who had rather a squeaky voice—said to him, "You have crawled out of a very small hole this time, Mr. Parker." To this Parker replied menacingly in his deep bass voice: "I will make a larger hole next time, Mr. Hallet."[18]

8

SHARP'S *RIGHTS* OF THE PEOPLE

P ARKER WROTE HOWE on April 17, 1853, stating his belief that the Disunion Abolitionists and the Free Soilers should have "a general unity of action." Parker pointed out that the two groups already had "unity of idea" in "denying that man can hold property in man." They also had "unity of aim, viz. the annihilation of slavery in America." The two groups had heretofore only differed in measures to be adopted toward this end. "Both agree in the *necessity of agitation.* . . . But there they separate—and differ as to the *special mode of operation. The Abolitionist* uses only the *moral machinery* of the community, the church; the *political tools of the state* he will not touch. *The Free Soiler* will. This is the difference between the two; that is all of it." Parker pointed out that the strict disunion position as enunciated in Garrison's *Liberator* and Howe's *Commonwealth,* which rejected all political compromise in the fight against slavery, was perhaps unrealistic. "In respect to denunciation [of the Constitution], we [Disunion Abolitionists] are all pretty much alone," wrote Parker.[1]

Parker's doubts about the efficacy of political compromise, and his out-and-out lack of faith in the Constitution, were soon revived the following year when the Free Soilers suffered a crushing defeat in Congress at the hands of Stephen A. Douglas. Called the "Squatter Sovereignty bill" by some abolitionists, Douglas's Kansas-Nebraska Act of 1854 signaled the opening of Kansas and Nebraska to the potential for slavery by declaring that the issue should be decided at some future date by a popular vote of those who settled there. Heretofore, the Missouri Compromise line of 1821 (latitude 36°30') had been considered an inviolable wall against slavery's spread through the northern section of the Louisiana Purchase lands. Now, suddenly, all of the western lands for as far north as the Canadian border seemed at risk.

Parker, like many others, saw the Kansas-Nebraska legislation as a critical turning point. Up to now, the political process had yielded a gradual increase in the territorial limits on slavery. The flow of American history had appeared to Parker to be progressive rather than regressive. Now, said Parker in a letter, the "healthy, procreative process toward liberty" seemed up for reversal. The embryo ideals expressed in the Declaration of Independence, defined yet unfulfilled, were threatened with "fatal miscarriage." After passage of the Kansas-Nebraska Act, Parker foresaw a host of dark possibilities that would "make stillborn the infant liberty": the expansion of the Slave Power majority in Congress, the addition of Cuba and Haiti to the Union as slave territories and then slave states, the revival of slave importation from Africa, and even the restoration of slavery as an institution in some free states.[2]

"The Slave Power," said Parker, "thus controlling the slaves and slaveholders at the South, and the Democratic party at the North, easily manages the government at Washington. The Federal officers are marked with different stripes—Whig, Democrat, and so on. They are all owned by the same master, and lick the same hand. So it controls the nation. It silences the great sects, Trinitarian, Unitarian, Nullitarian: the chief ministers of this American Church—threefold in denominations, one in nature—have naught to say against Slavery; the Tract Society dare not rebuke 'the sum of all villainies,' the Bible Society has no 'Word of

God' for the slave, the 'revealed religion' is not revealed to him. Writers of the schoolbooks 'remember the hands that feed them,' and venture no word against the national crime that threatens to become also the national ruin. In no nation on earth is there such social tyranny of opinion."[3] Now more than ever, said Parker, should *disunion* be the motto of all freedom-loving men. Now more than ever was a second American Revolution necessary to preserve the ideals of the first. And perhaps Kansas was the place for it to begin.

Parker was enthusiastic when a rich entrepreneur from Worcester, Eli Thayer, formed the New England Emigrant Aid Company, one of whose chief investors was the millionaire Boston industrialist Amos Lawrence. Under its charter, the Emigrant Aid Company was "to supply information, cheapen transportation, and set up saw mills and flower mills in the new territory" of Kansas, and in other ways encourage and facilitate the settling of the territory by antislavery homesteaders. The idea of the company was to win Kansas for the free-state movement while at the same time turning a tidy profit for investors. Thayer's dream was to send entire communities to Kansas all at once. The land and infrastructure owned by the company would in turn increase in value as the population grew. Charles Francis Adams, Sr., subscribed $25,000. Samuel Gridley Howe sat on the board of directors and committed what little of Julia's large inheritance he had not already lost through unshrewd real estate investments in and around south Boston. Theodore Parker extolled the genius of Thayer's plan to his fellow ministers.

The Emigrant Aid Company (and in fact, the entire Free Kansas movement) brought together a disparate group of backers with a range of political agendas. Many of the chief advancers of the New England Emigrant Aid Company—Thayer, Lawrence, and Parker among them—did not believe in social or political equality for blacks. In step with banning slavery in the territory, they also expected, if victorious, to ban black citizenship and property ownership. A large number of the settlers recruited by the company, many of whom were Irish Catholic immigrants such as worked in Lawrence's New England mills, supported the same notion.

There is no "truth in the assertion that those who go from New England to Kansas are abolitionists," wrote Amos Lawrence somewhat disingenuously to Missouri senator David R. Atchinson. "No person of that stamp is known to have gone from here." (Of course some, though not the majority, of the settlers sent by the Emigrant Aid Company were abolition-minded.) "I have been informed that you have an [annual] income of $100,000 . . . ," responded Atchinson to Lawrence. "I live within a few miles of Kansas, and have a few slaves; you have none, —*at least no black*

Industrialist Amos Lawrence, chief financier of the Free Kansas movement, who befriended Brown but later condemned him as a cold-blooded murderer. Photo courtesy Massachusetts Historical Society.

ones. . . ."[4] Atchinson remarked that 80 percent of the population in Lawrence, Massachusetts, worked in Lawrence's factories. And now Amos Lawrence was intent on exporting thousands more white wage-slaves to Kansas, to another town that would carry his name.

The Emigrant Aid Company sent two groups of free-soil colonists to found Lawrence, Kansas, beside the Kaw River in 1854. There on the low prairie, the company quickly built a number of substantial brick and stone buildings, including the massive Free State hotel, which was meant to double as a fortress should the need arise. Free-state emigrants flowed not only from the North but also from the South, looking to found a state where, in the absence of slavery, their labor would be in demand. One John Doyle, who was destined to have a fatal run-in with John

Brown, brought his family from Tennessee, recalled his widow, in order to "get to a free state where there would be no slave labor to hinder white men from making a fair day's wage." Her husband often said to her "that slavery was ruinous to white labor; and that they had a large family of boys and would go there [to Kansas] and settle and try to get comfortable homes for their children."[5]

Proslavery Missourians were enraged by what they characterized as a free-state invasion of Kansas. "Now if a set of fanatics and demagogues a thousand miles off," lectured Senator Atchinson at Liberty, Missouri, several days before the November 1854 Kansas election for a territorial representative to Congress, "can afford to advance the money and extend every nerve to abolitionize the territory and exclude the slaveholder, when they have not the least personal interest, what is your duty? When you reside one day's journey to the territory, and when your peace and quiet and your property depend upon your action, you can, without exertion, send five hundred of your young men who will vote in favor of your institutions."[6] And so they did, stuffing ballot boxes to elect a proslavery candidate as the territory's representative. It happened again on March 30, 1855. Five thousand Missourians stormed into Kansas to make sure that a proslavery territorial legislature was elected. The result was a host of slave codes and sedition measures based closely upon Missouri statutes that, among other things, made it illegal to speak publicly in opposition to slavery and declared that only those who recognized the "right" of slavery could hold elected office or sit on juries.

That September, angry free-state settlers formed a free-state party during a meeting at Big Springs, Kansas, where they repudiated the authority of the proslavery legislature. The free-state party was founded on a platform that, in line with the wishes of most free-staters, at once insisted Kansas ban both slavery *and black settlement*. The party called for its members to refrain from voting in the October 1 congressional election scheduled by the proslavery legislature and instead set a date of October 9 for election of free-state representatives and delegates to attend a constitutional convention in Topeka. Held in late October, the Topeka convention drafted a free-state constitution, soon to become known as the Topeka Constitution, that included, among other things, a "Negro Exclusion" clause. The Topeka Constitution was submitted for popular ratification in voting scheduled for December 15. Simultaneously, at Fort Leavenworth, proslavery settlers formed a "Law and Order" party, which endorsed the authority of the sitting legislature at Shawnee Mission and declared the free-state party elections invalid. The stage was set for an altercation.

In August of 1854, Higginson's college friend Edward Everett Hale, who now was a Worcester neighbor of both Higginson and Eli Thayer, published a 247-page volume entitled *Kansas and Nebraska: An Account of the Emigrant Aid Companies and Directions to Emigrants.* A copy of the book, inscribed "Jason Brown and John Brown [Jr.], Akron, Dec 20th 1854," is in the Sol Feinstone Collection at the Syracuse University Library.

The elder sons of John Brown, who migrated to Kansas in the spring of 1855, were a strange lot. John Brown, Jr., thirty-four, was fascinated by quack science and spiritualism. He'd once apprenticed with the New York publishers Fowler & Wells, leading propounders of phrenology, the popular pseudoscience whereby an expert would examine the lumps and bumps on a subject's head and from these deduce the characteristics of the subject's personality. (Young Brown was joined in his belief in phrenology by such worthies as Horace Greeley, Charles Sumner, and Samuel Gridley Howe. And he shared his belief in spiritualism with no less a personage than William Lloyd Garrison, who, it was said, once communicated with the departed soul of Nat Turner during a séance.) It was at John Brown, Jr.'s, urging that his father, in 1847, begrudgingly allowed the phrenologist Orson Fowler to "read" his head. Fowler's report was eerily accurate. "You have a pretty good opinion of yourself," wrote Fowler, "would rather lead than be led. You might be persuaded but to drive you would be impossible. You like your own way, and to think and act for yourself—are quite independent and dignified, open and plain, say just what you think, and most heartily despise hypocrisy and artificiality."[7] The son who shared his father's name was equally strong-willed, vain, and single-minded.

The next son in line was Jason. Thirty-two years old in 1855, Jason was peace-loving and gentle. "I never knew him to engage in a fight," his younger brother Salmon Brown recalled of Jason. Salmon remembered that Jason once refused to eat some quail because he "had seen the birds flutter as they were dying, and it so worked on his sympathies he could not eat them. . . . He could never endure the sight of suffering in either man or beast."[8] Jason was fascinated with machinery and fancied himself an inventor. (Jason, who was to live until 1912, would use many of the long years after Harpers Ferry tinkering with a heavier-than-air flying machine.) He flirted with Garrisonian pacifism and nonresistance and would later condemn his father for fostering undue bloodshed.

Owen, John Brown's third son, was thirty-one. He dreamed of being a humorist for the newspapers. He wrote long letters to friends filled less with day-to-day news than with rambling, fanciful tales of the absurd. Very shy, Owen was endlessly attracted to a host of women, but was never brave enough to do anything about it. Owen had a weak right arm, the result of a childhood accident. This would exempt him from participation at Harpers Ferry just as John Junior's, Jason's, and Salmon's family responsibilities would exempt them. (Owen would stay several miles away from the ferry, at a farm hideout, with a few other very lucky members of Brown's company, while Jason, John Junior, and Salmon would not be within a hundred miles.) Of his father and brothers, Owen was the most logical, the most reasonable, the most pragmatic. And he seems to have been respected within the family. "Owen's calm, philo-sophical way of thinking and speaking did not permit him to be impera-tively brushed aside," recalled a friend.[9]

Frederick, twenty-four in 1855, was the son the father called "wild" and even "insane." Like the father, he was fanatically religious. In Ohio, he had become interested in a beautiful young lady. Struggling with the sin of lust he felt rising within him, the confused young man attempted a radical penance. Frederick, wrote his father, "subjected himself to a most dreadful surgical operation but a short time before starting for

Kansas which well might have cost him his life." He had tried to emasculate himself.

Salmon, nineteen, can be quickly sketched. He was a simple carbon copy of the father: quick to unreasoned violence and easily able to cast a cold eye across blood that flowed in the name of righteous justice.

John Brown did not immediately follow his eldest sons to Kansas, although they urged him to. After years of trying to sort out the tangled affairs of Perkins & Brown, he had at last settled all the lawsuits by the summer of 1854. That autumn, Brown was near Akron, Ohio, on a rented farm where his wife and younger children had joined him, trying to sell his interest in some cattle there so as to have money with which to remove permanently to North Elba.

"Dear Children," he wrote in late September to his daughter Ruth, who was then living on the North Elba land with her husband, Henry Thompson, the son of a prosperous Essex County farmer, "After being hard pressed to go with my family to Kansas as more likely to benefit the colored people *on the whole* than to return . . . to North Elba; I have consented to ask your *advice & feeling* in the matter; & also to ask you to learn from Mr. [Lyman] Epps [a black community leader at Timbucto] & all the colored people (so far as you can) how they would wish and advise me to act in the case all things considered. As I volunteered in their service; (or in the service of the colored people); they have a right to vote as to the course I take. I have just written Gerrit Smith, Fredk Douglas[s], & Dr. McCune Smith for their advice. We have a new daughter now five days old. Mother & child are doing well to appearance."[10]

Gerrit Smith wrote Brown that he wished him to do the work that needed to be done at Timbucto. The wishes of Douglass, McCune Smith, and the people at Timbucto were the same. Thus, in June of 1855, John Brown started for North Elba after selling his cattle at Rockford, Illinois. He was heading to a plain but comfortable frame house that his son-in-law Thompson had built for him. He told his much relieved wife that he would leave the tense Kansas border country to others to tend. But it was just weeks later that John Brown changed his mind. He had not been at North Elba for more than a day—had not slept more than one night in his new house—when he received a long letter from John Brown, Jr., describing outrages inflicted on the free-state settlers, and what he and the other Browns in Kansas proposed to do about it.

"I tell you the truth," wrote John Brown, Jr., "when I say that while the interest of despotism has secured to its cause hundreds of thousands of the meanest and most desperate of men, armed to the teeth with Revolvers, Bowie Knives, Rifles & Cannon—while they are not only thoroughly organized, but under pay from Slaveholders—the friends of freedom are *not one fourth* of them *half armed,* and as to *military organization* among them *it no where exists in this territory* unless they have recently done something in Lawrence. The result of this is that the people here exhibit the most abject and cowardly spirit, whenever their dearest rights are invaded and trampled down by the lawless band of miscreants which Missouri has ready at a moment's call to pour in upon them. This is the *general* effect upon the people here so far as I have noticed; there are a few, and but a few exceptions. . . . Now the remedy we propose is that the Anti-Slavery portion of the inhabitants should *immediately, thoroughly arm,* and *organize themselves* in *military companies.* In order to effect this, some persons must begin and lead off in the matter."[11]

Brown took his son's letter with him to a large assembly of political abolitionists held at Syracuse on June 26. Gerrit Smith read John Brown, Jr.'s, letter aloud to the convention. Brown himself made a speech in which he offered his services to fight for a free Kansas and solicited funds to support that purpose. Frederick Douglass stood to endorse Brown and his self-assigned mission. The hat was passed, but only about $60 was raised. It appears Brown used most of the money that July to do finishing work on the house at North Elba and to lay in supplies for the family he was about to leave behind.

☆

The starlit, early-October evening was strangely quiet when John Brown pulled his small horse and wagon into his sons' Kansas settlement near Osawatomie. A sign, barely legible in the darkness, announced the place as "Brown's Station." It was a lonesome, desolate spot just south of the des Cygnes River and north and west of the meandering Pottawatomie Creek. The bookish, sixteen-year-old Oliver Brown sat beside his father in the front of the rig as it came to a stop at the cabin of John Junior. Looking into the back of the wagon, Brown's sons were pleased to find it loaded with revolvers, broadswords, rifles, and ammunition donated to Brown at stops in Ohio and Chicago. And they were somewhat shocked to find something else: a macabre surprise package tied up tightly in a blanket on the floorboards in between the boxed rifles. It was the body of Brown's grandson, Jason's four-year-old son, Austin, who had died of cholera and been buried in Missouri during the migration of the Brown boys and their families several months before. Brown had exhumed the little boy, believing, he said, that a reunion with the dead child "would afford some relief to the broken hearted Father and Mother."[12]

One of the first things Brown did in Kansas—after reburying little Austin—was to accompany his sons to the Pottawatomie precinct on October 9, where they were to vote for the free-state congressman and for delegates to the Topeka free-state constitutional convention. The Browns went heavily armed. As usual, the "old man," as his boys called him, was expecting trouble. But there was none. Brown surmised that a severe, early cold snap had kept the Missourians at bay and the local proslavery men at home. More likely, the proslavery elements simply saw no point in rigging or shutting down an election the results of which they did not plan to recognize. Whatever the reason, the Browns met no opposition going or coming from the polling place. Brown did not vote, as he owned no claim and was not therefore a legal resident. Brown stood to the side with his guns and saber and watched as his sons cast their ballots.

Shortly before the December 15 popular vote on the new free-state constitution, John Brown came within tasting distance of the trouble he seemed so much to crave. Early in the first week of December, the free-state town of Lawrence was surrounded by Kansas militia as well as several hundred heavily armed Missourians demanding the surrender of a free-state settler named Coleman, who was wanted for contempt of laws passed by the Shawnee Mission legislature. The citizens of Lawrence threw up earthworks, stockpiled ammunition and food, and prepared for a siege. The brief engagement just begun was to be called the Wakarusa War, after the nearby river where proslavery forces camped.

Brown and his sons journeyed to Lawrence at first word of the siege. They left Brown's Station on December 6 and arrived at Lawrence the next day. John Brown drove the wagon loaded with rifles, revolvers, knives, and ammunition. Poles stood "endwise around the wagon box with fixed bayonets pointing upwards" looking "really formidable," as one witness recalled. John Junior, Owen, Salmon, and Frederick marched beside the wagon. Each man had a short, heavy broadsword strapped to his side. And each was armed with "a goodly number of fire arms, and navy revolvers." At a bridge south of Lawrence they came upon a band of Missourians. The Browns moved onto the bridge with their rifles leveled at the invaders, who parted to allow them through. At Lawrence, the small contingent was welcomed by George Washington Brown, a man of no relation to them who was editor of the *Lawrence Herald of Freedom,* the official newspaper of the New England Emigrant Aid Company. George Brown was already acquainted with John Brown, Jr., who now introduced him to his father and brothers. It would take George Brown a little under an hour to realize that he did not care at all for John Brown, Sr.

At the fortresslike Free State hotel, John Brown met Dr. Charles Robinson, the Lawrence agent of the New England Emigrant Aid Company. With Indiana's James Henry Lane, Robinson was busy directing the Committee of Public Safety in the defense of the town. Robinson told Brown confidently that he was in the midst of negotiating a peace treaty; there would likely be no battle. Nevertheless, he welcomed Brown's support and appointed Brown a captain in the First Brigade of Kansas Volunteers. George Washington Brown would recall that it was a somewhat disappointed captain, discouraged at the scent of peace, who led his sons to the earthworks where men of Lawrence were busy drilling and where, according to the editor, Brown started to "make trouble" immediately.[13] Brown refused to execute orders from senior officers, saying obstinately that he and God were the sole commanders of his sons, and no one else.

Even more problematical in the face of Robinson's attempts at negotiating a truce, Brown insisted on formulating a plan to take a small band from Lawrence in the dead of night, sneak down to where proslavery forces were camped by the Wakarusa, and slaughter them in their sleep. He was stopped from doing so only through the direct inter-

Charles Robinson, Lawrence agent for the New England Emigrant Aid Company who later became Free State governor. Robinson at first questioned and then condemned John Brown's actions in the territory. Photo courtesy Massachusetts Historical Society.

vention of Robinson.[14] The coolheaded Robinson pointed out to the frustrated, annoyed Brown that thus far the free-state forces were guilty of no atrocities. They were perfectly positioned for a large propaganda victory over the proslavery Missourians, who were drinking heavily, vandalizing the countryside, and had killed a free-state settler in cold blood the evening before. It was only because of the despicable behavior of the Missourians (whom even the proslavery territorial governor Wilson Shannon was now calling a "pack of hyenas") that a negotiated settlement was possible for the outnumbered and surrounded free-staters. Should Brown give Governor Shannon an excuse to paint the free-staters as murderers, then he just might see fit to turn his hyenas loose on

Lawrence. Robinson would not allow that to happen; he would physically restrain Brown and his sons if necessary.

A truce was agreed to one day later. Brown's argument with Robinson did not stop him from supporting the man that January, when Robinson ran and won as governor in the free-staters' still-unrecognized Topeka government. John Brown, Jr., was elected to the shadow Topeka legislature in the same election.

☆

There were subarctic temperatures in Kansas that winter—as low as twenty-nine below zero. The season was an interminable expanse of snow and ice interrupted only by occasional outbreaks of violence and bad news more bitter than the Siberian winds that blew across the plains. The free-state government—with its own constitution, legislature, and governor in competition with the authorized proslavery versions of each institution—fostered extreme reactions from many fronts, all of them violent in intent if not in fact. Two free-staters were wounded and one proslavery man killed in fighting near Leavenworth at about the time of the free-state election. Shortly after, a free-stater named Brown (no relation to either John Brown or George Washington Brown) was hacked to death by proslavery settlers who tossed his bloody body on his doorstep and shouted "Here's Brown" to his horrified wife.

"War! War!" read an editorial in a proslavery paper endorsing the murder of the free-stater. "These higher-law men will not be permitted any longer to carry on their illegal and high-handed proceedings. *War! War!"*[15]In a speech before Congress, Pres. Franklin Pierce angrily called the Topeka constitution a farce, the Topeka legislature and Governor Robinson the same, and declared that any free-state resistance to "real" laws sponsored by "real" electors would be considered a "treasonable insurrection" and dealt with as such. In spite of the fact that the president said he would refuse to recognize their authority and might even muster federal troops to force them to disband, the Kansas free-state legislature convened at Topeka on March 4. John Brown, Jr., attended as the delegate from Pottawatomie. In that capacity he voted in favor of

senatorial nominations for both James Henry Lane and the former Kansas territorial governor Andrew Reader, whom President Pierce had fired because of his free-state sympathies.

More than one member of the Topeka legislature remarked the similarity between their gathering and that of the outlawed Continental Congress eighty years before. The analogy was one the free-state Kansans luxuriated in, confidently boasting of their links to the ideals, inspiration, and revolutionary instinct of the founders. "We seek communion with the spirits of 1775–76," wrote John Brown, Jr., to a group from Ohio who were contemplating Kansas emigration. Thus, he said, in the spirit of '76, they should "come *thoroughly armed*" and "bring plenty of ammunition." In the same letter, Brown's eldest son made a dark prophecy of what was to become the tragedy at Harpers Ferry. If the slave power persisted in "its aggressive acts" against the free-state majority in Kansas, wrote young Brown, "the war cry heard upon our plains will reverberate not only through the hemp and tobacco fields of Missouri but through the 'Rice Swamps,' [and] the cotton and Sugar plantations of the Sunny South." If "the first act in the drama of insane Despotism is to be performed here, you may look elsewhere for the theatre of other acts."[16]

In late December of 1855, shortly after the Wakarusa War, Sam Howe flirted briefly with the idea of assembling a troop of men to go west. Theodore Parker wrote him on December 27 suggesting several likely volunteers, including Nathaniel Bowditch, who "might be added to your list" and "would train in a Nebraska troop. I think of none besides."[17] Meanwhile, Parker declared from the pulpit that while he ordinarily spent $1,500 a year on books, he now intended to spend $1,300 of that amount to instead buy guns and ammunition for Kansas. ("I make all my pecuniary arrangements," he wrote, "with the expectation of civil war.")[18] Ironically, many of the boxes of Sharp's breech-loading rifles that Parker shipped illegally to Kansas were marked "Books." Parker even took to referring to the guns in his journal as if they actually were books, gleefully tallying up how many copies of *Rights of the People* he had personally sent west. (Parker wrote in his journal of seeing off a band of Kansas emigrants. "There were twenty copies of Sharp's *Rights of the People* in their hands, of the new and improved edition, and diverse Colt's six shooters also. . . . But what a comment were the weapons of that company on the boasted democracy of America! Those rifles and pistols were to defend their soil from the American Government, which wishes to plant slavery in Kansas!")[19]

Amos Lawrence, Samuel Cabot, and other Massachusetts aristocrats took it upon themselves to buy one hundred rifles each for the defense of Kansas.[20] The rifles cost $25 apiece when bought in quantity. "Dr. Howe and others [in the form of the Massachusetts State Kansas Committee] raised five thousand dollars one day last week to buy Sharp's rifles," wrote Parker. "We want a thousand rifles, and got two hundred in one day."[21] In New York, Henry Ward Beecher took up a collection at Plymouth Church, the proceeds of which he used to purchase twenty-five rifles that he shipped to Kansas in a crate marked "Bibles." The contents of the box, Beecher told a friend, would actually be of more use than Bibles "in an argument with wolves." The story got around. Soon Sharp's rifles were referred to as "Beecher's Bibles" throughout Kansas.[22]

$$9$$

GIDEON

HEN THE SNOWS melted, violence began to sprout green again across the Kansas prairie—first sparse and sporadic, then quickly more profuse. In April of 1856, a sheriff was assassinated by a sniper outside Lawrence after arresting several free-staters for failing to cooperate with laws passed by the Shawnee Mission legislature. "War to the knife," wrote a proslavery editor in response, "and knife to the hilt. *Jones's Murder Must Be Revenged!*" Things percolated. A drunken proslavery mob killed two free-staters. On May 8, a federal judge charged a grand jury at Lecompton to indict every member of the Topeka free-state legislature for high treason. On May 21, an army of approximately one thousand proslavery men invaded Lawrence and burned the Free State hotel to the ground. Governor Robinson was arrested and his home set afire. The presses of two newspapers, the *Free State* and the *Herald of Freedom,* were attacked with axes and hammers and rendered useless. On the afternoon of the following day, in distant Washington, Massachusetts senator Charles Sumner was savagely beaten on the floor of the Senate by Preston Brooks of South Carolina after delivering a speech about Kansas.

On May 23, following the burning of Lawrence and the beating of Sumner, John Brown mustered a fast, silent, yet fiery and deadly rage. After going to the forest to "converse with God," he returned home to Brown's Station and in a low, somber voice ordered his sons Frederick, Owen, and Salmon (and his son-in-law Henry Thompson, who had now joined them in Kansas) to take the broadswords he'd brought from Ohio and sharpen them for deadly precision. Then he marched his sons, son-in-law, and two other men off by night in the direction of the Pottawatomie Creek, where a ramshackle collection of settlers' cabins hugged the shore at an interval of about one every mile or so.

Brown's first stop was the cabin of James P. Doyle, a Catholic from Tennessee who had come to Kansas to get away from slavery, but whom the New England Calvinist John Brown seems nevertheless to have disliked, in part for his Catholicism and in part for his incriminating Southern drawl. Leaving Doyle's wife, a young daughter, and a fourteen-year-old son inside, Brown ordered Doyle and his sons Drury (twenty) and William (twenty-two) out of the cabin. Then Brown marched his prisoners out of sight of the house to a clearing where their heads were split open with the broadswords. (In addition, Drury's arms were cut off.) An hour later, Brown kidnapped and executed the proslavery settler Allen Wilkinson while his sick wife and several young children stood by helpless. (Afterward, one of Brown's sons returned to Wilkinson's house to steal two saddles from the terrified wife, these to go with some horses that Brown was taking from the barn.) Farther down the creek, Brown abducted and killed William Sherman, whose bowie knife and horse Brown stole. A friend found Sherman's mutilated body floating in the creek the next day. His left hand was cut off "except a little piece of skin." His skull was split open and "some of his brains" had washed away.[1]

Moderate free-staters were horrified by what came to be called the Pottawatomie Massacre. A "conciliation meeting" was held at Osawatomie on the Tuesday after the murders at which free-state and proslavery men joined together in denouncing the massacre, promising to cooperate in bringing Brown and his band to justice. Soon warrants

James Redpath, abolitionist newspaper editor from Scotland who first met Brown during the Kansas Civil War. He would publish a best-selling biography of Brown shortly after Brown's execution in 1859. Photo courtesy Massachusetts Historical Society.

were issued, and Brown was the subject of a manhunt by U.S. marshals assisted by Missouri militia and federal troops. In the face of nearly universal condemnation from proslavery men and free-staters alike, Brown and his small band retreated through the prairie wilderness to a squalid, desolate spot on Vine Branch Creek that Old Brown promptly named Camp Brown.

Within days of the massacre, Osawatomie was attacked by proslavery irregulars seeking revenge. Brown's Station (shrewdly abandoned by the various Brown wives and families) was reduced to rubble. The houses were burned to the ground; the horses and cattle were stolen; even the little wooden cross that marked Austin Brown's latest grave was set ablaze. John Brown, Jr.—who had played no part in the massacre and had no prior knowledge of it—hid in the woods behind the home of an uncle. He was finally arrested on May 31. The federal soldiers detaining young Brown tied him to a tent pole and beat him with rifle butts. Jason Brown—who like his older brother was not involved in the massacre and in fact condemned it—was also beaten before being exonerated and released.

James Redpath, a twenty-three-year-old native of Scotland with pronounced antislavery sympathies who served as Kansas correspondent for the *New York Herald,* managed to make his way to Camp Brown within days of the Pottawatomie Massacre. The camp, recorded Redpath, was "near the edge of the creek [where] a dozen horses were tied, all ready [*sic*] saddled for a ride for life, or a hunt after Southern invaders. A dozen rifles and sabres were stacked around the trees. . . . Three or four armed men were lying on red and blue blankets on the grass; and two fine-looking youths were standing, leaning on their arms, on guard nearby." Brown stood by "a great blazing fire with a pot on it. He was poorly clad, and his toes protruded from his boots." Several of Brown's men told Redpath that the old man would often "retire to the densest solitudes [of the forest], to wrestle with his God in secret prayer." After these prayerful moments, "he would say that the Lord had directed him in visions what to do." When Redpath tried to question Brown about the events along the Pottawatomie, Brown refused to answer. "He respectfully but firmly forbade conversation on the Pottawatomie affair," reported Redpath, who would ever thereafter argue that Brown was innocent of the atrocity.[2]

☆

In the collection of the Massachusetts Historical Society is a fine, leather-bound volume of manuscripts and letters. *Papers Relating to John Brown, Given to the Massachusetts Historical Society by Amos A. Lawrence, February 12, 1885,* says the gold stamping on the cover. "John Brown had been dead twenty years before many of his acts became known," reads Lawrence's careful script on the first page of the book. "His devotion to the cause of freedom, and his splendid death had checked inquiry. Meantime his fame had become worldwide. Should this ignorance be perpetuated by a concealment of facts? This would not be in accordance with the principles or the practice of this Society [the Massachusetts Historical Society]. The undersigned had never been unfriendly to him. His business firm had employed Brown to buy wool in the West as early as 1843. They parted with him because he spoke disloyally of the U.S. government. It was 13 years after this that he came to the writer, and asked to be sent to Kansas. His line of action was different from ours. But it did not prevent our interceding for him when a prisoner, nor assisting his family ever since whenever asked to do so."[3]

The first item in the little collection (evidently added to the book by Lawrence five years after he donated it to the Society) is a clipping from the *Lawrence* (Kan.) *Weekly Journal* of May 12, 1900. "Wednesday was the [100th] anniversary of the birth of John Brown, and it was celebrated by his worshippers," wrote the editor. "John Brown's worshippers for the most part are people who didn't know him. Those who were acquainted with him and were familiar with his career in Kansas are not among them. He did more harm to Kansas than Jim Lane, or any other of the fanatics who infested the territory in the early days. The men who came to Kansas for legitimate purposes, and who desired to employ peaceful and fair means in the settlement of the country, had about as much trouble with the disturbing elements encouraged by Brown and Lane as they had with the Missouri outlaws. The charitable thing to say of Brown is that he was a lunatic. He was a disturber even in the east, a dead beat, and swindler. He never became a bona fide resident of Kansas and was always a thorn in the side of the settlers. They never knew what moment his outlawry would bring the torch to their cabins and the knife of the Missourians to their throats. His hands were bloody, and his nature was that of a wolf. His desire was to kill and to slay, and he gratified his ambition when he could do so without danger to himself. It is time to remove the halo from the head of John Brown, and sell it to the junk man."[4]

This item is accompanied in Lawrence's dossier by another clipping from the same newspaper dated June 16, 1900, responding to a note from Franklin Sanborn endeavoring to interest "the people of Kansas in Henry Thompson, of Pasadena, Cal., son-in-law of John Brown, who ought to have a pension from Kansas." A correspondent disagreed. "Mr. Sanborn, if at all familiar with the actual situation in Kansas in the early days, should know that the free state men, the men who made Kansas free, were not in favor of the forcible emancipation of slaves or the murder of defenceless men. Mr. Sanborn's affected knowledge was well tested in the matter of the Pottawatomie massacre, denying until denial was made ridiculous by incontrovertible evidence that John Brown was a party to it, because Brown told him he was not."[5] (Indeed, it was not until the 1870s, when confronted with testimony from his friend John Brown, Jr., that Sanborn was forced to understand that John Brown had lied to him about his complicity in the Pottawatomie murders.)

Going a few pages deeper into Amos Lawrence's catalog of John Brown's crimes, we find an 1885 letter to Lawrence from one David N. Utter, a Unitarian clergyman of Chicago who'd recently traveled to Chattanooga to speak with Mahala Doyle, the wife and mother of the first three men killed in the Pottawatomie Massacre. "Concerning the provocation or reasons for the killing she said there were none whatever only 'just we were southern people, I reckon,'" wrote Utter to Lawrence. "Why, Mr. Utter," Doyle continued, "it was just as wicked and unjustifiable a murder as if a company of men should ride up to that gate this minute and come in here and kill you and me and this woman and little girl all right here just for nothing at all."

Utter told Lawrence he'd referred Mrs. Doyle to the fact that some said the Doyles were slave hunters in Tennessee, before they came to Kansas, and had brought their bloodhounds with them. "To this she replied simply that there was no foundation for it of any kind whatever. They had never owned slaves or blood-hounds, nor had any of her people ever been concerned in slave hunting; and she wished me to ask her neighbors about Chattanooga the questions I had asked her. I inquired about previous disturbances or quarrels in the neighborhood but she could not remember anything of the kind before the murder. Their particular settlement had been peaceable and quiet although she had heard of trouble at Lawrence and elsewhere. Mrs. Doyle's manner and appearance, her general intelligence and perfect sincerity impressed me very favorably and I believe she spoke the simple truth when she said that her husband and sons had never taken any part in politics or political matters, from the time they came to Kansas to the night of their death. Mrs. Doyle is now seventy-two years of age, has a perfect recollection of her life in Kansas, and although she does not think it worth while to stir up the old feelings of the war, she is yet willing to answer all reasonable questions for truth's sake, and it would not be difficult to get a full sworn statement from her."[6]

While Franklin Sanborn endeavored to provide support for the heirs of John Brown through the years—often taking contributions from Amos Lawrence toward this end—Lawrence himself became deeply involved with providing financial aid for Brown's victims. "Grandmother rec'd your [money] order . . . and was very thankful to you," wrote Maggie Moore, a granddaughter of Mahala Doyle, to Lawrence in the spring of 1885. "[Grandmother] asks me to say to you that her understanding was when they went to Kansas that it was to get to a free state where there would be no slave labor to hinder white men from making a fair day's wages; that they never owned any slaves, never expected to, nor did not want any." Lawrence's note of identification scrawled across the top of the letter reads: "Widow of James Doyle, who was murdered by J.B."[7]

Lawrence's clipping book also contains numerous letters from George Washington Brown, the old Kansas antislavery editor who had despised John Brown ever since he'd first met him during the Wakarusa War. Writing to Amos Lawrence in December of 1884, George Brown criticized Sanborn's recent biography of Brown as being "very inaccurate in many respects. I am in hopes that former [free-state] Gov. [Charles] Robinson will review him, as he is abundantly able to do, and [as he] is in possession of facts that would silence an *honorable* opponent. I have no hopes, however, of silencing Sanborn, for he has a point to make, and when driven from one untenable position flies to another and then to another, from which he will soon retreat. The only true defense for the friends of John Brown to make for his actions is that he was a monomaniac."[8]

In the final analysis, Lawrence had nothing but condemnation for Brown. "John Brown had no enemies in New England, but many friends and admirers," said Amos Lawrence in May of 1884, when presenting a miniature portrait of Brown to the Massachusetts Historical Society. "He was constantly receiving money from them. They little knew what use he was making of it, for he deceived everybody. If he had succeeded in his design at Harpers Ferry of exciting a servile insurrection, the country would have stood aghast with horror; his would have been anything but a martyr's crown."⁹

Eight days after the Pottawatomie Massacre, John Brown received word that a group of Missourians commanded by Henry Clay Pate (a native of Virginia, a captain of the Missouri militia, and a deputy U.S. marshal) was camped on the Sante Fe Trail at Black Jack Springs. Pate's mission was to search out Brown and other free-stater fighters on whom warrants were outstanding. Brown would subsequently tell Redpath that he envisioned the Missourians at Black Jack as akin to the Midianites who had camped near the Wall of Harod. And he viewed himself as Gideon, chosen to slay them and drive them back across the Jordan (or, in this case, the Missouri) River.

Early in the first week of June, Brown traveled to Black Jack and, with the help of a free-state volunteer militia from Prairie City, surrounded Pate's squad, launched a surprise attack, and killed four Missourians. What came to be called the Battle of Black Jack ended when Captain Pate, who still had plenty of men and ammunition at his disposal but hoped to avoid further bloodshed on either side, came out to speak with his attackers under a flag of truce. Brown drew his revolver and aimed it at Pate as they talked. "You can't do this," said Pate. "I'm under a white flag; you're violating the articles of war." "You are my prisoner," replied Brown matter-of-factly. "I had no alternative," wrote Pate, "but to submit, or run and be shot. Had I known who I was fighting, I would not have trusted to a white flag." Brown marched Pate back to his lines, whereupon Brown put the gun to Pate's head and ordered the Missourians to either surrender or watch their captain die.¹⁰ The victorious Brown intended to exchange Pate and his men for Governor Robinson and other free-state prisoners. However, on June 5, Brown and his little band were surrounded by fifty United States cavalrymen who demanded the release of Pate and all the Missouri militiamen. Such was the limit of Brown's brief victory in the Battle of Black Jack.

When Thomas Wentworth Higginson arrived in Kansas within days of the fight, he did not meet the fugitive Brown, but did hear glowing accounts about the events at Black Jack. Higginson was sent west as an agent of the newly founded Massachusetts State Kansas Committee. He carried with him what was literally a trunkful of money and instructions to aid two contingents of settlers from Massachusetts who had been disarmed, robbed, and turned back from the Kansas border by proslavery Missourians. "I almost hoped to hear," Higginson wrote in a report published in the *New York Tribune,* "that some of their lives had been sacrificed, for it seems as if nothing but that would arouse the Eastern States to act. This seems a terrible thing to say, but these are terrible times."

With the Missouri River blockaded against the passage of free-state emigrants, Higginson used Committee funds to rent a steamboat and send settlers from St. Louis up the Mississippi to Davenport, Iowa, from where they could continue to Kansas by coach, horse, or foot. Others he sent via stage to Council Bluffs, Iowa, from where there was about a hundred miles to traverse to Topeka. Martin Stowell, a Worcester man who had been involved in the Anthony Burns affair, led a group of settlers who "came and absolutely begged of me to let them go up the Missouri River . . . pledging themselves to die, if need be, but to redeem the honor of Massachusetts. From the bottom of my heart I felt with them; one word from me would have done it, but I did not feel authorized to speak that word, and therefore sent them on by the other route. Had they gone by the river I should have gone with them."

Higginson was back in his comfortable Worcester home by early summer. Meanwhile, through most of July and August, the fugitive John Brown laid low in the inhospitable Kansas scrub wilderness, while the free-state guerrilla militia from Lawrence, commanded by James Lane, mounted a series of raids on proslavery settlements at New Georgia, Franklin, Fort Saunders, Treadwell, and Fort Titus. Lane and his men burned buildings and confiscated livestock and guns. Toward the end of August, itching to get back into the southern Kansas civil war he had done so much to precipitate, Brown raised a seven-man company of "Regulars" in Lawrence. On August 22, joined by two additional contingents of free-state soldiers, Brown's Kansas Regulars marched to his old neighborhood of Osawatomie, where reprisal attacks from Missouri were expected shortly in exchange for the raids made by Lane several weeks earlier. In the Battle of Osawatomie that followed, Brown's son Frederick was killed—shot through the heart—and Brown's company, after being routed, failed to stop Missouri raiders from burning the town of Osawatomie to the ground.

Higginson again missed crossing paths with Brown when he returned to Kansas that September, ready to take up arms to facilitate free-state emigration. "At present no person, without actually travelling across Iowa, can appreciate the injury done by the closing of the Missouri River," he wrote in a letter intended for publication back East. "Emigrants must toil, week after week, beneath a burning sun, over the parched and endless 'rolling prairie,' sometimes seeing no house for a day or two together, camping often without wood, and sometimes without water, and obliged to carry with them every eatable they use. It is no wonder that they often fall sick on the way; and when I consider how infinitely weary were even my four days and nights of staging (after as many more of railroad travel), I can only wonder at the patience and fortitude which the present emigrants have shown." He wrote to his wife from Nebraska City: "I have been for a week in a forlorn little town, arranging a [wagon] train of emigrants to go into Kansas, armed and equipped as the law forbids." The wagon train was to be heavily armed. Several carriages carried nothing but Sharp's rifles, pistols, ammunition, and cannon under tarps.

In the course of his preparations at Nebraska City, he met the would-be free-state senator and erstwhile guerrilla leader James Lane. The belligerent and bitter Lane was in retreat from Kansas at the head of the ill-provisioned militia with which he'd conducted his July raids. Lane and his men—among whom was a future confederate of John Brown, Aaron Stevens—had just been ordered out of the state by Gov. John W. Geary. (Geary was appointed to his post in mid-August by Pres. Franklin Pierce, but only arrived in the territory on September 9. Geary was fair-minded and forthright. Along with expelling Lane, another of his first official acts was to release Governor Robinson and all other free-state politicians from the jail cells in which they'd been held since May.) Higginson regarded Geary as just another stooge of the slave power, as he wrote to the board of the Massachusetts Kansas Committee, adding that Lane would go down in history books as a great hero of abolition. Higginson used Committee funds to buy clothes for Lane's ragged army. Lane rewarded him with an honorary free-state commission as brigadier general. (The commission, it turns out, was an honor that Lane conferred liberally on virtually any and all sympathizers with the free-state cause.)

"I got here yesterday afternoon after six days' ride and walk (chiefly the former) across the prairies of Kansas," Higginson wrote to his wife from Topeka on September 24. "The rest of the [wagon] train will be in today and tomorrow." He asked Mary to imagine him patrolling "as one of the guard for an hour every night, in high boots amid the dewy grass, rifle in hand and revolver in belt. But nobody ever came and we never had any danger. Only once, in the day time, the whole company charged upon a band of extremely nude Indians, taking them for Missourians." The wagon train consisted of thirty wagons and included settlers from Maine, Massachusetts, Vermont, Illinois, and Indiana.

"Yesterday morning I waked at Topeka and found the house surrounded by dragoons," wrote Higginson to his wife on September 28. "To my amazement, on going out, the Captain addressed me by name. . . . He was very cordial, but their [orders were] to arrest the leaders of the party just arrived if they proved to be a military company. . . . Finally, Col. Preston, the young Virginia Marshal, decided to arrest no one, and he, Redpath, Gov. Robinson, and I rode down in one carriage to Gov. Geary at Lecompton, and after some talk with the pompous, foolish, conceited, obstinate Governor [we] were honorably discharged. If they had had wit to discover the Sharp's rifles and cannon we brought in with us, we should all have been arrested."

Higginson preached in Lawrence on the last Sunday in September. He took for his text that used by the Reverend John Martin the Sunday after he fought at Bunker Hill: "Be not ye afraid of them; remember the Lord, which is great and terrible, and fight for your brethren, your sons and your daughters, your wives and your houses." A few days later, beginning his journey home on the steamboat *Cataract,* which was now suddenly aground on a bank in the Missouri River, Higginson killed time by making a note in his journal book. "My best hope is that the contest may be at once transferred to more favorable soil, Nebraska or Iowa, and result in a disruption of the Union; for I am sure that the disease [of slavery] is too deep for cure without amputation."

He stopped at St. Louis for a few days during which he visited a slave market. When Higginson asked the proprietor of the establishment whence came most of his inventory, it was reported that it was not uncommon for families visiting Northern watering places to bring with them a "likely boy or girl" and sell them to pay the expenses of the jaunt. "This is a feature of the patriarchal institution which I think has escaped Mrs. Stowe," wrote Higginson. "Hereafter I shall never see a Southern heiress at Newport without fancying I read on her ball-dress the name of the 'likely boy or girl' who was sold for it." Before he left the place, Higginson watched as a tearful young black child named Sue was sold away from her two sisters. "So ended the bargain, and I presently took my leave," wrote Higginson. "I had one last glance at Sue. It is not long since I set foot on the floating wreck of an unknown vessel at sea, and then left it drifting away in the darkness alone. But it was sadder to me to think of that little wreck of babyhood drifting off alone into the ocean of Southern crime and despair."

Recording his trip to the slave market in an article that was reprinted in pamphlet form and distributed at antislavery rallies throughout the country, Higginson said he was publishing his account "in the faint hope of enlightening the minds of those verdant innocents who still believe that the separation of families is a rare occurrence, when every New Orleans newspaper contains a dozen advertisements of 'Assorted lots of young Negroes.'"[11]

☆

Whether Higginson liked him or not, John Geary was just the type of governor Kansas needed. Geary cracked down on both antislavery and proslavery guerrillas and brought an end to the civil war that had cost more than two hundred lives and over $2 million in damaged property. The Kansas border was closed to *all* brands of terror. Gradually, as more and more irregulars from both sides were either disarmed or sent packing, peace broke out. By Christmas of 1856, there were virtually no instances of invasion from Missouri. Geary was maintaining strict law and order; and the major preoccupation for both proslavery and free-state emigrants was a land boom.

John Brown, who was still a wanted man, found the new, placid climate of Kansas uncomfortable and inhibiting. He had been operating in the territory since October of 1855; but now was a good time to go east and raise money to support the next round in his holy battle. His daughter Ruth had written him with an enticing bit of abolitionist gossip. "Gerrit Smith has had his name put down for ten thousand dollars towards starting a company of one thousand men to Kansas."[12] Now the would-be Commander Brown set out toward New England, intent on collecting Smith's $10,000 and any other money he could to continue his war.

10

TO SHAME
INTO NOBLENESS
UNMANLY YOUTH

COMING TO BOSTON in quest of affluent supporters, John Brown must at first have been disappointed by the sight of the squalid, Dickensian space maintained by the Massachusetts State Kansas Committee. The committee's office was in the cold garret of a brownstone on School Street, not far from Boston Common. The tiny, cheerless place was a confusion of old, donated tables and rickety chairs. The tables were piled high with penny pamphlets on Kansas issues, old and new copies of the *Commonwealth* and *Liberator,* and "Past Due" notices from various suppliers of guns, tools, and other Kansas essentials. The lone occupant of the office was the young volunteer secretary of the committee, Franklin Sanborn, who wore a greatcoat and gloves as he labored with one small candle yielding the sum total of his light, and most of his warmth as well.

When Brown first met him that January of 1857, the twenty-six-year-old Sanborn had a certain dark celebrity around Boston. When still in his teens, the handsome, New Hampshire–born Sanborn had

Franklin Sanborn, John Brown's adoring young Boston friend, photographed in the mid-1850s. Photo courtesy Boston Public Library.

fallen in love with a daughter of the affluent Walker family. Slightly older than Sanborn, the fragile yet precocious Ariana Walker helped her young suitor with his studies at Phillips Exeter Academy and encouraged him to continue on to Harvard. Sanborn was still at Harvard when he received the grim news that Ariana was dying of a rare neurological disease. He married her on her deathbed, buried her within days of their wedding, and treasured her letters and a lock of her hair for the rest of his life. After his nearly simultaneous marriage and bereavement, the glum young man with the black band on his stovepipe hat, making daily visits to the churchyard, was much the talk around Harvard and in Boston society. He seemed the epitome of romantic Victorian mourning in an age that made a cult not just of death, but especially of tragic youthful death. Several months after Ariana's demise, Sanborn got an estimate of the expense for an exhumation. He wanted to look upon her just once more. His friend Emerson had once unearthed his young son for the same purpose. In Sanborn's case, however, the transaction does not seem to have gone forward. In time, Sanborn's grief gave way to the concerns of his continuing life: his career as a teacher and his growing involvement in the antislavery movement.

Sanborn's class at Harvard (the class of 1855) numbered among its members Phillips Brooks and Alexander Agassiz. Sanborn graduated seventh in his class and was elected to Phi Beta Kappa but declined the election, calling the society an "unjustifiable intellectual aristocracy."[1] After graduation, Sanborn moved to Concord and opened a college preparatory school. In writing a testimonial for Sanborn to include in the promotional brochure for his new venture, Bronson Alcott called Sanborn "sensible and manly" and said the young teacher "commands the respect of all who know him." He was, wrote Alcott, a "graduate of Harvard and a scholar, in politics a Republican." As Sophia Hawthorne recalled, the Sanborn School was soon "popular and prosperous," attracting "scholars from the best families." The sons of Emerson, Hawthorne, and Horace Mann were enrolled, as were the younger sons of Henry James, Sr.[2] Alcott, in a private journal entry, qualified his opinion of Sanborn with a word of caution. It might be that Sanborn was "something of a revolutionary in a quiet way." Sanborn's friend Henry Thoreau expressed a similar sentiment, saying Sanborn's "quiet, steadfast earnestness and ethical fortitude are of the type that calmly, so calmly, ignites and then throws bomb after bomb."[3]

It was the late Ariana's brother George, an abolitionist who had known John Brown in Springfield, who suggested that Brown seek out Franklin Sanborn. "[Brown] came to me in this city," Sanborn recounted for a Boston audience in 1897, "with a note of introduction from a kinsman of mine in Springfield, —both of us being Kansas committeemen, working to maintain the cause of freedom in that territory, —and Brown having been one of the marked fighting men there in the summer before. His theory required fighting in Kansas; it was the only sure way, he thought, to keep that region free from the curse of slavery. His errand was to levy war on it, and for that to raise a company of 100 well-armed men who should resist aggression in Kansas, and occasionally carry the war into Missouri. Behind that purpose, but not yet disclosed, was the intention to use the men thus put into the field for similar incursions into Virginia and other Southern States."[4] But to get the whole enterprise off the ground he needed two hundred Sharp's rifles and $30,000 in cash.

Sitting in the small, flickering glow of Sanborn's little light, Brown seemed larger than life as he spent several hours telling an awed Sanborn tales from the Kansas battlefront. He spoke of the Wakarusa War, omitting his fomenting of dissension among the free-state ranks. He told of his fleeting and almost accidental conquest at the Battle of Black Jack as if it had been a success born of strategic genius. And he described his dismal performance during the fight at Osawatomie in the same glowing terms. "[Brown's] victory at Black Jack . . . ," wrote Frank Stearns, who as a boy heard Brown recount his exploits within a week of when Sanborn did, "was as brilliant an affair as the Concord fight of 1775; and at the subsequent battle of Osawatomie he inflicted such a severe loss on the Missourians that they never invaded that section of Kansas again."[5] Brown did not mention the events along the Pottawatomie Creek. When Sanborn asked him what had happened there (for he had heard rumors), John Brown assured Sanborn of his complete innocence.

Knowing what would play best in Boston, Brown made sure Sanborn knew that he was descended from Peter Browne, a carpenter who had arrived on the *Mayflower* with some of Sanborn's forebears in 1620.[6] He also pointed out that his paternal grandfather was "a martyr" of the Revolution—killed while serving as commander of the Eighteenth Connecticut Regiment.

The *Mayflower.* The Revolution. The blood of the old Puritans flowing in the devout, resolute, and seemingly incorruptible Brown, who was so intent on fulfilling the promise implicit in the Declaration of Independence by eradicating slavery forever. It all seemed so right, so appropriate. Sanborn would say in a speech that he felt always there was something "inevitable" about John Brown, that Brown personally embodied "the salvation—the continuation—of the great American experiment. He was a fighter and a purifier such as was long overdue. We had felt in our heart to expect one such as he; it had somehow been foretold." Now the inevitable knocked on the door; and an enthusiastic Sanborn answered, anxious to embrace his and his country's destiny. By the end of that first meeting, Sanborn had agreed to help Brown get the money he needed.

Two of the first people Sanborn introduced Brown to were Theodore Parker and Sam Howe. Both men fully shared Brown's view that only civil war, first in Kansas and then countrywide, could bring an end to slavery. Parker was sufficiently impressed with Brown to offer to host a reception for him.

Brown seemed painfully uncomfortable, nervous, and out of place as Howe, making introductions, steered him around Theodore Parker's plush dining room. Brown was dressed in a cheap and worn corduroy suit. One lapel had a small rip. There was dirt under his fingernails. His hands were callused and scarred. Shorn short, the hairs on his head seemed to shoot up straight vertically from it, pointing toward the ceiling and making it appear as though he had just absorbed some sort of electrical shock. His energetic, nervous eyes wandered quickly from one fancy gentleman to another—all these finely dressed and manicured dandies whom he needed to seduce into supporting his revolution.

The bald, bespectacled William Lloyd Garrison was among those who met Brown at Parker's home. "He saw in the famous Kansas chieftain," Garrison's grandson would write, "a tall, spare, farmer-like man with head disproportionately small, and that inflexible mouth which as yet no beard concealed. . . . [Brown and Garrison] discussed peace and non-resistance together, Brown quoting the Old Testament against Garrison's citations from the New, and Parker from time to time injecting a bit of Lexington into the controversy, which attracted a small group of interested listeners." Brown's God was a jealous, unforgiving demander of an eye for an eye and a tooth for a tooth. Garrison's milder version of the same was a compassionate healer: a God who tended to frown, for example, on the splitting open of heads with broadswords. Wendell Phillips, whom Brown also met at Parker's reception, joined Garrison in being skeptical of the Kansas militiaman. The massacre at Pottawatomie, wrote Phillips to Garrison shortly after meeting Brown, "cannot be successfully palliated or excused." It was just the sort of outrageous act that the antislavery movement needed no connection with. Brown, Garrison and Phillips agreed, was a detriment.

Both Phillips and Garrison would publicly voice support for Brown after the debacle at Harpers Ferry, when it became clear that the doomed, messianic terrorist was bound to become a heroic icon of their movement whether they liked it or not. Phillips would even travel to the Adirondack Mountains after Brown's execution in Virginia in order to speak at the old man's funeral. And Garrison would grudgingly admit him a hero. "In recording the expressions of sympathy and admiration which are so widely felt for Brown," Garrison wrote in the *Liberator,* "whose doom is so swiftly approaching, we desire to say—once and for all—that, judging him by the code of Bunker Hill, we think he is as deserving of high-wrought eulogy as any who ever wielded sword or battle-axe in the cause of liberty; but we do not and cannot approve any indulgence in the war spirit."[7]

☆

Another guest at Parker's reception was George Luther Stearns. Stearns, who had actually been introduced to Brown by Sanborn several days before Parker's party, was by this time one of the chief financiers of the Emigrant Aid Company. He also served as chairman of the Massachusetts State Kansas Committee and sat on the executive board of the National Kansas Committee. In the six months prior, Stearns personally raised no less than $48,000 for the Free Kansas movement, and his wife, Mary, another $20,000 to $30,000 through a number of women's auxiliary benefits.[8] When Stearns first encountered John Brown, they met, recalled Frank Preston Stearns, "like the iron and the magnet." Stearns, the iron-willed abolitionist, was irresistibly attracted to Brown, the magnetic Calvinist seeker of justice. Stearns took satisfaction, wrote his son, in the way Brown "looked at the world with the eyes of a Puritan of the Long Parliament, and judged it accordingly. His ideas of morality, private and public, were not relative but absolute."[9]

George Stearns was not the only person to compare Brown to the heroes of the Reformation. "When I entered the parlor he was sitting near the hearth," wrote Mary Stearns of her first meeting with Brown when he spent a night at her house, "where glowed a bright open fire. He rose to meet me, stepping forward with such an erect military bearing, such a fine courtesy of demeanor and grave earnestness that he seemed to my instant thought some old Cromwellian hero suddenly dropped down before me."[10] Brown reminded Thomas Wentworth Higginson of Cromwell or some other "high-minded, unselfish, belated Covenanter; a man whom Sir Walter Scott might have drawn." Sanborn said of Brown that he well illustrated "the Puritan of Cromwell's time."[11] Julia Ward Howe called him "a Puritan of the Puritans, forceful, concentrated, and self-contained."[12] Shortly before Brown's execution, Wendell Phillips would compare him to Huss and Wycliffe, two martyrs of the Reformation, "who died violent deaths for breaking the laws of Rome."[13] It is important to keep in mind that these analogies to Cromwell and other heroes of the Reformation were not likely to be drawn lightly by men like Higginson and Stearns, who took the greatest pride in claiming descent from the seventeenth-century Puritan settlers of Plymouth and Salem. The Pilgrim fathers had, after all, separated from the Church of England precisely because they felt it had not completely fulfilled the cleansing mission of the Reformation. (Frank Stearns echoed his father's view of Brown when he called him "a Cromwellian ironside introduced in the nineteenth century for a special purpose." That purpose was "to take up the work of the English Puritans where it had ended with the death of Cromwell—the work of social regeneration."[14])

George Luther Stearns respected men who, like himself, had made their own way in the world. He saw himself reflected in those who started with nothing, persevered in the face of failure, and rose to conquer all obstacles. Brown was smart enough to sense this and seems to have depicted himself accordingly. Fifty years after the first meeting of the adoring Stearns and the shrewd Brown, the Stearns family would still believe Brown's misrepresentations about his past. In his 1907 biography of his father, Frank Preston Stearns reported as verbatim fact what Brown told George Luther Stearns in 1857: that Brown had been "a successful sheep-farmer" considered "trustworthy and judicious" by his neighbors in Ohio. Of course, nothing could have been further from the truth.

Sitting by the fire at Stearns's ornate Medford mansion on the evening of January 11, Brown entertained Stearns's young sons with a blow-by-blow account of the battle at Black Jack and also told of other Kansas border fights. He took out the long bowie knife he had taken from one of his victims in the Pottawatomie Massacre, explained that he'd confiscated it from a captured Missouri invader, and allowed the boys to pass it amongst themselves in silent awe. He positioned chairs around the sitting room to represent barns or mountains or lakes, as the case might have been, and then energetically hopped amongst them to simulate the checkmating moves of various free-state militias against proslavery forces, making laughing quips about the shades of color the scared proslavery men changed to every time they were routed and sent into retreat. (Indeed, the way Brown lampooned his adversaries, pointing out their utter lack of wit and bravery, it was hard to see how they could have been considered a threat in the first place.) Then Brown suddenly grew serious and told the boys of murders committed by proslavery "terrorizors," and of free-state families left hungry and shelterless after having their barns and houses burned by Missouri ruffians. Brown's stories inspired the twelve-year-old Henry Stearns to give Brown his savings—a few stray dollars in a shoebox—for the relief of free-state Kansans. Then the boy said: "Captain Brown, I wish you would tell me about your boyhood." Brown smiled and said, "My son, I cannot do that now, for I fear it would weary the ladies, but when I have time I will try to write something for you on that subject."[15]

Within weeks of their first meeting, wishing to support Brown's idea for a Kansas free-state army, Stearns instructed Brown to buy two hundred revolvers from the Massachusetts Arms Company at a total cost of $1,300 and paid the bill out of his own pocket.[16]

☆

"'Old Brown' of Kansas is now in Boston . . . raising and arming a company of men for the future protection of Kansas," Sanborn wrote Higginson on January 5. "He wishes to raise $30,000 to arm and equip a company . . . but he will as I understand him, take what money he can raise and use it as far as it will go. Can you not come to Boston tomorrow or next day and see Capt. Brown? If not, please indicate when you will be in Worcester so that he can see you. I like the man from what I have seen and his deeds ought to bear witness for him."[17] Higginson, who was recently returned from his own Kansas adventure, met Brown in Boston on January 9 at the United States Hotel. After the interview, Higginson told a friend that Brown appealed to "the untamable Gypsy element in me which gives me instant sympathy with every desperate adventure."[18] "Can anything be done for the good old man [Brown] in Worcester County among your friends?" asked Sanborn shortly after Higginson's meeting with Brown. Higginson, who was busy organizing a state dis-union convention to be held in Worcester on January 15, agreed to help. Like Howe and Parker, he hoped Brown's activities would provoke a major conflict on the Kansas border that in turn might lead to civil war. An amateur boxer, Higginson itched to see slave and free states go at it with the gloves off. And he was intrigued by Brown's propensity for making fists fly.

On January 7, the Massachusetts State Kansas Committee—which was dominated by Sanborn, Stearns, and Howe—appointed Brown their agent and assigned him two hundred Sharp's rifles along with caps and cartridges that were stored at Tabor, Iowa. The only complication was that the two hundred rifles had already been contributed by the Massa-chusetts Committee to the National Kansas Committee (also known as the Kansas Aid Society) based in Chicago, which now had to approve the gift to Brown. In a somewhat rancorous meeting of the National Kansas Committee held at the Astor House Hotel in New York City on January 24, Franklin Sanborn stood in as proxy for Sam Howe and Samuel Cabot on a vote to ratify the gift of the Sharp's rifles to Brown's militia. Brown, who was present, asked not only for the guns, but also for an additional $1,000 in military supplies and $5,000 in cash. Several western delegates, led by Henry B. Hurd of Chicago, objected to the idea. Hurd, recalled Sanborn, "had some inkling that Brown would not confine his warfare to Kansas."[19] But, as Hurd wrote later, the "more radical eastern members" of the committee won the vote, and the National Committee approved the gift of both the arms and the money to Brown.[20]

The success Brown had with the National Kansas Committee was not to be repeated a few days later when he visited Gerrit Smith at Peterboro. Brown found the unpredictable Smith in a dour mood: morose, pessimistic, suffering from what he once called one of his "periodic low and melancholy" states, and suffering also from a severe cold. As Brown enthusiastically laid out his plan for raising and arming a free-state militia, Smith sat stone-faced at his desk, coughing occasionally, a thick woolen scarf wrapped around his neck, gazing soberly out the window at the frigid blanket of snow that covered his enormous lawn.

At the end of the presentation, Smith announced somewhat sourly that he could do nothing for Brown. Antislavery work had taxed his cash reserves too much lately. He had already subscribed $1,000 per year to the National Kansas Committee. Meeting that pledge along with all his other obligations was almost too much for him to handle without going into his capital. Smith said he had to be careful of things. The country was on the cusp of a great financial panic, with inflation on the rise, businesses going bust, and what he called "the general prosperity of the east" evaporating. Money was tight and bound to get tighter. Besides, Smith reminded Brown, he had not yet received payment from Brown of the very modest sum owed for the North Elba lands. (There was similar tension when, leaving Smith, Brown stopped for a few days with his family at North Elba. Brown's son-in-law and confederate in the Pottawatomie Massacre, Henry Thompson, who had returned from Kansas the previous summer, complained he'd not yet been paid for the house he'd built on Brown's property. Brown assured him the cash would be coming soon.)

Brown was back in Boston by February 18, on which date Sanborn introduced him before the Massachusetts State Legislature's joint committee on federal relations. Brown's purpose was to speak in support of a $100,000 appropriation to go toward the protection of former Massachusetts citizens who were now free-state Kansans. "Such an appropriation had been voted in Vermont," remembered Sanborn, "and we came near carrying it here; but it was finally voted down. Brown spoke forcibly, — reading much from a paper describing the losses he had seen inflicted in Kansas on free-state men."

Toward the end of February, or early in March, Brown stopped in the midst of his increasingly frustrating round of Eastern fund-raising to visit Sanborn for several days at Concord. Sanborn was at that time renting the home of Higginson's cousin by marriage Ellery Channing. The Channing house stood across the street from the home of Henry Thoreau's father and mother, with whom Thoreau was living. "It was on a Friday night that Brown came up from Boston," remembered Sanborn, "and at noon we went across the street to dine with the Thoreaus. All Concord had heard of his fights and escapes in Kansas, the summer before, and Henry Thoreau was desirous of meeting him. As I had engagements after dinner, I left Brown talking with Thoreau, who saw what manner of man he was. . . . While they sat discoursing, in the spring afternoon, Mr. Emerson, who lived at the other (eastern) side of the village, came up to call on Mr. Thoreau, and was there introduced to John Brown. From this day's conversation, and what followed the next night, which Brown spent at Mr. Emerson's house, came that intimate acquaintance with Brown's character and general purposes which enabled Thoreau and Emerson, in 1859, to make those addresses in praise of him that did so much to turn the tide of sentiment in Brown's favor, after his capture in Harpers Ferry."[21]

Sanborn arranged for Brown to speak at the Town House in Concord, where both Emerson and Thoreau were among his listeners. It seemed as if virtually every citizen of the little hamlet was crammed into the hall to hear the famous Captain Brown. Sanborn played master of ceremonies, giving by way of introduction a long and grave recitation of Brown's many victories and sacrifices for the antislavery cause. Then the old man himself rose up to the dais lit by several oil lanterns in the otherwise dark room. He recounted the crimes of Missouri, the U.S. government, and the proslavery forces in Kansas and explained his radical military prescription for resolving the problem. As he had so many times before, he told of how he abhorred war and violence, but accepted it as God's will: the penance prescribed for an unjust nation engaged in the ungodly act of countenancing slavery. Standing just a few hundred yards from Concord bridge, and but a few miles from Lexington Green,

Brown announced that the two most sacred documents known to man were the Bible and the Declaration of Independence, and that it was "better that a whole generation of men, women and children should pass away by a violent death than that a word of either should be violated in this country."[22] Brown's dramatic talk brought enthusiastic applause from the townspeople, but few donations. Emerson pledged only a modest sum to the cause. Thoreau wrote in his journal that he had "much confidence in the man—that he would do right," and therefore "subscribed a trifle."

The Concord reception was similar to that which met Brown in most other communities of the Northeast where he stopped: In the midst of the growing financial panic, his listeners were enthusiastic but tight-fisted. At town after town, they pitched nothing but nickels and dimes into the collection box. After speaking at dozens of towns across New York, Connecticut, and Massachusetts, Brown wound up with only a few hundred dollars in cash and pledges. In early April, Henry Hurd, secretary of the National Kansas Committee, who had voted against giving Brown support, wrote a slightly tongue-in-cheek letter to Brown saying "the present state of the public feeling, evinced by the almost cessation of contributions," left the committee nearly bankrupt. Hurd could not send Brown any of the $5,000 that had been promised at the January meeting.[23] In turn, the millionaire Amos Lawrence—after calling Brown the "Miles Standish of Kansas" and promising $1,000—came through with a mere $70 in cash.

Some slight good news came first from Higginson, who had gotten together a small collection, and then from Stearns. "Please retain in your own hands the funds you speak of; as I expect to be at Worcester this week," wrote Brown to Higginson on April 1. "Should you wish to leave [Worcester] please leave it for me with Dr. Webb, Emigrant Aide Office, 3 Winter St. . . . My heart grows sad in the fear of a failure of the enterprise."[24] On April 15, Stearns wrote Brown with word that the Massachusetts Kansas Committee would give him one hundred Sharp's rifles to be sold to free-state Kansans—"at a price of not less than fifteen dollars" apiece—for their home defense. The proceeds from the sales were to be used at Brown's discretion "for the benefit of the free-state men." Also, the committee put $500 in cash at Brown's disposal.[25]

During the first and second weeks of April, Brown had plenty of time to tally his meager pledges when he retreated to the home of Thomas B. Russell, abolitionist judge of the Massachusetts Superior Court, there to hide from a U.S. marshal rumored to be coming to Boston to arrest him for his role in the Pottawatomie affair. Judge Russell's wife recalled that she turned "stiff with fright" when the smiling Brown nonchalantly pulled out "a long, evil-looking knife" and several revolvers, announcing that he would hate to soil her fine carpet but that he would not be taken alive. Brown spent all his days and nights barricaded in a third-floor bedroom, coming downstairs only for meals. He seemed, Mrs. Russell recalled, to take a strange, perverse delight in tormenting his protectors. There was something mocking in the way he observed and commented on her and the judge's house, society, and way of life. He clearly viewed himself, in all his plainness and poverty, as possessing a subtle superiority over them. At meal after meal he persisted with the topics of starvation and poverty, always "gravely mentioning . . . unspeakable articles upon which he said he had lived—joints and toes of creatures that surely no human being ever tasted."[26]

John Brown was wounded and resentful. He felt ill-used. New England had not responded adequately to his call. He would not let these millionaires salve their consciences by throwing him a few morsels from the banquet that was their life, or by giving him an occasional roof to sleep under. On one level at least, he despised them all with their wealth and refinement and comfort. Lying across a plush bed in the Russells' fine home, with expensive mahogany furniture stacked against the door lest he be surprised by intruders, Brown composed a brief public letter that summarized all his bitter dissatisfaction. In the statement, which he titled "Old Browns [sic] Farewell to the Plymouth Rocks, Bunker Hill Monuments, Charter Oaks, and Uncle Thoms Cabbins [sic]," he wrote of himself in the third person, saying that Brown "has left for Kansas."

Brown, the somewhat inarticulate essay said, "has been trying since he came out of the territory to secure an outfit or in other words; the means of arming and thoroughly equipping his regular Minuet [*sic*] men, who are mixed up *with the people* of Kansas, and *he leaves* the States, *with a feeling of deepest sadness:* that after having exhausted his own small means and *with his family and his brave men;* suffered hunger, cold, nakedness, *and some* of them sickness, wounds, imprisonment in *irons;* with extreme cruel treatment, *and others death:* that . . . after all this; in order to sustain a cause which every citizen of this 'glorious Republic,' is under equal moral obligation to do: *and for the neglect of which, he will be held accountable by God:* a cause in which every man, woman, and child; of the entire *human family* has a *deep* and *awful* interest; that when no *wages* are asked; or expected; he cannot secure, amidst all the wealth, luxury, and extravagance of this 'Heaven exalted,' people; even the necessary supplies of the common soldier. How are the mighty fallen."[27]

Brown drafted copies of the "Farewell" for Stearns and Parker. After reading the missive, Mary Stearns urged her husband to liquidate their entire estate and give the money toward Brown's "sublime purpose."[28] Brown's "Farewell" affected Stearns greatly. Stearns wrote Brown a letter of credit authorizing him to draw on Stearns "at sight" for $7,000 to be applied as Brown saw fit toward "the defense of Kansas."[29] Hearing of Stearns's promise, Parker told an associate that Stearns's name would be "written in the Lambs [*sic*] Book of life."[30] With Stearns's pledge added to the rest on the sheet in his pocket, Brown slipped quietly out of Boston in mid-April and headed for North Elba, where he rested for a week before starting a circuitous, three-month-long, stop-and-go return to the western territories via Ohio and Chicago.

Sanborn, too, was still in Brown's thrall. On the evening of April 27, shortly after Brown departed Boston, he whiled away some time by writing a sonnet in praise of his new hero.

JOHN BROWN OF OSAWATOMIE

In thee still sternly lives our fathers' heart,
Brave Puritan. Stout Standish had praised God
for such as thou, —of Mayflower *blood thou art.*
And worthier feet on Plymouth Rock ne'er trod.
Deep in thy pious soul devoutly burns
the Hebrew fire with Saxon fuel fed;
Thy honest heart all fear and cunning spurns.
Swift hand for action hast thou, and wise head;
O good old man! the vigor of thy age
Shames into nobleness unmanly youth.
Honor *shall write thy name on her fair page.*
Ere thou art dead, and ancient Faith and Truth,
Valor and Constancy thy fame uphold,
When our sons' sons shall hear thy story told.[31]

$$11$$

ENTER HUGH FORBES

J OHN BROWN HELD a secret meeting in Chicago in mid-June with a newly radicalized, refreshingly upbeat Gerrit Smith. Whether it was the exchange of winter doldrums for summer warmth, or the improvement of his personal financial position despite the oncoming financial panic, Brown did not know, but some shift in mood or the planets returned Smith to his old open, courteous, and—of most importance to Brown—*generous* self. There were, of course, some obvious pragmatic reasons for the change. Sitting in a restaurant on Dearborn Street, Smith told Brown he believed recent ominous events—most particularly the Dred Scott decision—signaled a renewed need for extra vigilance by antislavery men. Smith, who was in the Midwest to speak at antislavery meetings in Illinois and Wisconsin, said he was sure that Kansas would soon erupt in violence once again. He gave Brown $350 in cash at their meeting and promised more toward the support of Brown's free-state soldiers. When Brown mentioned, hesitatingly, that in addition to money for his movement he also needed some cash with which to settle his debt to Henry Thompson for the house he'd built on the North Elba property, Smith smiled confidentially, reached into his pocket, and produced an additional $110.[1] Brown still had not paid Smith for the land the house was built on, but this was not mentioned.

A month later, Smith showed his continuing support of Brown by playing host to the man designated as Brown's deputy military strategist, Hugh Forbes. Before going west to join Brown and his men, Forbes came up from Manhattan to visit Gerrit Smith and prevail upon him for an advance of $150 above and beyond some $600 he had already received from Brown four months earlier. (It is unclear whether Smith knew about the $600.) "Col. Hugh Forbes arrives at 11 A.M.," wrote Smith in his journal for July 24, "on his way to Kansas to assist my friend Capt. John Brown in military operations. I put some money into his hands. I have put some this season into the hands of Capt. Brown."[2] Smith wrote Thaddeus Hyatt, an agent for the National Kansas Committee, that he was favorably impressed with Forbes, who would "prove very useful in our sacred work in Kansas."[3] Frederick Douglass, whom Forbes called on about this same time and tried to borrow money from, wrote that his initial instinct was to dislike and mistrust the colonel, but that Forbes shortly "conquered" his "prejudice."

It had been in Manhattan, in March, that Brown first encountered Forbes: a bold, volatile man who was an acquaintance of Kansas journalist James Redpath. Twelve years younger than Brown, the forty-five-year-old Forbes fancied himself as being blessed with a military genius akin to that of Wellington. In real life, his past was just as checkered and riddled with failure as Brown's. Born in Scotland, Forbes spent time as a silk merchant in Vienna before fighting with Garibaldi in the abortive Italian Revolution of 1848. After his time with Garibaldi, Forbes settled in Paris where he married, started a family, and authored a two-volume manual on military tactics. Leaving his wife and several children behind in Paris, Forbes came to the United States in the mid-1850s, where he settled in New York and served briefly as editor of an Italian-language newspaper, the *European*. By the time he met John Brown, the unpredictable, alcoholic Forbes had been fired from the *European* and was just scraping by. He lived in a slum apartment beside a brothel on Delancey

Street and moonlighted as a fencing coach when not working as a free-lance reporter/translator for the *New York Tribune.*

Brown found Forbes at once fascinated by the prospect of guerrilla warfare and hungry for a break in the monotony of his hand-to-mouth existence. Brown invited Forbes to join him as military instructor for his Kansas battalion at $100 per month, with a $600 advance on salary payable immediately. Forbes agreed not only to serve with Brown but also to write a handbook of military tactics for Brown's new militia to be entitled *The Manual of a Patriotic Volunteer.*

To a friend Forbes wrote that this was his chance to become a "general in the revolution against slavery." What Forbes did not understand was that Brown was not looking for a general. He was only looking for a drillmaster. And he was looking for unquestioning loyalty. The first milestone of their relationship would be marked when Forbes disobeyed a direct order from Brown to report for duty and instead lingered several months in Manhattan without explanation, prompting Brown to send a friend to visit Forbes in mid-June and demand that the $600 be returned if he was not coming west immediately. The two men, alike in so many ways, were on a collision course from the start.

On the evening of July 15, by the fire at a little campsite somewhere near Red Rock, Iowa, John Brown sat down in the dirt and wrote young Henry Stearns the autobiographical letter he had promised. He entitled it "A Boy Named John." This, wrote Brown, "will be mainly a narration of follies & errors, which it is hoped *you may avoid."* The letter was also a self-portrait subtly devised to further convince Henry's father, George Luther Stearns, that Brown was essentially a warmhearted, God-fearing man who, if he did embark upon grave deeds, did them to further the work of the Lord. And so, wrote Brown, "there is one thing connected" with the story of John "which will be calculated to encourage any young person to persevering effort; & that is the degree of success *in accomplishing his objects* which to a great extent marked the course of this boy throughout my entire acquaintanceship with him."

The italics are Brown's own underlinings. He used them throughout "A Boy Named John" to highlight a host of phrases to which more than one meaning could be given. Once again referring to himself in the third person, Brown wrote of the boy John that he had been fond of "the hardest & *roughest* kind of play." He recounted how John had lost his mother at a young age and had grown up "in the School of adversity" on the Ohio frontier. He recalled how he had sworn an *"Eternal war* with slavery" when as a young man he'd seen an owner beat a crying slave boy mercilessly with an iron fire shovel. At about the same time that he witnessed the beating, he'd also become "to some extent a convert to Christianity & ever after a firm believer in the divine authenticity of the Bible."

Now, he concluded, a few of the things he had communicated to young Henry had a special purpose. "I would like to know that you had *selected those out;* & adopted them as part of your *plan* of life; & I wish you to have some *deffinite plan.* Many seem to have none: & others never stick to any that they do form. This was not the case with John. He followed up with *tenacity* whatever he set about so long as it answered his general purpose: & hence he rarely failed in some good degree to effect the things he undertook. This was so much the case he *habitually expected to succeed* in his undertakings. With this feeling *should be coupled* the consciousness that our plans are right in themselves." Brown went on to say that John's profession was more one of being a shepherd than anything else, this "being a *calling* for which in early life he had a kind of enthusiastic longing: together with the idea that as a business it bid fair to afford him the means of carrying out his *greatest principal object."*[4]

The greatest principal object—shepherding to freedom the lamb that was the black race—seemed far out of reach, however, when Brown arrived at Tabor, Iowa, on August 7. There was, according to plan, supposed to have been several thousand dollars waiting for him here. Instead, the Lawrence agent for the Massachusetts Kansas Committee, E. B. Whitman, proffered Brown a mere $110. Thus, when "A Boy Named John" was finally posted to Henry Stearns, it was accompanied by a scathing note to George Luther Stearns in which Brown demanded to know why his Massachusetts friends had failed him. "I am in *immedi-*

ate want of from five hundred to one thousand dollars for *secret service* and no *questions asked,"* Brown wrote Stearns on August 10. "Will you exert yourself to have that amount, or some part of it, placed in your hands subject to my order?"[5]The answer was to be an unequivocal no. And the reason for it, in no small measure, was a simple want of cash by Stearns and other involved parties. While Gerrit Smith had been able put together a few hundred dollars, most of Brown's other supporters were strained. The panic was at its very worst that August. Stearns, who was struggling to remain solvent, did not have a cash flow that would allow him to divert any more funds to Brown than he had already, this in spite of his previous pledge. And besides, he had already done a great deal to help Brown in recent months.

In April, Stearns began raising a fund with which Brown might pay Gerrit Smith the money owed on the North Elba farm. "Mr. Lawrence has agreed with me that the $1000 shall be made up, and will write to Gerrit Smith today or tomorrow to say that he can depend on the money from him," wrote Stearns to Brown at North Elba on April 29. "After you see Mr. Smith write me again if the arrangement is not satis-factory to you." Stearns was to contribute approximately one-fourth of the sum, Lawrence nearly one-third, and other subscribers the rest. A few days later, however, Lawrence announced that he could find no other subscribers. "Mr. Lawrence informs me," wrote Stearns to Brown, who was still at North Elba, "he has written to Gerrit Smith, asking him to accept the $600 now raised and to take a mortgage from you for $400."[6] Lawrence's total contribution eventually came to $340; Stearns provided $260.[7]

In early August, at about the same time Brown arrived in Iowa only to become furious that there was little or no cash waiting for him there, Sanborn carried the $600 to Smith. "I am delighted with Mr. Smith and the way of life here," Sanborn wrote from Peterboro on August 3. "I went yesterday to his church, of which he is sort of a lay bishop. It is a conference in which each person is expected to say something on such topics as come up for discussion; there is little formality and much earnestness." A friend of Sanborn's from Harvard, Plymouth-born

Edwin Morton, was at Peterboro serving as tutor for Smith's sons. Morton, wrote Sanborn, "is greatly pleased with his way of life here, and with reason, I think. . . . In this high and secluded village there is a perpetual Sabbath and a coolness such as I have not found elsewhere."[8] After Peterboro, Sanborn went to North Elba, where he conveyed the deed personally to Mary Brown. Shortly thereafter, a somewhat apologetic Brown wrote to thank Sanborn for going to look after his family, "and cheer them in their homely condition."[9] He also thanked Sanborn for promising to send whatever money he could raise privately, which did not promise to be much. The depressed economy was the worst in twenty years. "There has been no such pressure since 1837," wrote Sanborn, sending Brown a draft for $75.68, "if things were as bad then."[10]

For all Brown's annoyance about his procrastination, Hugh Forbes arrived at Tabor on August 9, just two days after Brown himself. Upon his arrival, Forbes was as agitated as Brown, if not more so, to discover that the promised Eastern money was not forthcoming. In addition, there was a noticeable want of recruits for Forbes to train. Many good men were on their way from Kansas, Brown promised. But for weeks Forbes busied himself by drilling one lone soldier—Owen Brown. Day after day, hour after hour, Forbes marched Owen up and down, back and forth, at John Brown's uncomfortable, dusty, and increasingly boring camp. They occasionally broke the monotony by having target practice, but this was hampered by the fact that the guns given Brown by the Massachusetts Kansas Committee were virtually unusable. Stearns had told Brown the cache of weapons at Tabor consisted of, among other things, two hundred Sharp's rifle carbines, four thousand ball cartridges, and thirty-one thousand military (or percussion) caps.[11] In fact there was one semi-usable field piece, about seventy of what Forbes termed "ancient" muskets dating from the 1790s, and twelve swords. The only "real arms" available, Forbes would later recall, were the two hundred revolvers recently purchased by Stearns.

One imagines the unhappy, tense atmosphere at the little camp as the two would-be generals, Brown and Forbes, jockeyed with each other for command of what was essentially nothing: a mercenary army characterized by no cash, no recruits, no guns, no war, and perhaps worst of all so far as Forbes was concerned, no *plan*. Already bitter and frustrated, Brown and Forbes argued heatedly over the details of Brown's idea, in the absence of belligerencies in Kansas, to activate his Subterranean Pass Way scheme in the Alleghenies. Brown told Forbes they and some twenty to fifty well-armed men should go "beat up a slave quarter in Virginia," preferably that near the federal armory and arsenal at Harpers Ferry, Virginia, which Brown would seize. Once the revolt began, hundreds of slaves would "swarm" to Brown, who would arm and muster them for deliverance. After "liberating" Virginia, said Brown, his quickly growing army of freed slaves would move on to Tennessee and northern Alabama to continue the work of the Lord. For his part, Forbes simply did not think that the blacks would swarm. Forbes, who viewed blacks as being childlike, fearful, and stupid, thought any rebellion that relied on slave action would be impossible to command and doomed to failure from the first. Forbes preferred the idea of armed bands of white men making brief, sporadic incursions into Virginia during which they would abduct as many slaves as possible and then "stampede" them north, through the Allegheny wilderness to Canada, just as one would any other brutish herd.

Forbes's growing displeasure and disillusionment with Brown was heightened by the fact that he was not getting paid. He needed money to send his struggling wife and family in Paris. And he needed money for the little pint bottles he found it hard to live without and had to smuggle into the camp of the teetotaler Brown. He was, he brooded with his whiskey, a great, talented, and good man made a failure by liars. Brown was one of them, with his promises of guns, authority, legitimacy, action. And those damned New Englanders, with their promise of financing, were equally culpable. *They* had made him into a joke instead of a heroic fighter for freedom. *They* had subverted his destiny.

In September, during a stopover at Nebraska City, Forbes convinced Brown he had pressing business in the East and received permission to return to Manhattan for a short period of time. It was agreed the two would rendezvous again in a few months, at a time and place of Brown's choosing. But given Forbes's subsequent behavior, it would appear that the drillmaster had no intention of returning to the command of Brown, for whom he no longer had any respect or trust. Nor did he intend to rely further on the charity of Brown's Eastern backers, for whom he felt little else than an urge to revenge.

☆

Higginson was impatient that Brown was not causing a row on the Kansas/Iowa border. While Brown lurked at Tabor, furtively eyeing his disappointing appropriation of guns, Higginson wrote Sanborn demanding to know what Brown was doing. If damnable peace still reigned within Kansas, then why wasn't Brown using the copious arms allotted him by the Massachusetts Kansas Committee to cross Kansas, render the Missouri border insecure, and "resurrect" blacks from the slave state, delivering them into Iowa? Sanborn answered that Higginson did not understand Brown's situation. "He is as ready for revolution as any other man," wrote Sanborn, "and is now on the borders of Kansas, safe from arrest but prepared for action, but he needs money. I believe he is the best Disunion champion you can find, and with his hundred men, when he is put where he can raise and drill them (for he has an expert drill officer with him) will do more to split the Union than a list of 50,000 names for your [Disunion] Convention—good as that is." Still, for all his demands, Higginson said he could not contribute anything to Brown's cause. Normally impoverished, the minister was even more so in the midst of the panic.[12]

Other events conspired with the dismal economy to hinder Brown's fund-raising. The Kansas territory's latest appointed governor, Robert Walker of Mississippi, surprised virtually everyone by continuing the evenhanded, fair-minded administration that had begun under Governor Geary. Despite pressure from President Buchanan to do the contrary, Walker allowed the free-state party to mount candidates and actively participate in the October elections for a new territorial legislature and

United States congressman. Charles Robinson and other moderate free-
staters campaigned hard and scored a great victory. A free-state man was
elected to Congress, and the free-state party took thirty-three out of fifty-
two seats in the new legislature.

It suddenly seemed to many in the antislavery movement that a free-
state militia was no longer necessary. Even Howe, who represented the
most fire-breathing and cynical antislavery faction, wrote Brown counseling preparedness but also urging peace. Howe and Stearns both suspected that the Missourians would not give up Kansas so easily, that it
would take more than a free and fair election to do the trick. Still, the
free-staters should take a strictly *defensive* stance. "The free-state party
should wait for the Border-ruffian moves, and checkmate them, as they
are *developed,*" wrote Stearns to Brown on November 7. "Don't attack
them, but if they attack you, 'Give them Jessie' and Fremont besides.
You know how to do it."[13]

By midautumn, the panic had slowly begun to subside and Stearns
was more confident of his fortunes; however he now had other reasons to
withhold his support from Brown. Stearns came away from the election
completely convinced that Kansas could now be gained as a free state
through peaceful, democratic means. "I gave J.B. authority to draw on
me for money in a certain contingency," wrote Stearns to E. B. Whitman
on November 14. "That contingency has not occurred, and I now believe
it would be very unwise to have any of my funds used for that purpose."[14]
Nevertheless, Stearns sent Brown $500 by way of Whitman for his
personal and family needs. The money did not prevent Brown, still
resentful of his benefactors' failings, from writing a letter to Stearns
complaining of the latter's "abandonment" of him. Annoyed, Stearns
replied on February 4, 1858: "The $500 was furnished you by Whitman
at my request. It was done because I thought you needed money for the
winter, not because I felt myself under obligation to you, for I had made
up my mind then, and still continue to believe that our friends need no
aid in defending themselves from all marauders, and that their true
course now is to meet the enemy in the ballot-box, and vote them down
on every occasion."[15]

❈ BOOK TWO ❈

12

TROUBLING ISRAEL

THROUGH THE AUTUMN, after Forbes departed, Brown slowly gathered around him an odd and interesting band of recruits to help him with his largely undefined mission. They were a strange mix—Brown's little squad of misfits, idealists, and charlatans.

John E. Cook was an ex–law clerk (and a former member of Charles Lenhart's free-state guerrilla force operating out of Lawrence) who'd been expelled from Yale for an unexplained indiscretion. A native of Indiana, Cook was quite well connected. His family was one of the most prominent in the state. His brother-in-law, A. P. Willard, was governor. With his long, curly, blond hair, the handsome Cook was a great favorite of the ladies. Cook presented a suave counterpoint image to that of Aaron D. Stevens, a fierce Connecticut-born veteran of the Mexican War. Stevens was a middle-aged, cynical giant of a man with large fists and a fast temper. He had tried to kill an officer in a drunken brawl near Taos, New Mexico, for which he was imprisoned at Leavenworth on a commuted death sentence. Stevens escaped during 1856, lived among the Delaware Indians for several months, and eventually joined James Lane's free-state militia under an alias.

He came to Brown as an experienced guerrilla fighter who was known to wield a sword with swift and terrible precision.

John Henry Kagi, a former schoolteacher and would-be writer who came west from Ohio during the summer of 1856 to help the free-state cause, was an unlikely close friend to the crude and irascible Stevens. In his twenties, Kagi was quiet, meditative, and completely dedicated to annihilating the institution of slavery. He served side by side with Stevens throughout the height of the Kansas civil war and was known to have killed at least one man—an Alabaman in the town of Tecumseh who came at him with a bludgeon. Another new recruit, Charles Plummer Tidd, an adventurer and mercenary from Maine, was hungry for action and anxious to confront slavery face-to-face. Also from Maine was seventeen-year-old William H. Leeman—an earnest, awe-struck recruit ready to follow Brown anywhere.

The soldier with the most interesting tale to tell was Richard Realf, a twenty-three-year-old Englishman. The son of a British rural constable, Realf was a poet (the author of an 1852 collection entitled *Guesses at the Beautiful*) and the former lover of Lady Noell Byron, widow of Lord Byron. He came to the United States in 1854 to satisfy, he said, "instincts [that] were democratic and republican, or, at least, anti-monarchical." He also became a radical abolitionist. At the time Realf met Brown at the end of November 1857, he was living in Lawrence, Kansas, and working as a correspondent for the *Illinois State Gazette*. He was introduced to Brown and recruited into his service by Cook.

There were several other followers. Charles Moffett was a shadowy, mysterious drifter from Iowa, wholly without ideology, content to tail along behind any leader capable of clothing and feeding him. Luke F. Parsons, who'd fought with Brown at various times since shortly after the Battle of Black Jack, was a petty thief and mercenary who liked to cloak his dubious professions under the cover of antislavery action. Richard J. Hinton was an abolitionist journalist turned guerrilla fighter who believed Brown to be the country's best hope for destroying slavery. And Richard Richardson, a fugitive slave, stayed with Brown simply because Brown was the first white in the world to treat him as an equal.

Through most of December, the little army traveled by coach and foot across Iowa from Tabor, heading slowly east in the general direction of an Ohio camp where, Brown told them, his drillmaster Forbes would train them for a special purpose. As they journeyed, Brown slowly revealed more and more of his plan to the men, some of whom thought more highly of it than others. By the light of nightly fires at what seemed an endless series of cold, windblown encampments amid snow and mud, Brown "made known to a certain, but not to any definite and detailed degree, his intentions," recalled Realf. "He stated that he proposed to make an incursion [to liberate slaves] into the Southern States, somewhere in the mountainous region of the Blue Ridge and the Alleghenies." During the passage across Iowa, said Realf, "Brown's plan in regard to an incursion into Virginia gradually manifested itself. It was a matter of discussion between us as to the possibility of effecting a successful insurrection in the mountains, some arguing that it was, some that it was not; myself thinking, and still thinking, that a mountainous country is a very fine country for an insurrection, in which I am borne out by historic evidence."

By the time the ragged group arrived at the Quaker community of Springdale, Iowa, on or about New Year's Day, a reluctant consensus had been reached. Through numerous evenings of discussion, Brown had finally succeeded in convincing his men that the Virginia project was both necessary and, more importantly, possible. It was agreed that they would "trouble Israel" come spring, with Israel in this case being the first lady of slave states: Virginia. But it was also agreed that Brown's tiny, exhausted militia could get no nearer to Virginia this season. The men rebelled against the idea of another two months marching east in the bitter cold. And for his part, Brown was running short of cash with which to support them. Upon arriving at Springdale, Brown tried to sell the mules and wagons belonging to his battalion in order to raise some money for their board. Failing in this, he instead traded the same items to a farmer named Maxom, who in exchange agreed to provide room and board for the men until spring. Brown, meanwhile, would travel east and there seek out support for the Virginia project.[1]

☆

The home of Frederick Douglass (on St. Paul Road, later named South Avenue) sat high on a hilltop two miles south of the center of Rochester, New York. The house was a handsome place filled with books and decorated with comfortable, store-bought furniture. The elegant dwelling was just the type of luxurious space John Brown would never allow himself, and could probably never afford. When Brown arrived at Douglass's house on January 28, he seemed as much out of place there as he had a year before in the plush parlors of the Boston intelligentsia. But the Douglass home was quite comfortable for Brown in some respects—especially in that it was a rather lonely and "neighborless" place where the secretive, paranoid Brown felt safe from observation. And he was relaxed in the company of the many fugitive slaves, travelers on the Underground Railroad, who came and went almost daily, spending their last night in the United States under the shelter of Douglass's barn before being ferried across Lake Ontario to Canada and freedom.

Brown shut himself up in a bedroom at Douglass's elegant house for a week while diligently laboring with pen and paper to begin the project that was to end less than two years later with bullets and blood. Lying across the soft, quilted bed, using a flat piece of board for a desk, he composed several remarkable documents—not the least of which was, of all things, a constitution for the new revolutionary state of runaway slaves he hoped to found in the mountains of Virginia. "Article 26: Property confiscated," he wrote across the top of a sheet while, perhaps, listening to the sound of Douglass's lilting violin that came from down the hall. "The entire personal and real property of all persons known to be acting either directly or indirectly with or for the enemy, or found in arms with them, or found willfully holding slaves, shall be confiscated and taken whenever and wherever it may be found in either free or slave States." "Article 27: Desertion," he jotted, perhaps as a smiling Mrs. Douglass placed a warmed cup of apple cider on the delicate table beside his bed. "Persons convicted on impartial trial of desertion to the enemy . . . acting as spies, or of treacherous surrender of property, ammunition, provisions, or supplies of any kind, roads, bridges, persons, or fortifications, shall be put to death, and their property confiscated."

The scheme associated with his constitution—Brown's grand agenda for making God's fierce justice real on earth—was something he described for an astonished Douglass in increasing detail at meals. Calmly chewing his ham and sweet potatoes, Brown explained all too matter-of-factly how the army of his phantom, wilderness state was to be turned loose on the slaveholders. Douglass found Brown's deadpan nonchalance almost frightening as he discussed the prolonged punitive slave uprising—with all its attendant violence, destruction, and terror—that had become his most cherished ambition. Douglass was horrified to hear what Brown had in store for Virginia, even though he had no objection, in theory, to the concept of an armed revolt against slavery. "I should welcome the intelligence tomorrow," Douglass had said nine years earlier in a Faneuil Hall speech, "should it come, that slaves had risen in the South, and that the sable arms which had been engaged in beautifying and adorning the South, were engaged in spreading death and devastation."[2]

Yet he did not expect to receive such intelligence; and a review of the details of Brown's plan did nothing to change his mind. Like Hugh Forbes, Douglass believed that Brown was overestimating the propensity of black slaves for rebellion. While Forbes thought it would be a certain innate childishness and foolishness that would prohibit blacks from becoming effective soldiers in the war for their own liberation, Douglass thought they would instead be held back by a steely, wise cynicism born of many years' abuse and broken promises. It was not that blacks did not want freedom, Douglass told Brown, it was just that they were generally averse to suicide.

And suicide it would be, Douglass said firmly. He pointed his finger down at a map that showed Harpers Ferry and the armory. The location of the armory was indefensible, said Douglass. Situated on a peninsula formed by the confluence of the Potomac and Shenandoah rivers, Harpers Ferry was surrounded on all sides by commanding heights.

Douglass said he thought John Brown's mystical mountains were bound to work against him, rather than for him, during an invasion of Harpers Ferry. But Brown laughed off Douglass's doubts. As Douglass quickly learned, Brown adhered to his own unique, garbled military analysis—a twisted logic that made him deem indefensible positions defensible, and vice versa. Less than a year before, in April of 1857, Franklin Sanborn and John Brown had spoken of battle strategy as they drove one Sunday morning from Concord through Lexington and

Frederick Douglass, abolitionist leader and friend of Brown's who thought his Harpers Ferry scheme to be suicidal and tried to talk him out of it. Photo courtesy Massachusetts Historical Society.

West Medford to the home of George Luther Stearns. Brown told Sanborn that the traditional military objective of seizing the high ground was often a mistake in practice, and that a ravine, well guarded on the flanks, was often a better military post than a hilltop. "This was strange doctrine to me," recalled Sanborn, "and I reminded him of the clansman's remark in Waverly, —'Even a haggis, (God bless her!) can charge down hill'; but he maintained his opinion."[3] At Harpers Ferry, Brown found a ravine on a grand scale and convinced himself that God had placed it there to be the stage for his sacred mission.

Ultimately, Brown's response to Douglass's concerns was a patronizing one. Douglass should have more faith and should not waste his worry. The scheme would work. It could not fail, for it had been formulated to transact the business of God. One of Brown's Kansas recruits, George B. Gill, was to recall that Brown's military planning always seemed to have one fundamental flaw. Convinced that he was God's chosen instrument for the liberation of the slave, Brown was equally convinced that "God would be his guard and shield, rendering the most illogical movements into a grand success."[4]

☆

On his way east to Rochester, Brown had briefly stopped at the Ohio home of his son John Junior. There, he received grim news of Hugh Forbes. A January 12 letter from Sanborn informed Brown that Sanborn was in receipt of an "exceedingly abusive" letter from Forbes in which the colonel "calls one a cheat and accuses one of lying and other iniquities— you know that I am not guilty of these things—why will you not write and tell him so?"[5] Forbes, Sanborn informed Brown, was also the author of notes to Samuel Gridley Howe and Massachusetts senator Charles Sumner accusing them of being responsible, as Sanborn recalled, "for the termination of his engagement with Brown; by which, he said, he had been reduced to poverty, and his family in Paris, deprived of pecuniary aid from him, had suffered great hardship."

Forwarding Theodore Parker the original of Forbes's recent letter, Sanborn commented that "if it were not for the wife and children, who are undoubtedly in suffering, the man might be hanged . . . for his whole style towards me is a combination of insult and lunacy. But I fear there was such an agreement between him and Brown, though Brown has told me nothing of it; and if so, he has a claim upon somebody, though not particularly upon us. Is there anything that can be done for him? I have written to Brown inquiring about the matter."[6] Within two weeks, while staying at the home of Douglass, Brown received yet another inquiry stemming from the activity of Forbes's poison pen. "Colonel Forbes has written several abusive letters to Charles Sumner, and Sanborn, claiming that you had made a positive contract to pay him money, based on promises made to you by the New England men," queried George Luther Stearns. "Is it so?"[7]

Realizing at last that Forbes would not be returning to the fold—that he had in fact become an enemy—Brown grimly wrote to the men at

Springdale, informing them of Forbes's dishonorable discharge. "We expected Colonel Forbes to be our military instructor," recalled Realf, "[but] in consequence of a disagreement between himself and John Brown, the latter wrote us from the east that Forbes would not become our military instructor, and that we should not expect him."[8] Brown further had John Junior send a vaguely threatening letter to Forbes in New York saying that Brown did not want any more "highly offensive and insulting" letters sent either to him or to any of his friends.

Brown did not mention to Douglass the problem he was having with Forbes. Therefore, in mid-February, shortly after Brown left Douglass's home for Gerrit Smith's house at Peterboro, the unwitting Douglass gave Forbes a warm welcome when he showed up at Rochester (probably looking for Brown). After cordially receiving Forbes, Douglass advanced him train fare to Manhattan. He also provided him with a letter of introduction to Ottilia Assing, who was prominent in New York City's relatively affluent community of liberal German refugees, most of whom were veterans from the 1848 revolution. The Germans, Douglass assured Forbes, could be a lucrative source of contributions for Brown's enterprise. Assing, for her part, quickly pegged Forbes as an extortionist. "Using God knows what kind of tricks," she recalled, Forbes began making insinuations that he would betray Brown—who was still wanted for the Pottawatomie murders—if he did not get prompt payment of moneys owed him. Failing to exact a large sum from Assing and her friends, Forbes then tried to sell all he knew of Brown's Virginia plan to Horace Greeley for publication in the New York *Tribune*. Greeley ignored his former employee (whom he described later as a "lunatic") and wrote off his story as bogus sensationalism.

After his rejection by Greeley, Forbes subsided for a number of weeks. Neither Brown nor any of Brown's intimate supporters would hear again directly from Forbes or see any sign of him in the press, until May. Through late February and early March, as the Secret Six became the Secret Six by energetically embracing and pledging virtually unconditional support to Brown's Virginia project, they would do so assuming that Forbes and the threat he posed had simply disappeared.

☆

Sanborn wrote to Higginson on February 11 to say that he had received "two letters from J.B. in which he speaks of a plan but does not say what it is. Still I have confidence enough in him to trust him with the moderate sum he asks for—if I had it—without knowing his plan." Sanborn further explained that "with from 5 to 800 $ J.B. hopes to do more than has yet been done; wishes to raise the money in two months." Sanborn discounted a letter from E. B. Whitman in Kansas saying that Brown had disappeared, had not been of much service in recent months, and was thought by some to be insane. "Of course this is not so," commented Sanborn to Higginson. "If you can aid Brown in any substantial way please do so—for I do not well see how I can, though I shall try. Mr. Smith has sent him $100. Has B. written to you? I judge so. I should not wonder if his plan contemplated an uprising of slaves—though he has not said as much to me."[9]

Sanborn was not being entirely candid with Higginson. He knew quite well that Brown's scheme contemplated a slave revolt. Edwin Morton, Sanborn's old Harvard classmate and tutor to the sons of Gerrit Smith, had written Sanborn in early February with word that a letter from Brown to Smith left little to the imagination. "This is news," confided Morton to Sanborn. "He 'expects to overthrow slavery' in a large part of the country." In writing to Smith, Brown was far more plain about things than he was in letters to his Boston friends. Notes to Sanborn, Higginson, Howe, Parker and Stearns announced on a *"strictly confidential"* basis a scheme that would be "BY FAR the most *important* undertaking" of Brown's life. Brown provided no further details for his Boston correspondents. In his note to Higginson, however, he hinted that the plan was radical enough to possibly deter even some of the most stalwart defenders of abolition.

John Brown soon had answers to his letters from several of the men who would become the Secret Six. Gerrit Smith was definitely interested in hearing more about Brown's undertaking. In addition to sending Brown $100, Smith invited him to Peterboro to discuss the plan and the possibility of Smith's further and larger donations. Stearns replied that he was willing to talk to Brown about the matter. Higginson answered, "I am always ready to invest in treason, but at present have none to invest. As for my [Worcester] friends, those who are able are not quite willing, and those who are willing are at present bankrupt."[10] Though pleading poverty, Higginson could not resist asking for more details, explicitly whether Brown's scheme was related to the "railroad" business. (Higginson was of course referring to railroad business of the underground variety.) "Railroad business on a *somewhat extended* scale; is the identical object for which I am trying to get means," replied Brown. "I have been connected with that business as *commonly conducted* from my boyhood: & never let an opportunity slip . . . but I have a measure on foot that I feel sure would awaken in you something more than a *common interest;* if you could understand it." Brown said he had written to his "friends" Stearns and Sanborn inviting them to Peterboro "for consultation." Brown asked that Higginson please come as well.[11]

Stearns, Howe, Parker, Higginson—and initially Sanborn—decided not to go to Peterboro. "Your last letter is at hand," wrote Stearns to Brown on February 12. "I have seen Mr. Sanborn and we have agreed to write to you to come to Boston and meet us here. If it is not convenient for you to meet the expense of the journey we will repay it to you here, or send the money as you may direct."[12] Brown refused. He insisted that someone was sure to recognize him in Boston, and that it was essential to the security of his plan that he keep his presence in the East a secret. Probably at Brown's direction, Edwin Morton wrote again to Sanborn from Peterboro, where Brown was now staying. "He said it is not possible for him to go east under the circumstances," wrote Morton. "He would very much like to see you. He is pleased to find Mr. Smith more in harmony with his general plan than he thought he might be."[13] (Morton was understating Smith's enthusiasm. At about the same time Morton was writing Sanborn, Brown sent an enthusiastic, victorious note to his son, John Junior, saying that Gerrit Smith was more than merely in agreement with his plan, he was "ready to go in for a share in the *whole trade.*"[14])

When Sanborn read that Smith was generally supportive of Brown's secret project, he changed his mind about going to Peterboro. Perhaps it would be advisable to speak personally with both Smith and Brown. He wrote Higginson that he would be leaving for Peterboro from Boston on February 20 and invited Higginson to come along. "I hope you will go if possible—for Mr. Stearns cannot. Can you not meet me at the depot at Worcester tomorrow?"[15] In a telegram, Higginson reiterated his interest in supporting the enterprise, but said he could not leave home at the moment. And so Sanborn traveled alone to consult with Smith and Brown.

As Sanborn would remember, Brown "first unfolded his extreme plans for attacking slavery in Virginia, on the evening of Washington's birthday, 1858, in an upper chamber of Gerrit Smith's villa at Peterboro." Smith, who had already been fully briefed and had read Brown's constitution, did not attend the meeting. Only Sanborn and Morton were present to watch Brown stalk back and forth before his bedroom fireplace as he read aloud "the singular Constitution which he had recently drawn up, in Frederick Douglass's house at Rochester, for the government of the territory, small or large, which he might rescue by force from the curse of slavery, and for the control of his own little band." Brown said he had received a message from God in a revelation. It was God's wish that he, John Brown, should go to Virginia and there incite insurrection. It was time now for God's wrath to descend; Brown and the army he would raise were to be God's tools, delivering swift justice to oppressed and oppressor alike. Unrepentant slaveholders deserved to be violently punished for their sins. True servants of the Lord must not shirk from His work, no matter how repugnant the task at hand might be. Brown declared that he must have at least $800 to launch his war for slave liberation. Smith was prepared to help. Could Brown count on Sanborn? And could he count on the other Massachusetts men?

Sanborn considered Brown's an "amazing proposition, —desperate in its character, seemingly inadequate in its provision of means, and of very uncertain result. Such as it was, Brown had set his heart on it; he looked upon it as the shortest way to the restoration of our slave-cursed republic to the principles of the Declaration of Independence; and he was ready to die in its execution, —as he did. We dissuaded him from what seemed to us certain failure; urging all the objections that would naturally occur to persons desiring the end he was seeking, but distrusting the slender means, and the unpropitious time. But no argument could prevail against his settled purpose, with many or with few, —and he left us only the alternatives of betrayal, desertion, or support. We chose the last."[16]

On the following afternoon, Sanborn and Smith went for a walk amid the snowy hills that surrounded Smith's mansion. Their topic of discussion was, of course, Brown and his incredible plot. Sanborn still had many reservations about Brown's plan. Yet he was irresistibly attracted by the image of an unrepentant South in flames. Smith said quite plainly that he was ready for war. Now that John Brown was mobilizing a force of men to pursue slavery into the South itself, to destroy the peculiar institution with a violent insurrection, Smith was ready to "go all lengths" to support him. "You see how it is," Smith said, turning to Sanborn, "our dear friend has made up his mind to this course, and cannot be turned from it. We cannot give him up to die alone; we must support him. I will raise so many hundred dollars for him; you must lay the case before your friends in Massachusetts, and ask them to do as much. I can see no other way."[17]

Neither could Sanborn. He left for Boston the very next day, February 24, to arrange a meeting between Brown and the Massachusetts men. Brown sent a note after Sanborn, a warm letter that thanked him for feeling "1/2 inclined to make this common cause with me. I greatly *rejoice at this;* for I believe when you come to look at the *ample field* I labor in: & rich harvest which (not only this entire country, but) the whole world during the present & future generations may *reap* from its successful cultivation: you will feel that you are out of your element until you find you are in it; an entire unit."[18]

On the evening Sanborn departed for Boston, John Brown took a hike about Smith's property with Edwin Morton. "The road stretching on before us was freshly covered with one of those quiet snowfalls which our feet were the first to disturb," remembered Morton. "At one point, affording a longer view, lighted by a thinly-clouded moon, there was a pause which I did not interrupt. Gazing thoughtfully forward upon the untrodden expanse, —and then silently and thoughtfully backward, where our footsteps alone in the fresh snow lay far behind, he broke the silence presently, —saying slowly and with feeling, as if partly to himself and partly to me, —'I like to see my tracks behind me.'" Throughout the rest of the long walk, Brown and Morton discussed theology. Brown spoke of God, man, predestination, and how he always let himself be guided by "a conviction absolute of the constant, instant Presence of an overruling Providence, and a trusting reliance thereon." At the close of the walk, as they came to the door of Smith's house, Brown stopped before going in "to nail our conclusions, that the final and utter perdition and eternal condemnation of some souls was perfectly consistent with the justice and goodness of a perfectly just and good God."[19]

Sanborn wasted no time in communicating details of Brown's plan to Higginson, Parker, and Howe, though not to Stearns. Brown had insisted that he wanted to bring the matter up with Stearns personally.[20] Sanborn was likewise expressly instructed not to raise the subject of Brown's scheme with Wendell Phillips, whom Brown did not trust and did not care to bring into his confidence.[21] After being briefed by Sanborn, Theodore Parker recommended that Brown be invited once again to visit Boston so that he could discuss his intriguing enterprise within the tight, closed circle of his chosen, potential supporters. An invitation was quickly posted, as was a check to cover traveling expenses. Brown, now suddenly willing to make the trip, arrived in town quietly on March 4. He wrote to Higginson from Boston on the same day, setting a meeting at the American House Hotel, on Hanover Street, with Sanborn "& other friends who have named the evening of Friday next. Should an earlier period be just as convenient it would perhaps be better. Please inquire for Mr. Brown *(not Capt. Brown)* of New York."[22]

At the meeting in Brown's room, the plot that culminated with the invasion at Harpers Ferry was formally launched. Higginson, Howe,

Parker, and Sanborn—each of them voiced virtually unconditional support. Even George Luther Stearns, who had spent so many recent months counseling the avoidance of violence in favor of electioneering, was enthusiastic. Stearns had now abandoned his hope that Kansas and other territories could be gained without bloodshed for the free-state cause by way of balloting. In the past month, Pres. James Buchanan had petitioned the proslavery majority in the Senate to admit Kansas to the Union as a slave state and to accept the old proslavery Lecompton Constitution. Buchanan's request came despite the obvious, demonstrated fact that the overwhelming majority of Kansas residents were free-staters. (Buchanan's proposal was so outrageous that even Stephen A. Douglas, the author of the Kansas-Nebraska Act, denounced the administration for its role in what came to be called the Lecompton Swindle.) For Stearns, the administration's action, coming on the heels of the Dred Scott decision, was an ominous sign that there was to be no peaceful way to emancipation. Time now to buy more guns.

The courage and enthusiasm evoked by Brown as he described his plan, Higginson would recall, were both invigorating and contagious. Howe was especially intrigued. "The project of a slave stampede on a large scale was quite in Dr. Howe's line," recalled Higginson, "and he . . . entered into it quite cordially."[23] Howe liked the logic of using the mountain wilderness to confuse and elude pursuers. He remembered seeing superior numbers of Turkish troops defeated by small Greek bands in the mountain passes of Arcadia. He believed the same approach could succeed in the Blue Ridge and Alleghenies. By the time Brown left Boston on March 8, his friends had formed a secret committee of six—including the absent Gerrit Smith—to advise him and raise the capital he needed for his Harpers Ferry expedition.[24]

"Hawkins [Brown] has gone to Philadelphia today, leaving his friends to work for him," wrote Sanborn to the ever-busy Higginson, who had left town before Brown did. "$1000 is the sum set to be raised here—of which yourself, Mr. Parker, Dr. Howe, Mr. Stearns and myself are asked to raise $100. Some may do more. Perhaps you can not come up to that

nor can I."[25] When apprised of the result of the meetings with Brown in
Boston, Gerrit Smith was ecstatic. On March 25 he wrote Joshua Giddings gleefully that "the slave will be delivered by the shedding of blood,
and the signs are multiplying that his deliverance is at hand."[26] The
Secret Six, as a formal clandestine unit, was now a reality.

Stearns sent a note to Higginson on March 18, requesting his attendance at a meeting to be held at Howe's house in Boston on the following
Saturday.[27] Higginson, busy with a dozen different projects in Worcester,
could not make it. Sanborn wrote again to Higginson on March 21 to
describe the meeting, at which it was decided Stearns would serve as
"Treasurer of the Enterprise." Stearns, reported Sanborn, was giving
$100 and promised $200 more, "but holds it back for a future emergency." Parker had already raised his $100 and would probably do some-
thing more. Howe put in $50 and promised an additional $100. (Howe
had expected to be able to get $500 from "a third party," but the $500 fell
through due to the "unwilling wife" of the individual in question.) Sanborn gave Brown $25 directly, but was unable to raise anything else at
the moment. "It was informally agreed at the meeting—all being there
but yourself—that the first $500 could easily be made up and the second
in time. And that this should be done. And as much more as possible,"
Sanborn wrote.[28] Stearns, sometimes assisted by Sanborn, took his duties
as treasurer quite seriously. He kept in regular contact with all of the
group, carefully tallying the money collected and also providing gentle
reminders that more was needed. "$375 collected to this time," he wrote
to Higginson on April 1.[29]

They were all so well organized, meticulous, and circumspect—
Brown's businesslike backers with their regular meetings, carefully
tended ledger book, and tidy assignments of dues schedules. And they
were so unlike the carelessly organized Brown, who spent most of March
wandering vaguely from one antislavery gathering to another along the
Philadelphia/Manhattan corridor, vainly trying to raise funds for his
project, which he described for his audiences as simply an "experiment"
in slave deliverance: not an invasion, not a revolt, not an insurrection. No

details were given; few dollars were raised. By and large, the antislavery community of the Northeast was getting tired of Brown, his promises of dramatic results, and his constant requests for money.

Brown stopped briefly at North Elba for what seems to have been more of a recruiting foray than a family visit. Here he collected several family members to join him in his adventure. Brown's daughter Ruth dissuaded her husband, Henry Thompson, who had served with Brown at the time of the Pottawatomie affair, from going away with him once again. But Henry's brothers Dauphin and William Thompson signed up to be a part of Brown's experiment, as did Brown's sons Oliver and Watson. After North Elba, Brown made a flying visit to Syracuse, where he rendezvoused with a black leader, the Reverend J. W. Loguen, and traveled with him to St. Catharines, in Canada, where there was a large community of fugitive slaves whence Brown intended to recruit even more men. At St. Catharines, Brown met and gained the favor of Harriet Tubman, who even then was something of a legend in abolitionist circles. Tubman was told most, if not all, of what Brown's scheme involved. Endorsing Brown's project, Tubman agreed to use her influence among the Canadian fugitives to help Brown gather what he had taken to calling shepherds. She also told him all she knew about the area of Virginia where he planned to launch his action—which must have been not much, she being a Carolinian who'd spent very little time in the neighborhood of Harpers Ferry.

"I have lately had two letters from Mr. Hawkins [Brown] who has just left Canada for the West on business connected with his Enterprise," wrote Sanborn to Higginson on April 20. Brown was on his way to Springdale, Iowa, to pick up the men and feeble arms he'd left there in January. "He has found in Canada several good men for shepherds," reported Sanborn. Brown had received $410 of the $500 dollars promised, "but wants more, and we must try to make up to him the other $500. Part of it is pledged and the rest ought to be got, though with some difficulty. I believe Dr. Howe and myself are the delinquents at present—I for $40 and the Dr. for $50." Sanborn asked whether Higginson might contribute anything beyond what he had already. "Hawkins's address is Jason Brown, under cover to [in care of] John Jones, Chicago, Illinois. He has gone West to move his furniture [guns] and bring on his hands. A letter to him at Chicago would give him pleasure—his last letter I will send you when it returns to my hands, as I have sent it to Boston. He has received $260 from other sources than our friends and is raising more elsewhere, but got little in N.Y. and Phila."[30]

$$\widehat{13}$$

AN EVIL HOUR

N. H. [JOHN BROWN] will be at Chatham, Canada West some day next week with a company of 12 to 20 shepherds and would like to meet some friends," wrote Sanborn to Higginson on May 1, 1858. "Can you make it convenient to see him there? It will be an 'interesting time' he says. All goes well with him so far, but the other day I got a letter from Hugh Forbes. . . . Whether Forbes knows where H. [Brown] is or what he is now doing, I can't say, but it would be a bad thing to have the N.Y. *Herald* . . . quoting him . . . while we are hoping to steal a march. . . . Forbes has also written to the Chevalier, but I have not seen the letter."[1] Forbes's letter to Sanborn was his second, although Sanborn did not say as much to Higginson. Shortly after receipt of the May notes from Forbes to Howe and Sanborn, the two men, somewhat rattled, met with Stearns to discuss Hugh Forbes and the threat he presented.

"Last Tuesday I had a conference with our friends S. [Stearns] and Dr. H. [Howe] on the new aspect of affairs presented by Forbes's letters, and have written to Hawkins [Brown] informing him of the worst of the matter," wrote Sanborn to Higginson on May 5. "It looks as if the project must for the present be deferred—for I found by reading F's epistle to the Dr. that he knows the details of the plan, and even knows what very few do—that the Dr. and S. [Stearns] and myself are informed of it. How he got *this* knowledge is a mystery. He demands that Hawkins be discharged as agent, and himself or some other be put in his place. . . . I had yesterday a letter from H. [Brown] at Chatham, C.W. where he wishes friends to meet him on the 8th next Saturday." Sanborn said he could not attend, but hoped that Higginson would be able to make it. "Mr. S. [Stearns] will probably go. And I have written urging G.S. of P. [Gerrit Smith of Peterboro] to be there. At this conference the whole can be decided. H's men are at Chatham, and it is a fine chance to see what material he has got, and what sort of shepherds. . . . T.P. [Theodore Parker] and G.L.S. [George Luther Stearns] think the plan must be deferred till another year. The Dr. does not think so. And I am in doubt—inclining to the opinion of the two former. It is a bad business and I wish Forbes had been at the bottom of the sea before he ever got an agency for the wool business."[2] Howe would shortly change his mind and join the others in demanding postponement.

Higginson wrote Sanborn that he did not know the details of exactly who Hugh Forbes was or why he mattered. "H.F. is Hugh Forbes," answered Sanborn on May 7, "an Italieo English hothead whom N.H. [Brown] last year in an evil hour admitted to his councils. He has now quarrelled with [Brown] and knowing his plans for 'fresh fields and pastures new,' he threatens to expose them if our Boston friends allow the flock to be turned out. He wrote this in so many words to H. [Howe] and in much the same terms to me, and he is now at Washington where he can do great harm. I thought you knew of the man but I wish I were as ignorant of him as you. He is either a madman or a villain, and in either capacity can, and is inclined to, do great mischief." Forbes had made things so uncertain, wrote Sanborn, that Parker had already written Brown to say the enterprise must stop for the present. Forbes, Sanborn wrote to Higginson, "has a grudge against all New England, and especially against me; but I have never seen him."[3]

Howe later said he received three "ill-natured and spiteful" letters from Forbes. Howe burned all of Forbes's missives, but remembered the longest and most vicious of his notes, in which Forbes said that "he had been engaged during the active war in Kansas by Captain Brown, or by, as he called them, the Northern Abolitionists, to go to Kansas and drill men; that he never got any money for it; that he was in great distress; that he must have money; that Captain Brown was not a reliable person; that his plans, if entrusted to a man of head and prudence, might come to something; and he seemed to intimate that he, Captain Forbes, was a man of head and prudence; that if Captain Brown was allowed to go on it would be disastrous; that he would denounce it; and other things to that effect. It was a letter rather threatening in its general character. I did not heed it so much. It was a very long letter, full of vituperation and abuse. I had never seen Captain Forbes, nor heard of him before."[4]

Higginson, who had yet to hear from Forbes, was vehemently opposed to delaying Brown's experiment. "Sanborn writes me of a certain H.F. who wishes to veto the proceedings of our veteran friend," wrote Higginson to Parker from Brattleboro, Vermont, where he was in the midst of a lecture tour, on May 9. "I have only time to say that I regard any postponement as simply *abandoning the project*—for if we give it up now at the command or threat of H.F. it will be the same next year. . . . When the thing is once started, who cares what he says? I *protest* against postponement."[5] Parker told Higginson he was wrong. "If you knew all we do about 'Col.' F. you would think differently," wrote Parker.[6]

"I enclose a letter from Gerrit Smith, whose view of the matter agrees with that of our Boston friends," wrote Sanborn to Higginson on May 11. "There is much sense in your arguments, but I cannot quite yield to them, though I wish I could. [Forbes plans to] remove the terror of the thing by a complete exposure of the small resources of the group, and thus it would lose its main strength. Whether he is base enough to do this I still doubt, but the risk is too great to own. A year hence . . . he will know less of movements here and have less means to inspire confidence. . . . But his preaching now would spoil the scheme forever. . . . I am glad you stand 80 strong for the other side, for the matter will thus be fairly argued. But I think when [Brown] comes to see F's letters and knows how minute his information is, he will attach more importance to his opposition than he did on the 5th May when he wrote me saying that he would go on if supplies did not fail him. But the opinion of P. H. & S. [Parker, Howe, & Smith]—and G.S. [George Stearns]—who are such large stockholders, will prevent them raising money now. And the rest of us can do little in that way."[7]

Gerrit Smith led the arguments not just for a delay in the project, but for its complete abandonment. "It seems to me that in these circumstances Brown must go no further, and so I write him," said Smith in the note of May 7 that Sanborn forwarded to Higginson. "I never was convinced of the wisdom of this scheme," wrote the man who'd previously said he stood "foursquare" behind Brown. "But as things now stand, it seems to me it would be madness to attempt to execute it. Colonel Forbes would make such an attempt a certain and most disastrous failure. I write Brown *this evening.*"[8]After reading Smith's forwarded note, Higginson responded testily to Sanborn that Smith's opinion should not count because he was at heart too nervous for revolution and too likely to surrender at even the slightest sign of a problem. Higginson said they should all be wary of the less than stable Smith. His passions, commitments, and points of view shifted too quickly and easily for him to be relied upon. How could he honestly say he was never convinced of the wisdom of the scheme? asked Higginson. If that were the case, then why had he ever supported it?

☆

While all of this frantic bickering and backpedaling was going on in Massachusetts and New York, John Brown was at Chatham, located some forty-five miles east of Detroit on the Thames River in what is today Ontario and was then called Canada West. The town had a large, militant population of fugitive slaves. There, for several days commencing on May 8, in a hotel owned by a black man, an odd rite of passage took place: a meeting that was meant to be both a reaffirmation and a symbolic, revolutionary reanimation of the Declaration of Independence.

Sitting in a big chair at the center of a long table, Brown surveyed the disappointing turnout. All six of his principal Eastern backers were, of course, nowhere to be seen. Frederick Douglass and Harriet Tubman, both enthusiastically invited to participate, were also conspicuous in their absence. Brown's little Springdale militia stood about the room heavily armed, looking weary and cynical. (Charles Plummer Tidd, who'd "ruined" a young Quaker girl during his winter stay at Springdale, had to be spirited out of town under cloak of darkness. Tidd's crime was not one the puritanical Brown would normally have countenanced, but he was drastically short of men. With all his original Springdale recruits counted in, he still had only about twenty fighters committed to join him in the destruction of Virginia.)

The faces of a few new, desperately needed recruits now joined those of Tidd, Owen Brown, John Kagi, and the other Springdale soldiers. Among them were the young Canadian Stewart Taylor, twenty-six-year-old George B. Gill (who'd been a seaman on Pacific whaling ships before migrating to Kansas in 1857), and Barclay and Edwin Coppoc (Quaker brothers from Springdale). Also new to John Brown's service were James H. Harris, Osborn P. Anderson, and G. J. Reynolds—three eerily quiet, imposing representatives from a secret, unnamed black paramilitary organization.

These men of violence and death were joined in Chatham by several gentlemen whose usual businesses were peace and healing. William Charles Munroe, a black minister from Detroit, sat at the table near Brown, as did a black physician by the name of Delany and several other local black professionals and church leaders. Each held a copy of Brown's draft "Provisional Constitution and Ordinances for the people of the United States"—his apology, charter, and blueprint for governance of the new revolutionary state he would found in the mountains of the South. Each man that could—for many of them, black and white, were illiterate—followed the printed text as John Brown read aloud.

"Whereas slavery," recited Brown, reading from the preamble, "throughout its entire existence in the United States, is none other than a most barbarous, unprovoked, and unjustifiable war of one portion of its citizens upon another portion—the only conditions of which are perpetual imprisonment and hopeless servitude or absolute extermination—in utter disregard and violation of those eternal and self-confident truths set forth in our *Declaration of Independence:* Therefore we, citizens of the United States, and the oppressed people who, by a recent decision of the Supreme Court [the decision on Dred Scott], are declared to have no rights which the white man is bound to respect, together with all other people degraded by the laws thereof, do, for the time being, ordain and establish for ourselves the following Provisional Constitution and Ordinances, the better to protect our persons, property, lives, and liberties, and to govern our actions."[9]

Brown's constitution was shortly approved by a vote of all present. Two days later, at a second meeting, John Brown was appointed commander in chief. John Kagi was made secretary of war. The new man Gill was named secretary of the treasury. And Richard Realf, perhaps because of his British connections, was appointed secretary of state. When both Munroe and then the Syracuse minister Loguen, not present, refused the presidency, it was decided the post would be filled temporarily by a fifteen-man council with Brown at its head. The flag of the provisional government would be "the same that our Fathers fought under in the Revolution."

Higginson wrote Brown from Brattleboro, Vermont, on May 7, asking his views with regard to Forbes and the delay of the project recommended by Parker and the others. Brown answered on May 14, a few days after the close of his convention, writing from Chatham. "None of our friends need have any fears in relation to *hasty* or *rash steps* being taken by us," wrote Brown. ". . . We beg our friends to supply two or three hundred dollars without delay: *pledging ourselves not to act* other than to secure perfect *knowledge* of facts in regard to what F. has *really done; & will do:* so that we may ourselves *know how we ought to act.*" It would be foolish, counseled Brown, to decide the course to be taken while "under an excitement."[10] Based on the messages he was receiving from the East, Brown unhappily assumed his mission would have to be put off indefinitely.

Forbes was in Washington during the first weeks of May, seeing and speaking with any and every government official who would listen to his story about John Brown. Among those whom he visited was William H. Seward, senator from New York. "Forbes was a stranger to me," recalled Seward, "and came to my house in Washington, during the session of Congress, and asked to see me. I saw him alone. He began with a story of great personal distress, involving himself and family, and stated that he had come to me on that account. I supposed that the object of his visit was to solicit charity. I found it very incoherent, very erratic, and thought him a man of an unsound or very much disturbed mind."

Forbes pulled out the book he had written, "to show me how important a person he was." Seward thought the book "strange and absurd . . . giving the art of exciting or getting up military revolutions." Forbes told Seward that Brown was "a very bad man, and would not keep his word; was a reckless man, an unreliable man, a vicious man" who had betrayed Forbes. The furious Forbes stalked up and down before the seated Seward, pounding a fist into a palm as he recounted his story of how Brown had connived for him to come to Kansas to instruct an army that did not exist and aid in a war that was waged only within the old man's addled mind. "He said that his family was at the time in Paris, and that he was in business in New York—what business I do not remember—which paid him, I think, a salary of $1,200; that he went to Kansas on the understanding that he should be indemnified for the loss of this business; that he met with delays in getting to Kansas and in reaching John Brown, with whom he was to cooperate." But "there was no longer anything for him to do there. He was penniless and Brown refused to pay him anything."[11] Forbes then went on to enlighten Seward on John Brown's plans for "troubling Egypt" in Virginia—but this was a part of the conversation that Seward would deny when testifying before the Mason Committee in May of 1860. (At the time that he met Forbes, Seward thought him crazy and his tale of Brown's Virginia project too wild to be a true possibility.)

Forbes also visited Henry Wilson, senator from Massachusetts. Wilson was at his desk on the Senate floor when Forbes walked up and introduced himself. The Senate was not in session at the time; Wilson was busy franking documents and writing letters. Wilson had never before heard of Forbes. "He said that he had been employed the year before, I think he said about a year before that, by Brown to go to Kansas, or somewhere near there, to drill some men for the defense of Kansas," said Wilson in his testimony before the Mason Committee. "He seemed to be in a towering passion, greatly excited; said he had been abused and treated badly. Brown had discharged him or they had parted; Brown had failed to pay him what he ought to be paid; that he thought those persons in the East, and he mentioned Dr. Howe among them, who had made contributions for Kansas were under obligations to pay him; that his family was suffering in France. . . . He said his family was starving. He spoke very nervously and excitedly about it." Though Wilson would not admit it to the Senate investigating committee, Forbes also seems to have alluded to Brown's plans for offensive action against slavery via an armed incursion into slave territory. We gather this from the fact that immediately after his meeting with Forbes on the floor of the Senate, Wilson wrote his friend Howe on May 9 that the arms sent to Brown "for defense, ought not to be used for any illegal or aggressive purpose; that it was illegal and wrong so to use the arms, and so far as the men were concerned who contributed the arms, they ought to take them out of Brown's hands, and give him no encouragement, but keep clear of him." Wilson did not mention to Howe that he had met with Hugh Forbes.

"I received a letter [from Howe] within three or four days," recalled Wilson, "I think as soon nearly as the mail could carry my letter and bring his back."[12] Howe's letter was dated May 12. "I understand perfectly your meaning," said Howe, prefatory to a clever combination of words that lied without lying. "No countenance has been given to Brown for any operations outside of Kansas by the Kansas committee." (No, the committee certainly had not authorized any irregular action, though the Secret Six had.) "There is," added Howe, "in Washington a disappointed and malicious man, working with all the activity which hate and revenge can inspire, to harm Brown, and to cast odium upon the friends of Kansas in Massachusetts. You probably know him. He has been to Mr. Seward."[13]

Before Howe responded to Wilson, he wrote a scathing note to Forbes. Forbes had written three letters to Howe that had gone unanswered. Now with the senator from Massachusetts querying his relationship with this madman, the doctor determined to scare Forbes off. "The Dr. has written to F. an adroit and stringing letter, intended to baffle him," wrote Sanborn to Higginson.[14] As many of Howe's friends knew all too well, he was quite talented in the art of "adroit and stringing" letters. The smug, leering attacks he'd published so regularly in the *Commonwealth* were evidence enough of his prowess with insults. So were the curt and often ingeniously cruel notes he was capable of sending friends whom he imagined guilty of some slight. Now he trained his verbal fire on Hugh Forbes.

"I infer from your language that you have obtained (in confidence) some information respecting an expedition which you think would be commendable provided *you* could manage it, but which you will *betray* and *denounce* if Brown does not give it up!" wrote Howe to Forbes on May 10. "You are, sir, the guardian of your own honor; but I trust that for your children's sake at least you will never let your passion lead you to a course that might make them blush. In order, however, to disabuse you of any lingering notion that I, or any of the members of the late Kansas Committee (whom I know intimately) have any responsibility for Captain Brown's actions, I wish to say that the very last communication I sent him was in order to signify the earnest wish of certain gentlemen, whom you name as his supporters, that he should go at once to Kansas and give his aid in the coming elections. Whether he will do so or not, we do not know."[15]

Actually, the letter to Brown had not yet been written. And it was not Howe, but George Luther Stearns who addressed Brown on May 14. "Enclosed please find a copy of a letter to Doctor Howe, from Hon. Henry Wilson," wrote Stearns to Brown. "You will recollect that you have the custody of the arms alluded to, to be used for the defense of Kansas, as agent of the Massachusetts State Kansas Committee. In consequence of the information thus communicated to me, it becomes my duty to warn you not to use them for any other purpose, and to hold them subject to my order as chairman of said committee. A member of our committee will be at Chatham early in the coming week, to confer with you as to the best mode of disposing of them."[16] The subtext was plainly there for Brown to see: the Virginia experiment was off.

Howe wrote a second note to Senator Wilson on May 15, this one indicating far more comprehension and cooperation than did his May 12 letter. "When I last wrote to you I was not aware fully of the true state of the case, with respect to certain arms belonging to the late Kansas Committee," wrote Howe. "Prompt measures have been taken, and will be resolutely followed up, to prevent any such monstrous perversion of a trust as would be the application of means raised for the defence of Kansas to a purpose which the subscribers to the fund would disapprove and vehemently condemn."[17]

About a week later, on May 26, Howe wrote to a George Wood of Washington, an abolitionist leader who had met with Forbes and then wrote Howe to query his legitimacy.[18] In a note marked "Confidential" Howe made Wood a veiled offer to buy Forbes off. "I know nothing of Captain Forbes personally. I never saw him and never heard of him until within last month. I am told that he is, or was, a gentleman, and I conclude he has become intemperate or insane, because he makes the most preposterous claims upon persons who never directly or indirectly incurred the slightest obligation to him and upon whom he has no *legal* or *moral claims whatsoever.* I say what I know. . . . [However] if he is in distress, he has claim upon every humane man, and his abusive language to me and my friends shall not cut him off from our sympathy. Let me know how without hurting his feelings we can help him. Probably he will not accept aid; and we cannot admit any claim for pay, for we owe him nothing but good will."[19]

On May 16, two days after his initial letter to Brown saying a committeeman would come to him shortly in Canada to coordinate liquidation of his arms, Stearns wrote once again. No member of the committee could spare the time for the trip to Canada. Brown should come to New

York sometime in the next week to meet with several of his supporters. "A letter to me, directed to care of John Hopper, 110 Broadway, New York, will be in season. Come as early as you can. Our committee will pay your expenses."[20] At first it was hoped that Parker and Higginson would join Stearns and Howe in meeting Brown at New York, although it turned out they did not. Sanborn suggested that Higginson and perhaps Parker could look up Forbes, who was quite possibly returned from Washington and back in Manhattan.[21] When Higginson and then Parker decided not to go to New York, Stearns and Howe in their stead made a formal attempt to arrange a meeting with Forbes. An invitation was issued but Forbes did not reply.[22]

☆

Howe at first vacillated, but as we have seen ultimately came down for postponement of Brown's experiment. But under the impression that Howe was still for proceeding, Higginson wrote to Theodore Parker of the Forbes problem on May 18: "I find from Dr. H. that he, at least, agrees with me about H.F. & the policy to be pursued. I am entirely satisfied of the correctness of the following positions. *1st.* Postponement is abandonment, because F. can do as much harm next year as this. Indeed he will probably let it out at any rate before long & the question is whether to act before or after betrayal. The latter alternative is impossible, or nearly so. *2nd.* He can do no harm if we can steal a march on him, of which there is little doubt. Any betrayal *afterward* will only *increase the panic* which is one element of the operation. S. [Sanborn] has a theory that F. can injure the operation by disclosing the smallness of its resources. He seems to forget that by the original programme, it was to be regarded (at first) as a mere local flurry with *no resonances at all.* . . . The more I think of it, the more amazed I am at the view which you and the other two S's [Smith and Stearns] have taken. . . . If I had the wherewithal I would buy out the other stockholders and tell our veteran [Brown] to go on: As it is, I can only urge it to the extent of my investment."[23]

Higginson believed that once Brown's insurrection was embarked upon, it would gain tremendous popular support from constituencies that would have denounced the scheme as impractical or inappropriate before the fact. "For one man who would consent to the *proposition* of a slave insurrection, there are ten who would applaud it, when it came to the point," Higginson wrote. "People's hearts go faster than their heads."[24] In other words, it would be foolish to allow practicalities to stop the program from getting under way. In Higginson's view, the apparently impractical and unrealistic scheme would become an entirely pragmatic exercise with achievable goals the moment it was set in motion. This view was fundamental to the psychology whereby Higginson convinced himself that viability lurked somewhere in a plan that seemed in fact to be characterized by its absence. To Higginson, Forbes was just one more major logistical problem that, in the twisted logic of Higginson and Brown, should be taken as a cause for hope.

Higginson wrote to Brown on the same day he'd written Parker, voicing support but adding that he had no money to send. "The sum raised by me was all I can possibly provide, but I have written to the others, strongly urging them not to give up the ship."[25]

"Wilson, as well as Hale [senator from New Hampshire] . . . and God knows how many more have heard about the plan from F.," wrote Sanborn to Higginson in a letter that, like Higginson's two notes to Parker and Brown, was composed on May 18. "To go on in the face of this is mere madness and I place myself full on the side of P. [Parker] S. [Stearns] and Dr. H.—with G.S. [Gerrit Smith] who *does* count. . . . Mr. S. [Stearns] and the Dr. will see Hawkins [Brown] in New York this week and settle matters finally." After the signature on the note, Sanborn wrote: "Please return this letter."[26]

Higginson now wrote Stearns to try to convince him that delay was a bad idea. "Your letter sent to me from Boston was received this morning," responded Stearns on May 21 from New York. "I [am fully convinced] by reasons that cannot be written to recall the arms committed to B.'s custody. We are all agreed on that point. And if you come to Boston I think I can convince you that it is for the best." Stearns did not sign the letter.[27] Brown stood up Stearns and Howe; he never came to New York City.

14

THE REPUTED
NEW ENGLAND
HUMANITARIANS

GERRIT SMITH CAME to Boston on or about May 24, 1858, to discuss the Forbes situation with other members of the Six. "We meet G. Smith today at Revere House at two o'clock—Come down," telegraphed Sanborn to Higginson at Worcester.[1] Feeling completely isolated in his opinion that the enterprise should proceed unhampered, and evidently thinking he had already done all he could to change his friends' minds, Higginson did not attend the meeting, where more than one fateful decision was made.

It was five of the Six, then, that gathered in the former home of Paul Revere on Hanover Street, at that time a tavern that offered private meeting rooms. As a clock ticked loudly on the wall, Smith—anxious, annoyed, and giving off the air of a busy man being greatly inconvenienced by nonsense—bitterly criticized the ineptitude of Brown in taking one so unreliable as Forbes into his confidence. The entire enterprise, Smith announced with the gruffness of one used to having his wishes acted upon instantly and without debate, would have to be abandoned immediately. Brown himself, after his failure to give his supporters the courtesy of showing up for the New York conference, should be censured, condemned, and cut off. He would see the end of Brown, Smith said—would give him no more support, would have him off the Adirondack lands, would give him whatever recompense was required to send him packing.

Calming the agitated Smith, Messrs. Sanborn, Stearns, Howe, and Parker urged a more moderate approach, which eventually prevailed. The decision was to definitely postpone the Harpers Ferry adventure until the following winter or spring, thus in the short term making Forbes's wild forecast of rebellion appear to be a canard. Brown would be instructed to return to Kansas for the summer and autumn. Then, early in the new year, two or three thousand dollars would be raised for him to finance the Virginia invasion. Furthermore, the group formulated a new "blind" arrangement whereby Brown was not, in the future, to provide the Six with any details on his precise plans nor "burden" them with "knowledge that would be . . . both needless and inconvenient," thus affording the group a plausible amount of deniability in the event of criminal charges ever being filed.[2]

Brown came to Boston a week later, after receiving a letter from Sanborn that contained the essence of the Revere House decisions. "Hawkins is here at the American House, Room 86. Can you not come down tomorrow and see him?" telegraphed Sanborn to Higginson on May 31.[3] Higginson, who had refused to allocate time a week before to meet with Brown's now hesitant supporters, quickly sought out Brown himself at the American House on the day after receiving Sanborn's telegram, June 1. Sitting on the bed in his room and talking to Higginson for more than three hours, the earnest Brown seemed exhausted, depressed, and pessimistic. Brown showed Higginson the letter from Sanborn announcing the results of the Revere House meeting. "On questioning B.," recalled Higginson, "I gradually found he agreed entirely with me, considered delay very discouraging to his 13 men and to those in Canada." But Brown was not surprised by the decision of the group. "G.S. [Smith] he knew to be a timid man, G.L.S. [Stearns] and T.P. [Parker] he did not think abounded in courage, H. [Howe] had more." Overall, said Brown, they were not "men of action" if they could be intimidated by the mere threat of "a Forbes."[4]

Higginson subsequently learned from Howe that Brown at least left Boston with something. "I went to see Dr. Howe and found that things had ended far better than I supposed." At a meeting with Howe, Stearns, and Sanborn, Brown had agreed to go into the West and stay there for several months. "The Kansas committee put some $500 in gold into [Brown's] hands and all the arms with only the understanding that he should go to Kansas and then be left to his own discretion. He went off in good spirits."[5] Acting without the formal knowledge of any of the Six, Brown was to do what he could to establish and secure Underground Railroad lines out of Missouri, across Iowa, and north to Canada. It was suggested that he, in the course of this activity, be just heavy-handed enough to publicly establish his presence in Kansas—thus giving the lie to any rumors he was lurking about the borders of Virginia. It was with this clear understanding that Brown was given the $500—which in fact was the absolute last of the cash in the Kansas Committee's small war chest. "The most disagreeable work I ever do," wrote Howe to Martin Conway, Kansas agent for the committee, on May 30, "is to go begging . . . and with our staunch friend Stearns, to go round like a highwayman and bid friends stand and deliver. . . . We cannot get any more except in case of actual hostilities, which I trust will not occur."[6]

Looking back, and realizing that Brown was a madman who would lead all who marched with him to certain death, one is tempted to think that perhaps Forbes had been a voice of reason at the camp in Kansas, and that later he was not trying to destroy the experiment but rather salvage it by rendering it from Brown's command. However, the one letter from Forbes to survive the fireplaces of any of the Six—an absurd, rambling note he sent to Higginson on June 6—indicates something else altogether. Sanborn had written Higginson that Forbes "has a grudge against all New England, and especially against me." And both Howe and Sanborn hinted to Higginson that the letters they'd burned revealed an unstable personality capable of anything. One gets a sense of this reading Forbes's note to Higginson. There is paranoia here, laced with shrewd manipulation as well as the most thinly veiled suggestion of blackmail. Forbes was writing from Philadelphia:

My Dear Sir:

I was in hopes that I should have left Washington in season to have seen you at the New York May meetings. Important business which called me to Washington detained me longer than I anticipated—besides certain financial difficulties throw obstacles in my way. I have much to say—*very much*—so much that I can hardly find time to write even a tithe to you & several others with whom I wish to communicate—& moreover I am little disposed to trust certain letters by the U.S. mail addressed to obnoxious individuals. You can get from F. B. Sanborn of Concord, Mass. & Dr. S. G. Howe of Boston a sight of my letters to them, unless Dr. H. may have thrown them behind the fire as he said he would do if he did not like their tone—as if he thought himself the Pope or the Autocrat of Austria, Japan, or China.

I have been grossly defrauded in the name of Humanity and Antislavery. At the earnest request of certain Committees and Humanitarians, I in the spring of 1857 consented to go West, provided a monthly provision were made for my family dependent upon me for support. While in the West on the Antislavery service, the New England promisers broke their engagements toward my family, & on my return to New York in Dec. last (so ill as to be there for a long time confined to my bed) I learned the dreadful tidings that my family in Paris had actually been turned destitute into the street. But for the indomitable energy of Mrs. Forbes & the assistances of some Italian Refugees (themselves very poor) my family must have perished, & the guilt . . . must have rested on the reputed New England Humanitarians.

I have for years laboured in the antislavery cause . . .
[therefore] if my family were from any circumstance to be in
distress, that distress ought cheerfully & effectually to be alle-
viated by the antislavery men of every school. When however that distress arises from my having been, through the
falsehood & fraud of committeemen & their agents, induced
to leave my then existing means of supporting my family
that I might go West in the cause of Humanity & Antislavery, then I say that the claim of my family is immeasurably
increased. I do not beg for charity. I demand redress from
those who have robbed me. And Humanity, Justice, & Com-
monsense require that no precious time be squandered by
the culprits in contemptible shuffling to shift their responsibility on other shoulders.

. . . Let them not flatter themselves that I shall eventually
become weary, & shall drop the subject. It's as yet quite at its
beginning. The Massachusetts Senators Sumner & Wilson
wrote to Boston about it: but Howe, Lawrence, Sanborn &
associates prefer to accumulate injury on injury rather than
acknowledge their fallibility by redressing the wrong they
have committed.[7]

It is interesting to note from the text that Forbes does not seem to cen-
sure Higginson as one of his nemeses. Forbes addresses Higginson as
more of a bystander and potential ally than a culprit. Also interesting is
Forbes's assumption that Amos Lawrence was a backer of the Harpers
Ferry plot, which he definitely was not. Lawrence knew nothing about it.

There is no record of Higginson responding to Forbes's note. Forbes,
as all the rest of the Six had anticipated and counted upon, soon faded
when the slave insurrection of which he warned failed to materialize.

☆

Forbes was not the only vulgar opportunist the Secret Six had to deal
with. Brown had come to Boston carrying with him a letter directed to

the Six from Richard Realf, the young Englishman recently appointed secretary of state for his vaporous government in exile.

"In view of the temporary postponement of a certain enterprise," Realf wrote the Six, "I avail myself of the kindness of our mutual friend, the bearer of this, to say the following: solely (I hope) with the desire of forwarding the interests of the Association with which I am identified. During the six or nine months which may now elapse before any active measures can be taken, an energetic agent could collect at least $2,000, clear of all expenses, in England. Indeed, without claiming the possession of any extraordinary activity, I think I could secure such an amount myself. I am an Englishman by birth; and, prior to my emigration to this country, which occurred several years ago, I was a protege of Lady Noel Byron, Charles Kingsley, and others of the aristocracy and literati. I have some acquaintance with men of wealth, letters, and position; and I used to possess an influence among the more educated of the working classes. I believe I have sufficient ability to collect funds without disclosing our plan, or the names of any of its adherents." If the Six would underwrite Realf with $250 and "accept my simple word that all monies received (except such portions of them as I should have to devote to my own support) should be delivered into the hands of our friend, the bearer of this, I beg, respectfully, to offer myself for this service."[8]

Realf's word was taken, his offer accepted. It seems likely that Stearns supplied most of the requested $250. Realf left for England in the late spring. In his January 1860 testimony before the Select Committee of the Senate investigating the affair at Harpers Ferry, Realf would deny that his mission to England was purposed to raise funds for Brown, that Brown had any prior knowledge of his trip, or that Brown or any of his backers endorsed or financed the journey. This was a less embarrassing scenario to articulate than the truth: that Realf took the money of Brown's friends and, after arriving in England, reneged on his promise to them, making absolutely no attempt to raise any donations toward the enterprise.

It seems possible that some sort of personal religious crisis experienced after Realf left Brown's company but before he arrived in Britain was the cause of his change of plan. In any event, Realf did not do what he'd promised the Secret Six in asking them to fund his trip. Instead of visiting leading abolitionists and intellectuals in the United Kingdom to solicit funds for Brown, Realf made an extended visit to his parents, trying in vain to procure their consent for him to convert to the Roman Catholic Church. Departing for the United States from Le Havre on March 2, 1859, he did so with little money in his pockets and certainly none for John Brown. Once back in the States, Realf made no attempt to contact either Brown or any of the Secret Six. He instead got himself to New Orleans, where he briefly considered applying to be received into the Jesuit priesthood. For his part, John Brown had no hint of the whereabouts of his secretary of state.

"I saw a statement in a paper," Realf told the Senate inquisitors in 1860, "I do not remember what paper, but sometime ago, I saw a statement that the internal evidence of the letters of Brown and his friends plainly revealed the fact that, though they could trace my departure for England, they could not learn anything of me or my movements since. That, therefore, is evidence that I was not collecting money for them in England, or that if I did, they did not get it; which, so far as implicating me is concerned, amounts to about the same thing."[9]

MANIFESTO

O N HIS WAY west from Boston, after brief layovers first at North Elba and then at the home of Ohio relatives, Brown stopped at Cleveland on June 20 and 21. According to his orders, his men were waiting for him there. Brown distributed to each a portion of the $500 he'd been given in Boston— just enough to see them to their homes in places as various as Canada, Ohio, Illinois, and Iowa. Richard Realf went to New York, whence he would travel to Britain on his supposed fund-raising mission. Stevens, Gill, and the Coppoc brothers were dispatched to Springdale. The handsome, well-spoken Cook was sent to Harpers Ferry as an advance agent. His instructions were to get a job, settle into the community, and learn everything he could about the population and terrain. All the men were firmly instructed that they were to return to Brown, at whatever location and time he prescribed, immediately upon command. Kagi and Tidd traveled with Brown to Kansas.

Brown's men had to look twice at him when he arrived in Cleveland. Upon leaving Boston, he'd begun to sprout the long, white, Moses-like beard that he would be buried with. He told Tidd he wanted the beard as a disguise; it made him look considerably older than his years. He told Kagi the whiskers had been ordered by God in a vision. And he was to tell Redpath that life "away from home, in the camp and on the trail," simply did not lend itself to keeping clean-shaven. In the final analysis, the beard seems to have been more one of convenience than of either disguise or divine inspiration. The beard was long and full by the time Brown, operating under the alias Shubel Morgan, arrived quietly in Lawrence, Kansas, at the end of June.

"I send you a copy of a letter from [Brown] who, in accordance with the decision of two meetings in Boston late in May and early in June at which all . . . were present except yourself, went with a few companions to Kansas to look after matters," wrote Sanborn to Higginson on July 6, 1858. The plans for the Harpers Ferry enterprise "hold good, and it is to be put in action next spring. . . . I have seen and heard nothing from you for long. Where are you to be this summer?"[1]

The unsigned letter from Brown that Sanborn forwarded to Higginson, dated June 28, was intended as a round-robin to all of the Six. "I reached Kansas with friends on the 26th inst; came here last night, and leave *here today* for the neighborhood of late troubles," wrote Brown. "It seems the troubles are not *over* yet. Can write you but few words now. Hope to write you more fully after a while. I do hope you will be in earnest now to carry out *as soon as possible* the measure [establishment of an Underground Railroad route out of Missouri to Iowa] proposed in Mr. Sanborn's letter inviting me to Boston *this last Spring*. I hope there will be *no delay* of that matter. Can you send me by Express care E.B. Whitman Esq. half a doz. or a full doz. whistles [guns] such as I described? at once? Write me till further advised under sealed envelope directing stamped ones to Rev. S.L. Adair [Brown's brother-in-law], Osawatomie, Kansas Ter."[2]

Late troubles. At first glance, it was hard to find a region of Kansas where there had been some. Despite occasional outbursts, the region was far more peaceful than it had been in years. Pres. James Buchanan had fired Governor Walker due to his evenhanded approach to dealing with the free-state majority; but Walker's replacement, the Virginian James

Wilson Denver, turned out (annoyingly enough for Buchanan) to be equally fair and just in his management of the territory. Moreover, Buchanan's bill accepting Kansas into the Union as a slave state, and authorizing adoption of the proslavery Lecompton Constitution, was defeated soundly in the House of Representatives after being approved by the Senate where the slave-state majority dominated.

The one area of Kansas where there had been any fighting of late was in the southeastern section, around the towns of Trading Post and Fort Scott. There, a little over a month before Brown's return, a proslavery man from Georgia named Charles Hamelton led a band that kidnapped eleven free-staters and attempted, ineptly, to execute them by gunfire in a ravine close by the Marais des Cygnes River. Only five of the hostages were actually killed. Shortly thereafter, the free-state guerrilla leader James Montgomery tried, just as ineptly, to burn the town of Fort Scott to the ground. The silent, bearded Brown rode through a slightly charred Fort Scott on his way, with Tidd and Kagi, to meet with Montgomery in a cabin at Sugar Mound during early July. John Brown liked Montgomery, writing that his fellow burner of towns and taker of hostages was "a very intelligent, kind gentlemanly and most excellent man and lover of freedom."[3]

Not long after the meeting with Montgomery, Brown and several of his men built a log and stone fort at a high, conspicuous location close by the site of the Marais des Cygnes massacre. Brown named the place Fort Snyder after the man, a blacksmith named Eli Snyder, on whose claim it was located. From the fort's elevated lookout, Brown and his men had a commanding view of the surrounding countryside. In a letter addressed to "F.B. Sanborn Esq. & Friends at Boston and Worcester," John Brown did his best to make the placid landscape sound like a tinderbox. "I am here with about 10 of my men located on the same quarter section where the terrible murders of the 17th May were committed, called the Hamilton [sic] or Trading Post murders," wrote Brown. "Deserted farms & dwellings lie in all directions for some miles along the line, & the remaining inhabitants watch every appearance of persons moving about with anxious jealousy & vigilance. Four of the persons wounded or attacked on the occasion are staying *with* me. . . . A constant fear of new troubles seems to prevail on both sides of the line & on both sides of the companies of armed men. Any little affair may open the quarrel afresh. Two *murders* and cases of robbery are reported of late. . . . I have concealed the fact of my *presence pretty much* lest it should tend to create excitement, but it is getting leaked out & will soon be known to all. As I am not *here* to *seek* or to *secure revenge,* I do not mean to be the first to reopen the quarrel. . . . We shall soon be in *great want* of a small amount in a draft or drafts on New York *to feed us.* We cannot work *for wages,* & provisions *are not easily* obtained on the frontier."[4]

In an election on August 2 the Lecompton Constitution was defeated by a vast majority, 11,300 to 1,788. As even President Buchanan was quick to admit, this in effect closed the book on the question of slavery in Kansas. The fight was over; the free-staters were victorious. In response to this success, Brown continued to recruit soldiers and train a growing band of men at his fort—seeing to it that word leaked into Missouri that "old Brown" was busy "improving a claim" dangerously near the border. Still, no Missouri raiders took the bait. Brown's frustration at the continuation of peace was compounded by a health problem: he suffered from an extreme case of the ague through most of August and into September. When the correspondent Richard Hinton came to visit Brown on his sickbed, Kagi used the opportunity to inform Hinton of Brown's plan for invading Virginia. An astonished Hinton told Kagi bluntly that the action would not be an invasion, but a suicide. Brown, Kagi, and all who joined with them would die.

After Brown finally recovered from the ague in mid-September, he summoned most of his old Springdale squad back to him at Fort Snyder, adding to them two of Montgomery's men: Jeremiah Anderson, a young Indianan, and Anderson's equally young friend from Pennsylvania, Albert Hazlett.

Following his call for men, Brown sent out a call for money. "Your kind & very welcome letter of the 11th July was received a long time since," wrote Brown to Franklin Sanborn in the autumn, "but I was sick at the time & have been ever since until now so that I did not even answer the letters of my own family or anyone else before yesterday when I began to try. I am very weak yet but gaining well." Brown asked Sanborn for money; the $500 given in Boston that spring was not proving enough to launch the Missouri slave-delivering scheme. "It now looks as though but little business can be accomplished until we get our mill in operation. I am *most* anxious about that, & want you to name the earliest date possible as near as you can learn when you can have your matters gathered up. *Do let me hear from you on this point* (as soon as consistent;) so that I may have some idea how to arrange my business. . . . *Dear friends do be in earnest.* The harvest we shall reap, if we are only up & doing."[5]

"I received the enclosed letter from our friend a week or two since," wrote Sanborn to Higginson on October 13, forwarding Brown's note. "You see he's anxious about future operations. Can you do anything for him before next March, and if so what? The partners in Boston have talked the matter over, but have not yet come to any definite proposal. *Please write me fully* about this."[6] Higginson had nothing to send; neither did Sanborn. And the majority shareholders Smith, Stearns, Parker, and Howe were not willing to advance Brown any more money before spring. Thus, the Six should not have been surprised when Brown joined James Montgomery two months later, on December 16, in a raid on Fort Scott during which a proslavery man was killed and his store plundered. Brown was looking elsewhere for the sustenance his Eastern backers procrastinated in supplying.

☆

One thing inhibiting contributions from the more nervous members of the Six was an alarming broadside published in the autumn of 1858 by Boston attorney Lysander Spooner and several other abolitionists. Addressed "To the Non-Slaveholders of the South," the broadside was entitled "A Plan for the Abolition of Slavery." The plan elucidated by Spooner was "to make war (openly or secretly as circumstances may dictate)" upon slaveholders. The large sheet, printed on both sides—which Spooner called a Manifesto—endorsed the kidnapping of slaveholders, the arming and training of blacks for guerrilla warfare, and other acts to disrupt the system of slavery and encourage black insurrection. The hope of Spooner's Manifesto was that, when distributed throughout the South, it would give rise to "a movement that shall result not only in the freedom of the blacks, but also in the political, pecuniary, educational, moral, and social advantage of the present non-slaveholding whites."[7]

The Secret Six were not happy with the appearance of Spooner's open call for revolt. With their own plan for inciting revolt under way, the last thing they wanted was someone calling attention to the idea. Nothing should be done, wrote Sanborn to Higginson, that might put the slave-holders on their guard and thus make general insurrection more difficult. Higginson wrote Spooner a discreet note on November 30.

Dear Sir:

. . . The increase of interest in the subject of slave insurrection is one of the most important signs of the times. It is my firm conviction that, within a few years, that phase of the subject will urge itself on general attention, and the root of the matter be thus reached. I think that this will be done by the action of the slaves themselves, in certain localities, with the aid of *secret* co-operation from the whites.

This is greatly to be denied. The great obstacle to anti-slavery action has always been the apparent feebleness & timidity of the slaves themselves. Had there been an insurrection every year since the American Revolution, I believe that slavery would have been abolished ere this. . . .

In place therefore of forming a society or otherwise propounding insurrection as a *plan,* my wish would be to assume it as a *fact.* The concrete will arouse sympathy more than the abstract.

Were I free to do it, I would give you assurances that what I say means something, & that other influences than these of which you speak are even now looking to the same end. I am not now at liberty to be more explicit.

You may however say, the public mind need [*sic*] to be prepared by the promulgation of bold theories, so that the facts
whenever they come, will be better received. This I admit to
be true, and, in this point of view, I see the value of your circular. The fugitive slave cases and the Kansas excitement
have prepared the public mind for it, in some degree, and I
always advise anti-slavery speakers to suggest the matter & do
it myself. Still, it will be some time before a statement as
exceedingly frank as yours will be received without a shudder. Yet, it asserts important principles & will do good. . . .[8]

Higginson met with Spooner in Boston at Monk's Bookstore, 14
Broomfield Street, during early December. At this meeting, Higginson
was more candid than he was willing to be in a letter. He evidently
explained in detail exactly why Spooner's circular might not serve well
the cause for which it was intended. Parker, who was sick in bed, also
urged Spooner to withdraw the document, writing him a note that did
not specify details as to reasons but simply said, "When I am well enough
I will come & talk with you about it."[9]

Writing in 1878, Spooner recalled that after publication of the Manifesto, he was given to understand that Brown "was sorry for it, lest it
should put the slaveholders on their guard, and make his main enterprise more dangerous. For this reason, the Manifesto was suppressed so
far as it could then be. Not a great many copies had been issued—
perhaps two hundred, or thereabouts; mostly among the slaveholders
themselves." In the same 1878 letter, Spooner explained that the Manifesto "was gotten up by one [himself] who knew nothing of Brown's
scheme, until after the Manifesto had been printed, and some copies of it
issued. It was suppressed, as I said, as far as it could be, in deference to
the wishes of Brown, or at least of some of Brown's friends."[10] (Spooner
would have a meeting with Brown himself in Boston during the first
week of May in 1859, at which Brown would personally request further
suppression of the well-intentioned broadside.[11])

There was similar dissatisfaction among the Secret Six slightly later when, five months before the Harpers Ferry invasion, the journalist James Redpath (Brown's old Kansas friend) wrote and published a book that prescribed black insurrection with the aid of white armed allies from free territory. Redpath, who was by this time advised of Brown's scheme, even went so far as to dedicate the book to Brown. "You, Old Hero!" wrote Redpath, "believe that the slave should be aided and urged to insurrection and hence do I lay this tribute at your feet."[12]

☆

Theodore Parker was never to be well enough to visit Lysander Spooner. He had suffered premonitions of mortality for several years. On August 24, 1853—his forty-third birthday—he'd written, "Certain admonitions of late warn me that I am not to live to be an old man."[13] Three years later, in 1856, he wrote mournfully to a friend in Germany, "I fear you would hardly know me, I am grown so old in look. My head is bald and my beard is gray. . . . I have grown very old within the last three years; too much work and too many cares have done this to me."[14] He almost fainted while lecturing at New Bedford in April of 1858. "[I] tried to speak," he recalled, "but was so ill, that I could not hear or see or speak well. I left the room, and went . . . to an apothecary's and took about a spoonful and a half of sherry wine, which helped me. Spoke but with great difficulty. Am better today, but slenderly and meanly. *I take this as a warning,* —not the first."[15] He was feeling increasingly tired. "I don't know what is to come of it," he wrote. "Sometimes I think of knocking at earth's gate with my staff, saying, 'Liebe Mutter, let me in.' "[16]

It was in October of 1858, while a frustrated Brown eyed the quiet Kansas landscape and pondered how to shake things up, that Parker first started to bleed in his lungs. The minister, whose family had been prone to tuberculosis for generations, came to Howe's office one day in December and said, pointing to his chest, "Howe, that venomous cat which has destroyed so many of my people has fixed her claws here."[17] Soon after, in February of 1859, Parker and his wife departed by steamship for the warmer, healing climates of Cuba and Santa Cruz. They were accompanied on the first leg of their journey by Sam and Julia Howe. Their friend George Ripley, formerly a principal in the Brook Farm commune and lately affiliated with the *New York Tribune,* for which Julia Ward Howe would shortly start writing, saw them off.

The ailing Parker was a "wretched sailor," Julia remembered. Parker spent many days sick in his cabin before appearing on deck at last, "limp and helpless, and glad to lie upon a mattress." In Havana, Parker was able to tour a bit with Dr. Howe, but remained quite weak. Julia recalled seeing Parker off on the boat that was to take him to Santa Cruz. From there, after a stay of several months, he was scheduled to go to Europe. She knew she would never see him again. "It was dusk already as we ascended [the] steep gangway . . . ," wrote Julia. "Dusk too were our thoughts at parting from Can Grande, the mighty, the vehement, the great fighter. How were we to miss his deep music, here and at home. . . . And now came silence and tears and last embraces; we slipped down the gangway into our little craft and, looking up, saw bending above us between the slouched hat and the silver beard, the eyes that we can never forget, that seemed to drop back in the darkness with the solemnity of a last farewell."[18]

Writing to Francis Jackson, the Boston historian and abolitionist who had been instrumental in helping evacuate William and Ellen Craft several years before, Parker described his new life in temperate Santa Cruz. The house where he lived, wrote Parker, was "a little piece of outdoors with a roof over it. . . . If I don't get better here you must make up your mind to let me go, for if the air of Santa Cruz does not help me nothing will or can." He did not trouble Jackson with the news that, so far, the warm air was doing nothing at all to improve his condition. "A few months will determine my fate," Parker wrote to his church committee, "and I shall know where I stand—whether I am to recover entirely or partially or pass quietly away. . . . My chance of recovery is not more than one in ten."[19]

He heard nothing of John Brown's enterprise after leaving Boston. But Brown's experiment was evidently still very much on Parker's mind as he quietly waged his private fight for life under the palms of the

Caribbean. Writing again to Francis Jackson, he dwelt not on his infirmities but rather on a particularly relevant piece of Santa Cruz's history. "Slavery continued here until 1848 when all over the little island the blacks rose, took possession of all except the two forts, & demanded their freedom. There were 3,000 whites & 25,000 blacks on the island. The negroes *did not shed a drop of blood.* They burnt a few houses but destroyed very little property & took no man's life. Imagine the consternation of the whites who knew what *they* would do under like circumstances."[20]

16

THE STUFF OF WHICH MARTYRS ARE MADE

FIVE DAYS BEFORE Christmas, 1858, John Brown led his men on a raid into Missouri during which the homes of two slave owners were plundered. One of the slaveowners was executed—shot in the head. Eleven slaves were liberated. Brown also liberated several wagons, many horses and mules, five guns, and nearly $100 in cash. The Missouri General Assembly condemned the incursion and suggested the possibility of violent retaliation. Moderate free-state Kansans such as Charles Robinson and George Washington Brown of the *Lawrence Herald of Freedom* criticized Brown's action, saying that it invited the resurgence of border war by giving Missourians an excuse to invade and terrorize free-state communities under cloak of searching for the stolen property. The governor of Missouri offered $75 for Brown's capture. And President Buchanan was so enraged that he personally put a $250 price on Brown's head. (Brown, in turn, mockingly offered a reward of $2.50 for Buchanan's capture.) Back East, the unpredictable Gerrit Smith surprised his wife by being delighted with the news of Brown's activity.

"Do you hear the news from Kansas?" asked Smith. "Our dear John Brown is . . . pursuing the policy which he intended to pursue *elsewhere*."[1]

Sanborn wrote to Higginson on January 19, 1859, with news of Brown's adventures in Kansas, passing along an exaggerated report of Brown's success in abducting slaves from bondage. "Mr. Parker has rec'd a letter from [Kagi in] Lawrence, describing the operations of our friends of the Underground R.R. . . . of which perhaps you may be informed; if not, let me say that according to [Kagi] there were on Dec. 28th about 20 fugitives in and about Lawrence . . . seven of those set free by J.B. were expected in Lawrence on the 28th, while others were known to be en route from Leavenworth. The immediate cause of this stampede is the constant sale of slaves to go South from western Mo. . . . [Unless Brown's operations are somehow stopped, he will] release many more of our black sheep. For R.R. [railroad] purposes money is wanted. . . . Can you raise any? And are these facts new to you? I have no private advice from J.B. since I wrote you. He has begun the work in earnest, I fancy, and will find enough to do where he is for the present. I am glad of what he has done. . . . You are busy, I know. But can you not write me a word? Or hopefully I can meet you in Boston, where I shall be next Saturday and Friday, and a week after also."[2] Brown was to liberate only the eleven sheep he then had in his custody, and no more.

This is one of several letters to Higginson of the period in which Sanborn specifically queries Higginson's refusal to respond to his notes. Higginson, still annoyed at the delay of the Virginia scheme imposed by the other stockholders, seems to have been unwilling to play any part at all for several months. He had, he told Sanborn, decided that the entire project was too "chimerical" to warrant further attention. He would waste no more of his time; no more of his money. Yet it seems that the demonstration of productive activity on the part of Brown in Kansas that December made Higginson rethink things. Throughout late January and all of February, while Howe accompanied the dying Parker on his steamship journey south, Higginson sent what money he could in response to Sanborn's entreaties. By March, Higginson was as much an active player as he ever was. And thus Sanborn wrote him

when the Virginia project
started to become a reality
once more.

"Your X was rec'd and forwarded to Lawrence . . . ,"
wrote Sanborn to Higginson
on March 4. "Brown . . .
was at Tabor on the 10th
Feb. with his stock in fine
condition, as he says in a letter to G. Smith. He also says
he is ready . . . to set his will
in operation, and seems to be
coming East for that pur-
pose. Mr. Smith proposes to
raise $1000 for him, and to
contribute $100 himself. I
think a larger sum ought to
be raised for his operations,
but can we raise so much as
this? Can you do anything
towards it? B. says he thinks

John Murray Forbes, railroad magnate and financier of Boston who joined in giving financial support to Brown without knowing—or wanting to know—the details of the Harpers Ferry scheme. Photo courtesy Massachusetts Historical Society.

any one of us . . . might raise the sum if we should set about it; perhaps
this is so; but I doubt it. As a reward for what he has done, perhaps
money might be raised for him. At any rate I think he means to do the
work; and I expect to hear of him at Peterboro within a few weeks. Dr.
Howe [writes that he] thinks John Forbes and several others not of our
party would help the project if they knew of it."[3]

On April 6, Sanborn wrote Higginson to say that both Judge
Ebenezer Rockwood Hoar—a Concord neighbor of Sanborn's—and
John Murray Forbes had contributed small amounts without learning
the whole story of exactly what Brown had planned. At forty-six years of
age, John Murray Forbes was a millionaire many times over. An inheritor of wealth, Forbes made new fortunes of his own in the China trade

and then as a developer of railroads. He was a nephew of Thomas Hansyd Perkins, the affluent Boston merchant who'd been the original benefactor of the Perkins Institute for the Blind. After successfully petitioning Forbes and Hoar, Sanborn had less success with another man of money. "I called on [Samuel] Cabot last Tuesday thinking I might open the whole matter to him, but found it not advisable to do so. Nor did I ask him to raise money, as I suppose he might do. He has all confidence in J.B., however." Howe had yet to return from his trip to Cuba, but would by mid-April. "When the Dr. gets home he will do something I have no doubt, but I fear not very much."[4]

Sanborn wrote Higginson on April 19 to thank him for a donation of $20. "Brown himself is in Boston, or soon to be so, and I hope you will look him up if you can, at the American House or the U.S. or else Dr. Howe or Mr. Stearns will tell you if he has come. He was in Peterboro a week ago, and Mr. Smith sent me word he would soon be in Boston. I shall go down to meet him I suppose, probably tomorrow night. But if I do not hear from him I shall not go down tomorrow night. If you don't see Brown pray see Dr. Howe if you can, or Mr. Stearns. G. Smith has subscribed $400."[5] Sanborn did not have the entire story about Smith's contribution. Smith gave Brown nearly $160 in cash, a note for an additional $285, and a pledge to provide another $400 *if* the balance of a total fund of $2,000 were raised among other Eastern supporters.[6]

A few years later, when Smith was busy denying his complicity in the raid at Harpers Ferry, Sanborn would write that "with some of this [money], or with money afterwards sent by Mr. Smith, Brown paid in part for his pikes, at Collinsville, Connecticut, to arm the slaves of Virginia. I presume Mr. Smith never knew that his gift would be so used; but he put no restrictions on its use, and he knew that Brown was then on his slow way to execute the plan unfolded to us at Peterboro the winter before."[7] In August of 1859, when John Brown, Jr., visited the Syracuse area and spoke to Edwin Morton, Morton categorically reaffirmed that Smith had "his whole soul absorbed in" the Virginia invasion.[8] During Brown's brief stay at his house, Smith was unequivocal about his support and respect for Brown. At a gathering of friends at which Brown was present, Smith announced loudly: "If I were asked to point out—I will say it in his presence—to point out the man in all this world I think most truly a Christian, I would point to John Brown."[9] It was only a few months prior to this that Smith had denounced Brown at the Revere House meeting of the Six.

It actually took John Brown another few weeks to make it to the Boston area after his visit to Smith, as he stopped for a time at North Elba, where he became sick with an ear infection and a return of the ague. Brown was in Concord by May 8, however, where he spoke at a meeting in the evening. "He goes to the U.S. House in Boston today," wrote Sanborn to Higginson on May 9, "and I go down this noon to meet him at Dr. Howe's office at 3 P.M., where I have [arranged for] a few friends to meet him. Can you not go down and meet us there? In the evening it is not unlikely we may go out to John Forbes's at Milton. . . . I must return here, while Brown will stay in Boston a day or two longer. So try to see him."[10]

Back on February 5, just as he was about to sail with Parker, Howe had written out a note of introduction for John Brown to bring to John Murray Forbes. "I have carefully watched the movements of Brown for two years, and have considerable personal knowledge of him," wrote Howe to Forbes. "He is of the stuff of which martyrs are made. He is of the Puritan order militant. He is called fighting Brown, because under his natural and unaffected simplicity and modesty there is an irresistible propensity to war upon injustice and wrong. He is cool, fearless, keen, and ready with all his mental and bodily powers, in the most sudden and imminent dangers. If you would like to talk with him *upon the square,* and hear what he has to say about what might perhaps seem at first to be treason, he will be glad to talk with you. So far as one man can answer for another whom he has not known very long and intimately, I can answer for Brown's honesty of purpose."[11] The note of introduction still was not used by the time Howe returned to Boston from Cuba. And before Brown had a chance to show the letter to Forbes, Howe would decide to revise his enthusiastic recommendation.

Back in Boston in May, Howe had a private meeting with Brown. Howe, who had been entertained by several Southern plantation owners during his return trip from Cuba, said that he was having second thoughts about a key aspect of the Virginia plan. If blacks should not be kidnapped, Howe told Brown, perhaps neither should whites. And neither should any property of whites be stolen—excluding, of course, the slaves, who were not legitimately anyone's property but their own. Howe asked Brown to moderate his plans to exclude kidnapping as well as the theft of merchandise and cash. Brown respectfully refused to do so, whereupon Howe announced that *he* would respectfully refuse to provide any further financial assistance to Brown's venture.

"It was after father became weary (and even discouraged) with begging for money and men to help carry out 'his plan,' that he made up his mind to confiscate property that the slave, and his ancestors, had been compelled to [create] for others—property that he needed to subsist on, and to enable him to free himself and others," remembered Brown's daughter Anne. "I think that Dr. Howe and father were both right—only they viewed the situation from a different point. I cannot see anything inconsistent in either one's opinion on the subject. They just believed what was best for them." In lieu of cash, remembered Anne, Howe gave Brown "a little walnut pot, with a fine Smith and Wesson revolver in it. (Father gave me the pot; I have it still in my possession.) Now, Dr. Howe fully expected father to break the law prohibiting the carrying [of] concealed weapons, and possibly the Commandment that says, 'Thou shalt not kill' if he was attacked."[12]

In her statement, Anne Brown made it seem that theft was a new and recent item in the operating principles of her father as of 1859. As we have seen, this is certainly not the case. Wherever Brown traveled, whatever fight he found, he had always doubled as a thief. There were numerous thefts throughout his time in Kansas, beginning with the stealing of horses, arms, and saddles belonging to the victims of the Pottawatomie Massacre. For justification, as Anne Brown recalled, Brown went to Deuteronomy: "All that is in the city," God told Moses, "even all the spoil thereof, shalt thou take unto thyself; and thou shalt eat the spoil of thine enemies, which the Lord thy God hath given thee."

What is puzzling is the incendiary Howe's sudden reluctance to allow Brown to wreak havoc on the proprietors of the plantation system. It was so out of character. He had always been such a strong advocate of armed action against slavery. "The *word* must be *emancipation,* and [we must wage] war upon slaveholders as such—as a distinct class—as the authors of all the present ills," he would write just two years later, at the beginning of the Civil War. At the time, he would be flirting with a plan reminiscent of Brown's at Harpers Ferry, this one substituting swamps for mountains. "The public need something, or somebody, some word, or some blow, to magnetize them, or else they will be fearfully demoralized in a month," wrote Howe to John Murray Forbes early into the war. Howe suggested "an expedition to land in or about Albemarle Sound, composed mainly of blacks, who would go into the Dismal and other swamps and raise the thousands of refugees there to go out and make sallies and onslaughts upon the [slaveholders]; and so make a diversion. . . . There are plenty of men in Canada, resolute and intelligent refugees, who would enlist in such an enterprise."[13]

What accounts, then, for Howe's reticence during his meeting with Brown in the spring of 1859? It is safe to assume he held no genuine protective emotion for the fathers of the slave system. So what was the real reason behind Howe's new and perplexing reserve? An argument can be made that Howe's reluctance to be a benefactor was caused by a simple, sudden want of cash. As a spate of correspondence between Martin F. Conway, agent of the Massachusetts Kansas Committee, and Samuel Gridley Howe archived in the Howe Papers at the Massachusetts Historical Society documents, Howe was in dire financial distress at just this time, frantically trying to recoup large sums invested in Kansas real estate. The proud Howe was not likely to plead poverty to the beggar Brown; he'd most certainly prefer to plead scruples. It is interesting to note that later, when Howe's investment horizon proved brighter, his scruples dissipated almost instantly and he again began to contribute to

Brown's cause. Further evidence of subtext in Howe's position is that, despite all his supposed newfound reservations about Brown's methods, he invited Brown to tea with Julia.[14] And he continued to facilitate Brown's fund-raising through other channels although refusing on principle to put any of his own money into the pot. (He told Higginson that his decision against further investment was a personal one he would not "impose on any other gentlemen by doing anything to limit their access to Brown, or Brown's access to them."[15])

Thus, on May 9, the day of his meeting with Brown, Howe wrote out another note about Brown to John Murray Forbes and sent it to Forbes directly. This one was less glowing in its recommendation, but was still a recommendation. "Captain Brown (old J.B.) is here," wrote Howe. "If any one desires to get the $325 reward offered for his apprehension by the Governor of Missouri and the President of the United States, he has only to go to the hotel in Beach Street, and try to take the old fellow. He is a character, I assure you and if you are disposed to have a conversation with him, he will call at your house, or your office, as you may appoint. He knows more about the question of practical emancipation than anyone I have seen."[16]

"When I received the last of Dr. Howe's letters," recalled Forbes, "I was busy in town, and wished to show the captain to the rest of my family; so I invited him and Mr. Frank Sanborn out to Milton to tea, and one rainy night they appeared. We summoned such neighbors as we could easily reach, among them William Hunt [the painter], and had a most interesting evening, and indeed night; for, the storm continuing, we kept them over and sat up talking until after midnight." Brown impressed Forbes as "a grim, farmer-like looking man, with a long gray beard and glittering eyes" that had "a little touch of insanity about them." In their long discussion of abolition, Brown rejected "almost with scorn" Forbes's suggestion that "firmness at the ballot-box by the North and West might avert the storm; and said it had passed the stage of ballots, and nothing but bayonets and bullets could settle it now." Early the next morning, Forbes's maid was startled to find "the grim old soldier" Brown sitting bolt upright in a chair by the front entry of the house, fast asleep. "When her light awoke him," remembered Forbes, "he sprang up and put his hand into his breast-pocket, where no doubt his habit of danger led him to carry a revolver."[17]

Before Sanborn and Brown left Forbes's house the next morning, Forbes pledged a contribution. "Sorry not to see you," wrote Forbes to Howe on May 12. "Call me good for $100. . . . Possibly Mr. Rob. G. [Robert Gould] Shaw might give something if properly approached."[18] Responding to Forbes's note, Howe urged pursuit of Shaw and other would-be contributors. "You mentioned that perhaps Mr. R. G. Shaw would help [Brown]. The old man is still several hundred dollars short of the sum necessary for an outfit, and I should like to have him see Mr. S. or any others likely to help him. I do not know him [Shaw], however, and write to ask if you can bring about a meeting."[19] It does not appear that any such meeting ever materialized.

"I came down from Concord this afternoon . . . ," wrote Sanborn to Theodore Parker, now in Europe, on May 18, "for the sake of seeing Capt. Brown, who is at the United States hotel, while his friends are trying to raise money for him, —with no very great success so far. Mr. Stearns and Mr. Smith are ready, and John Forbes has subscribed $100, —but Dr. Howe will do nothing at present, pleading scruples of conscience, etc., and Phillips says he can do little. Still I hope the required sum may be raised, and the plan carried out." (In an unpublished memoir, Sanborn was to remark dryly that "Howe's scruples of conscience came and went."[20])

Through Stearns, Smith, John Murray Forbes, and a succession of smaller subscribers that included Lewis Hayden and Harriet Tubman, Brown managed to raise the $2,000 he was looking for by the end of the month and was preparing to leave Boston. Still, Higginson had not seen him. "I wonder if you have rec'd two letters from me about Capt. B. who has been here for three weeks and is soon to leave, having got his $2000," wrote Sanborn to Higginson on May 30. "He is at the U.S. Hotel, and you ought to see him before he goes, for now he is to begin. Also you ought to see Harriet Tubman, the woman who brought away 50 slaves in 8 journeys made to Maryland; but perhaps you have seen her. She is the heroine of the day. She came here Friday night and is at 168 Cambridge St."[21] Higginson did, finally, come into town for a private session with Brown during which he gave the old man some $60 collected for him among Worcester abolitionists.

Shortly before Brown left Boston, he had dinner with George Stearns at the Parker House Hotel, just up the street from the little tenement on School Street where he had first met Sanborn two years before. As usual, the poorly dressed Brown seemed terribly out of place in elegant surroundings, but by now he was relaxed within them. He appeared to Stearns to settle back for a moment, the old puritan allowing himself one brief moment of comfort and relaxation before he resumed the hard living of his holy war. At the end of the pleasant dinner during which Stearns and Brown discussed such nonpolitical topics as fatherhood, the migratory habits of starlings, and the future of steam transportation, Brown casually remarked to Stearns that he suspected he would not live much longer. And he thought it possible that, like Moses, he would not make it to the promised land of an emancipated United States. Pulling out the bowie knife he had taken from William Sherman before decapitating him during the Pottawatomie Massacre, Brown said, "I think it probable that we may never meet again in this world, and I want to give to you in token of my gratitude an article which may have, at a future time, some little historic value." The knife, Brown lied, was a "spoil of war" from the Battle of Black Jack.[22]

Brown left Boston on or about May 30. "[Brown] got the needful," telegraphed Howe to Kagi on June 4, "and left three (3) days ago, direction unknown."[23] Once more, a letter from Sanborn to Higginson fills in the blanks. "Brown has set out on his expedition having got some $800 from all sources except from Mr. Stearns, and from him the balance of $2000 . . . ," wrote Sanborn on June 4. "B. left Boston for Springfield and New York on Wednesday morning at 8½ and Mr. Stearns has probably gone to N.Y. today to make final arrangements for him. He means to be on the ground as soon as he can—perhaps so as to begin by the 4th July. He could not say where he shall be for a few weeks, but a letter [may be] addressed to him under cover to his son John Jr., West

Andover, Ashtaboola Co., Ohio. This . . . is not far from where B. will begin, and his son will communicate with him. Two of his sons [Oliver and Owen] will go with him. . . . Within the next two months the experiment will be made."[24] In fact, Oliver and Owen were not to be the only Brown family members involved in the enterprise. Watson Brown would also be in attendance, as would Dauphin and William Thompson, brothers of Ruth Brown's husband, Henry, who had served with Brown since the time of the Chatham convention. All of them save for Owen and the old man himself were to die at Harpers Ferry.

☆

It was in July that Brown first came to the neighborhood of Harpers Ferry. He settled on a rented farm in Maryland—a place owned by a man named Kennedy—which was located across the Potomac from Harpers Ferry. Cook had been in the area since May, reconnoitering. When Brown arrived, he presented himself as a New York farmer named Isaac Smith. He and his slowly growing number of men kept to themselves, but nevertheless aroused curiosity amongst their neighbors. When the number of hands around him became conspicuous and Brown was asked just what he needed so many men for when he seemed to farm so little, he answered sardonically that he expected to mine rich deposits of a precious metal in the nearby mountains. Hundreds of miles away, Gerrit Smith was so confident as not to bother with analogies. "No wonder," Smith wrote in a letter to the "Jerry Rescue" Anniversary Committee on August 27, that "intelligent black men in the States and Canada should see no hope for their race in the practice and policy of white men. No wonder they are brought to the conclusion that no resource is left to them but in God and insurrections. For insurrections then we may look any year, any month, any day. A terrible remedy for a terrible wrong! But come it must unless anticipated by repentance and the putting away of the terrible wrong!"[25]

But the terrible remedy was slow in coming. To the surprise of the Six, Brown was still biding his time in August. During August, he tried to convince Frederick Douglass to join him in recruiting and organizing slaves for the rebellion. During the second week of that month, John Brown, Jr., traveled from Ohio to Syracuse to invite Douglass to a secret meeting with Brown at Chambersburg, Pennsylvania—a spot some fifty miles to the north of Harpers Ferry where Brown kept a store of guns. Brown Junior gave Douglass $22 to cover the expenses of Douglass's journey there and back.[26] Shortly, Douglass traveled to meet Brown, bringing with him Shields Green, a young fugitive slave whom Brown had met at Douglass's house in January.

The place of meeting was an abandoned quarry near Chambersburg. Douglass remembered that he approached the old quarry "very cautiously, for John Brown was generally well armed, and regarded strangers with suspicion." The two men moved slowly around the edge of the lonesome, echoing place, the sound of their bootsteps bouncing eerily off the high rock walls. It seemed like a long time before they finally came upon the brooding figure of Brown seated on a ledge halfway up a chasm, a rifle across his legs. From here he had a good view to see whether Douglass had been followed. Slowly, Brown climbed down to greet his guests. "Come with me, Douglass," said Brown. "I want you for a special purpose. When I strike, the bees will begin to swarm, and I shall want you to help hive them." Douglass, however, stood by his previously voiced reservations about Brown's plan. Brown, Douglass was convinced, was doomed to both political and personal failure. Armed attack on the federal government would, argued Douglass, be a disaster. It would array the entire country against the abolition movement. His purpose in meeting Brown was not to allow himself to be recruited, but rather to try one last time to dissuade Brown from a course that would bode well for no one.

Douglass said Harpers Ferry was a "perfect steel-trap." "You will never get out alive," Douglass told Brown. Virginia would blow him and any hostages he might take sky-high, rather than he should hold Harpers Ferry one hour.[27] Just as he had several months earlier, Brown shrugged off Douglass's doubts. Douglass left Brown in the quarry with his delusion of divinely assured success. He also left him with another soldier: Shields Green.

$$17$$

HARPERS FERRY

ALL THROUGH THE late summer and early fall of 1859, the cash requests from Brown, and the correlative fund-raising in Boston, went on at a steady pace even though the invasion never materialized. More money, and then more money again, was needed by the secretive Brown, who, it must be remembered, had carried $2,000 away with him at the end of May. Sanborn was now the chief collector for the fund set aside to service Brown's requests. And the relatively poor Higginson, so often delinquent on payment of his pledges, was the main focus of Sanborn's attention. "I enclose a note [a request for money] from our friend which you must return to me directly," wrote Sanborn to Higginson on August 24. "Can you do anything?"[1] Dr. Howe—whose scruples had now subsided, in step with the improvement of his financial position—sent Brown $50 after reading the same solemn, imploring letter, dated August 18, that Sanborn now sent to Higginson. "Our friend from Concord called with your note," wrote Howe to Brown. "I begin the investment with fifty dollars inclosed, and will try to do more through friends."[2]

Another thing that may have helped sway Howe was a visit from John Brown, Jr., in mid-August. The younger Brown was making a furtive fund-raising tour on behalf of his father, stopping at Boston after his mission to Frederick Douglass at Syracuse. "While in Boston," wrote John Junior to Kagi, "I improved the time in making the acquaintance of those staunch friends of our friend Isaac [Brown]. First, called on Dr. H.—, who, though I had no letter of introduction, received me most cordially." Howe gave young Brown a letter of introduction to Stearns, who in turn took him home to dinner. "The last word he [Stearns] sent to me," recalled young Brown, "was 'Tell friend (Isaac) that we have the fullest confidence in his endeavor, whatever may be the result.'"[3]

Stearns was nearly as impressed with young Brown as he'd been with his father. "[John Brown, Jr.] seemed to be interested in what I had about my house," remembered Stearns, "and I was particularly struck with the fact that he inquired about some bas-reliefs I had put into the walls. He criticized them in a most remarkable manner. He looked at the garden, and picked one or two flowers, and asked that he might take them home to his wife. I told him that he might take as many as he chose. In a few minutes, I found that he was holding them up and contrasting the colors—what not one man in five hundred would do. I was struck particularly with the natural love he showed not only for art but for nature."[4]

Sanborn wrote John Brown on August 27 from Springfield, Massachusetts, where he was stopping. Brown had recently requested an additional $300. "Yours of the 18th has been received and communicated," wrote Sanborn to Brown. "S.G.H. has sent you fifty dollars in a draft on New York, and I am expecting to get more from other sources, perhaps some here, and will make up to you the $300, if I can, as soon as I can, but I can give nothing myself just now, being already in debt. I hear, with great pleasure, what you say of the success of the business, and hope nothing will occur to thwart it. Your son John was in Boston a week or two since, and I tried to find him, but did not; and being away from Concord, he did not come to see me. . . . All your Boston friends are well. Theodore Parker is in Switzerland, much better, it is thought, than when he left home. . . . I conclude that your operations will not be delayed if the money reaches you in course of the next fortnight, if you are sure of having it there. I cannot certainly promise that you will; but I think so. Harriet Tubman is probably in New Bedford, sick. She has staid [*sic*] here in N.E. a long time." Sanborn wrote Brown again on August 30, enclosing a draft for fifty dollars from Mrs. Russell and the promise of $100 more from Gerrit Smith.[5]

Higginson's response to Sanborn's requests for money was that he could not help any more than he had already. "Yours was rec'd at Springfield," responded the persistent Sanborn on September 4. "You *must* raise $50 if possible."[6] Higginson sent only $20. There was another plea from Sanborn to Higginson on September 14: "I enclose a letter from J.B. Jr. which will interest you. I have a later one but have sent it to S.G.H. & C. Your . . . $20 is rec'd. I have added $30 and sent a draft . . . for $50 today. There is still $50 to make up."[7] And on the same day, again to Higginson: "I enclose the letter [from Brown] I spoke of this A.M. I have sent $55 and have $10 more tonight. . . . Return this to me please."[8]

During the last week of September, Brown sent a final urgent request for cash. Wearily, the stockholders eyed the letter. They did not want to abandon Brown; but neither did they want to ceaselessly invest without getting any results. They'd been expecting an outbreak in the late spring or early summer. Now it was already fall, and a damnable peace still reigned. It was decided to send an emissary to join Brown, deliver the requested money, and report back to Boston on the general state of affairs. "Tomorrow or next day a Francis Meriam of Boston . . . will start for the pastures where [Brown] is," wrote Sanborn to Higginson on October 6. "He goes to look into matters a little for the stockholders."[9]

Twenty-two-year-old Francis Jackson Meriam was the grandson and namesake of Francis Jackson, the Boston historian and abolitionist to whom the ailing Theodore Parker had written several months earlier from Santa Cruz. Meriam, who had only one good eye, was a troubled and troubling young man. He was highly unstable, prone to bouts of depression and fits of sudden temper. Samuel Gridley Howe, who made his first acquaintance with Meriam at about this time, did not believe it wise to send Meriam to Brown, for he thought the young man "in a state of mental excitement bordering on insanity."[10] Lewis Hayden later claimed to have been the one who recruited Meriam to go to Brown; however, it appears that it actually was James Redpath—who had moved to Malden, Massachusetts, and who by this time was one of many in Boston's radical abolitionist fringe who knew of Brown's plan—who arranged for Meriam to undertake the mission.[11] (Redpath and Meriam had traveled together to Haiti and across the south the previous winter, gathering material for the book Redpath dedicated to Brown, *The Roving Editor; or, Talks with Slaves in the Southern States,* in which Redpath recommended slave insurrection as the fastest possible route to emancipation.)

Meriam was anxious to join Brown. Almost a year before, on December 23, 1858, Meriam had written Brown that Redpath and Hinton "have told me of your contemplated action, in which I earnestly wish to join you to act in any capacity you wish to place me as far as my small capacities go. . . . Of course I shall pay all my expenses, and shall acquire the use of the proper tools for the work which I have bought."[12] Now, Meriam was to convey $600 to Brown from the stockholders.[13] On his way out of Massachusetts, the young man stopped at Worcester to see Higginson, who, reported Meriam to Sanborn, "had nothing to urge but what will be done shortly." Sanborn wrote Higginson on October 13 to say that Meriam had "seen Hawkins, given him money, and is to join him in his . . . operation," which was set to "commence next Saturday. . . . I think we may expect some news next week or soon after."[14]

Meriam's grandfather, Francis Jackson, probably did not know of either Brown's scheme or his grandson's involvement with it. Jackson was an avowed Garrisonian abolitionist, steeped in the culture of nonresistance. He was a close friend of Garrison's, who named one of his sons after him. Less than a year before young Meriam joined Brown, when Lysander Spooner asked Jackson to endorse his "Plan for the Abolition of Slavery," Jackson refused to do so. "I believe that the doctrine of Non-Resistance is true . . . ," Jackson wrote to Spooner. "I have arrived at my three score & tenth year, —have labored a quarter of a century with the Garrisonians to put an end to slavery. I accept most fully their plans of operation. I am loaded down to the gunwales with their apparatus." Jackson could not and would not condone or encourage violence as a means for eradicating slavery.[15] Jackson's impetuous grandson, however, had other ideas.

☆

Lewis W. Washington, a forty-six-year-old great-grand-nephew of George Washington, possessed a large and prosperous farm some five miles from Harpers Ferry in Jefferson County, Virginia. Washington was a retired career cavalry officer, debonair and sophisticated. He was a special assistant to Gov. Henry A. Wise of Virginia, a crack shot, and an unapologetic slave owner. Like most bear-

Francis Jackson, Garrisonian abolitionist of Boston whose addled grandson and namesake Francis Meriam participated in the raid at Harpers Ferry. Photo courtesy Massachusetts Historical Society.

ers of famous names, Washington was used to some measure of intrusion by both the curious and the reverent. Some wanted to shake a hand through which the blood of his famous forebear flowed. Others wanted to touch some trifle of the general's, of which Lewis Washington owned not a few.

Thus Washington was unsurprised when John Cook, secretly survey-ing Harpers Ferry for his commander John Brown, stopped him on the street in mid-September. "I believe you have a great many interesting relics at your house; could I have permission to see them if I should walk out someday?" asked Cook. Washington, as was his habit on such occasions, answered in the affirmative. "At that time I supposed he was an armorer, engaged in the public works at Harpers Ferry, almost all of whom know me, though I do not know them; but I am familiar with the faces of most of them. I had not seen this man before, or I should have recognized him."

The encounter on the street was followed within a few days by a visit from Cook. "While [at my house] he was looking at a pistol that General Lafayette had presented to General Washington about the period of the Revolution," remembered Washington. "He asked me if I had ever shot it. I told him I had. He asked, 'Does it shoot well?' I told him I had not shot it for six or eight or ten years, that I had merely tried it, cleaned it, and put it in the cabinet, and, I remarked, it would never be shot again." Washington also showed Cook a sword that had been presented to the general by no less than Frederick the Great. After handling Lafayette's gun and Frederick the Great's sword, Cook pulled back his coat and showed Washington two fine Colt revolvers with his name engraved on their breeches. Cook invited Washington to try the guns. "We went in front of my house, and under a tree we stuck up a target, and fired some twenty-four shots. He then told me that he had a rifle, a twenty-two shooter, that he would like me to look at, as he saw I had some fondness for firearms." When, a few days later, Washington tried to call on Cook and see the gun, he was informed that Cook had suddenly disappeared from Harpers Ferry; no one in town knew his whereabouts.

But Washington was to see Cook again, and soon. At about half past one in the early morning of Monday, October 17, there was a knock at the door of Washington's bedroom. Being a widower, Washington was alone in the house save for several of his slaves, his daughter having left the morning before for Baltimore. "My name was called in an under tone," remembered Washington, "and supposing it to be by some friend who had possibly arrived late, and being familiar with the house, had been admitted in the rear by the servants, I opened the door in my night-shirt and slippers. . . . As I opened the door there were four armed men with their guns drawn upon me." The men at Washington's door were Stevens, Cook, Taylor, and Tidd. (Shields Green, also part of the party, was standing guard outside the house.) Three of the men at Washington's chamber door held rifles and had revolvers stuck in their belts. The fourth held a large flambeau, which was burning. "The person in command turned out to be [Aaron] Stevens," remembered Washington. "He asked me my name, and then referred to a man of the name of Cook, who had been at my house before, to know whether I was Colonel Washington. On being told that I was, he said, 'You are our prisoner.'"

The haughty Washington remarked to his invaders that they were a "very bold looking set of fellows, but I should doubt your courage; you have too many arms to take one man." Pulling his nightcap from his head, Washington continued, "I believe with a pop-gun I could take any of you in your shirt tail." At that point, the flambeau began to drop flames. Washington lit some candles and asked his captors to douse the flambeau, "so as to prevent my house from being burnt." As Washington hastily got dressed, he addressed Stevens: "Possibly you will have the courtesy to tell me what this means. It is really a myth to me." Stevens answered that they had come to Virginia to begin freeing all the slaves of the South.

After Washington dressed, his captors collected Lafayette's pistol, several other guns, and also the sword of Frederick the Great. Then Stevens asked Washington, "Have you a watch, sir?" Washington replied, "I have." To this Stevens responded, "I want it, sir." And Washington answered, "You shall not have it." Annoyed, Stevens aimed his rifle casually at Washington and said, "Take care, sir." A similar exchange followed involving whatever cash was in the house. "I am going to speak very plainly," said Washington to Stevens. "You told me your purpose was philanthropic, but you did not mention at the same time that it was robbery and rascality." Washington did not choose to give up either his watch or his money. "I told him [Stevens] there were four there with arms, and they could take it [the watch, the money, or both], but I would not surrender it." Stevens yielded the point; the attempt at petty theft proceeded no further.

Changing the subject, Stevens said to Washington, "I presume you have heard of Osawatomie Brown?" Washington said he had not. "Then," said Stevens, "you have paid very little attention to Kansas matters." Washington remarked to Stevens that he had become so disgusted with Kansas, and everything connected with it, that whenever he saw a newspaper with "Kansas" at the head of it, he turned it over and did not read it. Stevens then informed Washington—speaking, as Washington remembered it, with "great glorification," as though Washington ought to be mightily impressed—that he would be meeting Osawatomie Brown that very morning. With that, Washington was loaded into his own carriage along with several of his male slaves (leaving the women and children). The next stop of Brown's men was the home of Washington's neighbor John H. Allstadt, who in turn was kidnapped along with his nineteen-year-old son, a number of horses, and several male slaves.

Washington was amazed when, once at Harpers Ferry, the carriage pulled up to the gates of the federal armory and arsenal. It was about 3:30 A.M. One of Washington's captors addressed a sentry with the phrase: "All's well." The gates opened. The carriage stopped in the courtyard close by the armory's fire engine house, and Washington was soon greeted by Old Brown. Pointing Washington toward the watchhouse, connected to the armory's engine house, Brown said politely, "You will find a fire in here, sir; it is rather cool this morning." Once inside the watchhouse, Brown said, "I presume you are Mr. Washington. It is too dark to see to write at this time, but when it shall have cleared off a little and become lighter, if you have not pen and ink, I will furnish them to you, and I shall require you to write to some of your friends to send a stout, able-bodied negro; I think after a while, possibly, I shall be enabled to release you, but only on the condition of getting your friends to send a negro man as a ransom." A bit later, Brown told Washington he had made it a point to have him as a hostage, because "of the moral effect it would give our cause, having one of your name as a prisoner."

Brown had easily seized the armory (including several million dollars' worth of guns and munitions) earlier that same night, protected as it was by one lone watchman. Brown had eighteen men with him. (Owen Brown, Barclay Coppoc, and Francis Meriam remained behind at the Kennedy farm with a horde of guns.) At about five on Monday morning, after the delivery of Washington and the Allstadts, Brown ordered Cook, Tidd, Leeman, and several blacks to take Lewis Washington's horses and carriage to the Kennedy farm, there to collect the remaining men along with arms that included two hundred Sharp's rifles, two hundred revolvers, and close to a thousand pikes. They were to bring these to a schoolhouse about a mile from Harpers Ferry, on the Maryland side

Harpers Ferry, Virginia, now West Virginia. Photo courtesy Massachusetts Historical Society.

of the river, where neighborhood slaves would supposedly know to go to partake of them. (The fact was that precious little had been done to prepare the blacks for uprising; very few local slaves knew anything was planned, and consequently virtually none would rally to Brown.)

Eventually, Lewis Washington and the Allstadts were joined by about thirty additional hostages: craftsmen and officers of the armory who were gradually taken into custody as they began to show up for work.[16] It took a few hours of daylight before the town awoke to the fact that it had invaders in its midst. At first, the gunfire was scattered, sporadic. By eleven o'clock in the morning on Monday, a steady though irregular fire was being leveled at the armory from Bolivar Heights, back of Harpers Ferry, to which armed citizens and local militiamen had evacuated with their families at the first terrifying word of a slave rebellion. From the heights, while waiting for neighboring militias and federal troops to come attack the raiders, the people of Harpers Ferry trained their sights on Brown and his men—afraid to come too close, but furious enough to snipe. A number of roughs passed jugs around in between potshots, congratulating themselves on the unexpected holiday from work, the opportunity for free target practice, and the inevitable defeat of the invaders down below. The liquor flowed. The population of militiamen and regular soldiers grew. The mood of all turned increasingly vicious. And the odds for Brown and his men became slimmer and slimmer.

Sometime before noon, the Jefferson Guards from Charles Town, Virginia, arrived on the Maryland side of the Potomac. Charging across the Harpers Ferry bridge, they routed the sentinels Oliver Brown and Dangerfield Newby, a forty-eight-year-old mulatto. Oliver made his way back to the armory, but Newby was killed, "his throat cut literally from ear to ear" by a bullet. He was shortly dragged into the street by a militiaman, who cut off his ears as souvenirs. Angry citizens beat Newby's dead body. Hogs were driven to root on his corpse.[17]

The severe handling of Newby was a sign of things to come. The townsmen of Harpers Ferry, as well as many of the steadily arriving militia units (from Martinsburg, Shepherdstown, Winchester, and Hammtramck, Virginia, and also from Fredericktown and Baltimore, Maryland) were, as the day wore on, increasingly enraged and increasingly drunk. Gradually, hundreds of troops surrounded the engine house and an adjacent building above the armory called Hall's Rifle Works, where Kagi and the two blacks Leary and Copeland were trapped. It quickly became obvious that the invaders were at a great disadvantage. Brown's slave insurrection was a fizzle. The soldiers relaxed; the victory party went into full swing. The scene in the streets around the besieged armory was one of bloodthirsty festivity. The atmosphere became carnivallike; and the battle became a turkey shoot. A chant arose: *Kill them, kill them.* Osborn Anderson would remember that Brown seemed "puzzled" as he watched the whites of Virginia swarming in the way the blacks, in his dream, were supposed to have done.[18]

Of the men whom Brown sent out of the armory to collect arms, only Leeman was so unwise as to return. Tidd stayed at the schoolhouse with Owen Brown, Barclay Coppoc, Francis Meriam, and the guns. Cook wound up climbing a tree on the Maryland side of the Potomac, overlooking Harpers Ferry, from there to survey the carnage to be inflicted on

Brown and his little band. The few neighborhood slaves who had been successfully recruited into Brown's service stayed at the schoolhouse but briefly. ("The slaves were ready & glad to be armed against the masters . . . ," Tidd told Higginson. "But when they heard firing & then [the] rumor that all [were] killed, they slipped back and joined their masters."[19])

When Brown sent Will Thompson to negotiate under a flag of truce, the crowd took Thompson away at gunpoint and put him under arrest. Thompson was lucky, at least for the moment. When Brown tried once again to negotiate, this time sending out his son Watson with Aaron Stevens, both raiders were shot down. Watson managed to crawl back to the engine house where he curled up, groaning in agony. The wounded Stevens was seized by the Virginia militiamen and placed under arrest. William Leeman—who at twenty was the youngest of the raiders—panicked, ran out of the armory, and dashed for the Potomac. He did not stand a chance. Two militiamen overtook him and shot him point-blank. His body lay for several hours on an islet in the river. Marksmen from the town amused themselves by using the cadaver for target practice. The last of what seemed an infinite number of potshots pushed the body into the river to float in slow, bloody circles downstream. Sometime after this, a party of townsmen attacked Kagi, Leary, and Copeland at the Rifle Works. The three men made a run for it, heading down toward the Shenandoah. Running into the river, they were trapped in crossfire. Kagi was killed instantly and left to float grotesquely in the river. Leary was shot several times and then arrested. He died the following morning. Copeland, miraculously having not been wounded in the hail of bullets, was taken prisoner and narrowly avoided being lynched by his captors when a rival militia unit insisted on taking custody of the prisoner.

A few well-aimed shots from within the engine house added to the crowd's rage. The first person killed by Brown and his abolitionist militia was a free black. Hayward Shepard, the baggage master at the Harpers Ferry train station, was shot in the back. The second killed was a farmer and slave owner: George Turner. Then the mayor of Harpers Ferry, Fontaine Beckham, took a bullet and died. In retaliation, a militiaman from Charles Town by the name of Hunter, who was kin to the mayor, led a mob that dragged the prisoner Will Thompson down to the Potomac, shot him in the head, and cast his body into the river to join that of Leeman. Like Leeman, the floating Thompson became the object of target practice. Once the body had absorbed enough lead and water, it sank. As one horrified reporter remembered, Thompson could be seen for a day or two after, lying white and silent at the bottom of the clear river, "his ghastly face still exhibiting his fearful death agony."[20] In the midst of the confused bloodletting, Albert Hazlett and Osborn Anderson—who'd been trapped not in the engine house with Brown but rather in the armory proper—were able to escape. They ran from the armory, paddled across the Potomac in a stolen boat, and dashed off through the Maryland woods.

The night came. The temperature dropped. Rain—which had started and stopped all day long—now steadied to a constant, cold drizzle. Inside the engine house, there was no fire, no warmth, no light. The desperate Brown sent out a note, signed with his real name, offering to release his eleven hostages in return for safe passage for him and his men across the Potomac. The note was ignored. Outside, Brown could hear the hoots and hollers of nearly a thousand rowdy, victorious militiamen. The drunken soldiers shot their guns in the air and seemed only to aim their fire at the besieged engine house as an afterthought. Inside the engine house, the body of Brown's man Stewart Taylor lay in a corner. He'd been shot in the forehead. One of the hostages turned Taylor's face toward the wall, so that the gross wound would not have to be looked at. In another corner the nearly dead Watson and Oliver Brown lay whimpering and choking in their agony while a hostage, Joseph Brua, did his best to tend them. Oliver begged his father to shoot him in the head, but Brown refused. "If you must die," the old puritan told his son, "die like a man." Later, in the darkness, when Oliver fell silent, Brown called to him. The silence continued. "I guess he is dead," Brown said matter-of-factly to Washington.[21]

By Tuesday morning, Bvt. Col. Robert E. Lee, in command of the Second Cavalry, and Lt. J. E. B. ("Jeb") Stuart of the First Cavalry arrived in town to take command at Harpers Ferry. Placed in command by President Buchanan himself, Colonel Lee had a personal connection to at least one of the hostages. Lee's father, the Revolutionary cavalry hero Henry "Lighthorse Harry" Lee, had been one of George Washington's closest friends; and Lee himself was married to a great-granddaughter of Martha Washington by her first marriage. As the sun rose, Lee swiftly marshaled his large force to surround the little engine house. Thus when Brown and his remaining raiders—Edwin Coppoc, Jeremiah Anderson, Dauphin Thompson, and Shields Green—looked outside, they saw an imposing contingent: hundreds of marines armed with rifles, bayonets, sledgehammers, axes, and battering rams. Behind the soldiers were rows of cannon. And behind the cannon stood a howling mob of more than two thousand enraged spectators, crying for blood.

Lee sent Jeb Stuart to the door of the engine house, under a flag of truce. Stuart delivered a terse note from Lee. The colonel would assure the safety of Brown and his men should Brown choose to surrender immediately and unconditionally. Upon Brown's refusal, which Lee had expected, Stuart abruptly leapt away from the front of the engine house and waved his cap. Brown slammed the thick oak door shut as several storming parties, commanded by Lt. Israel Green, dashed toward it. Brown's raiders fired out at Green's men, two of whom fell dead before the door finally gave way. When the soldiers charged into Brown's tiny, last redoubt, they found a chokingly small space filled with gunpowder smoke. Jeremiah Anderson was quickly pinned to the wall with a bayonet. Dauphin Thompson was run through as he tried to crawl under a fire engine. (Both would die from their wounds.) Coppoc and Green were, amazingly, arrested unhurt. Brown was stabbed and then beaten unconscious by Lieutenant Green, who was furious at the loss of two of his men. Watson Brown, who would soon be dead from the wounds he had sustained on Monday, lay groaning in a corner amid the carnage. The body of Stewart Taylor took two more bullets in the melee.

Brown and his men—living, dead, and nearly dead—were dragged out onto the grass beside the engine house. Copeland and the severely wounded Stevens, captured the day before, were brought and thrown down beside the cadavers of Oliver Brown and Stewart Taylor. The fatally wounded Watson Brown, moaning softly, curled up on his side with his head close to his knees. Jeremiah Anderson and Dauphin Thompson, each slashed open at the waist, cried in agony and struggled to hold in their vitals while being unceremoniously tossed down with the others. Edwin Coppoc was brought out with his hands tied behind him, while the black Shields Green was placed in irons immediately. The crowd jeered and chanted, "Hang them, hang them." Lee's guards closely surrounded the exhausted, wounded raiders, less to guard them than to obscure them as targets. Brown's revolution had lasted less than thirty-seven hours. Inside the engine house, Lewis Washington found Frederick the Great's sword, which Brown had carried with him throughout the last day and a half, lying on a fire engine.[22]

18

THE STEEL TRAP

I N THE EARLY 1880s, Edwin Morton would write an essay portrait of Brown in which he compared himself, the Secret Six, and other Northern supporters of Brown to the apostles who abandoned Christ at the time of the crucifixion.

"It occurs to me," wrote Morton, "that you may say, (or some one not knowing the facts, as nobody as yet does, may say,) 'Yes, you have sketched a picture of human nature . . . and human nature is always the same. For in those hours of terror and panic of half a nation, and of profound emotion of all, in those dark days and nights of tragedy when a trembling and passionate populace clamored hungrily for the swift sacrifice of your friend Brown, —he likewise alone with them, and nigh stricken to death with wounds, he repeating also to his accusers the words of Jesus, the golden Rule of conduct, he likewise found by them to be a just man and so gaining even their respect and admiration, —yes, you yourself, in those dark and cold hours of that falling and sympathizing season, you yourselves, his single handful of friends in a whole nation, kept far away, at a safe distance, deserted, fled, were concealed, or departed to the ends of the earth.' True, quite true, all perhaps too true."[1]

As we shall see, Morton's first act upon hearing about Harpers Ferry would be to leave the country for an extended visit to Europe.

☆

Sanborn was alarmed and astonished to read newspaper reports saying that Jeb Stuart had confiscated a large cache of documents at the Kennedy farm shortly after the arrest of Brown and his men at Harpers Ferry. Letters from Sanborn, Howe, Stearns, and Smith were found strewn about the little farmhouse. Sanborn asked his sister Sarah how Brown could be so foolish as to leave such documents accessible. How could the lucky survivors of Brown's squad, in departing the farm, abandon to fate the incriminating papers and, with the papers, those whom they implicated? It was a dishonorable act, said the frightened and infuriated Sanborn. It was a betrayal and a breach of faith.

Somewhat reassuringly, it seemed Brown was evasive when asked about the financing for his little army. On Tuesday afternoon, reported the *New York Herald,* the weary and wounded Brown was questioned at the jail in Charles Town, Virginia, by a committee that included Robert E. Lee, Jeb Stuart, Rep. Clement L. Vallandigham of Ohio, Lewis Washington, Virginia's Gov. Henry A. Wise, and Sen. James Mason of the same state. "Can you tell us, at least, who furnished the money for your expedition?" asked Mason. Brown shook his head. "I furnished most of it myself," he replied. "I cannot implicate others." Vallandigham, a proslavery Democrat who suspected that his Ohio nemesis Joshua Giddings might be involved, pressed the issue again, rephrasing the question. Who had sent Brown to Virginia? "No man sent me here; it was my own prompting and that of my Maker, or that of the Devil— whichever you please to ascribe it to. I acknowledge no master in human form." Later, Vallandigham tried once more. "Who are your advisers in this movement?" he asked. "I cannot answer that," replied Brown, adding, "I have numerous sympathizers throughout the entire North."[2]

Fatalistically confident that he would eventually be implicated in the fiasco at Harpers Ferry, Franklin Sanborn went to Boston the day after Brown's arrest to consult attorney John Albion Andrew. Andrew, who

would soon be elected governor of the Commonwealth,
was a complex and often
stern man whom Julia Ward
Howe oversimplified as "a
benevolent cherub in specta-
cles."[3] Andrew was one of
the finest lawyers on the Eastern seaboard, quick to grasp
facts and characterizeed by a
calm deliberation and cool
pragmatism he brought to
bear in all aspects of politics
and life. He was also an
avowed abolitionist and a frequent congregant at black
churches where, he told a
friend, he found a refreshing
atmosphere that was "more
than nine parts God and less
than one part hypocrisy, —
this ratio being much at vari-
ance with what is found at so

John Albion Andrew, the attorney who advised Stearns, Sanborn, and Howe after the collapse of the Harpers Ferry endeavor. Andrew later became govenor of Massachusetts. Photo courtesy Massachusetts Historical Society.

many other houses of worship." Andrew was horrified at what he called
the "madness" at Harpers Ferry. The "cherub" was severe with Sanborn,
calling him a fool for involving himself with so insane an act.

Without being given time by the anxious Sanborn to properly
research the legalities of the situation, Andrew suggested that for safety's
sake Sanborn leave the country immediately. "Acceding to advice of
good friends and my own deliberate judgment I am to try change of air
for any old complaint," wrote Sanborn to Higginson in an unsigned note
mailed from Portland, Maine, on October 21. "By this means it is
thought that others will benefit as well as I. Whether my absence will be
long or short will depend on circumstances. Yours of the 19th was rec'd

yesterday before I left home. Should you have occasion to write me again, I have a friend in Quebec named Frederick Stainley, to whom you can write. Burn this. Yours Ever."[4]

In South Boston on Monday evening, Julia Ward Howe was startled when she saw one of the first newspaper reports of the Harpers Ferry invasion. The report—an early one—said only that a disturbance involving Brown was in progress, not that it had ended in defeat. When Julia told Sam what she had read, he took it nonchalantly, as though he had been expecting headlines involving Brown to appear at any moment. "Brown has got to work," was all he said before returning to his book. Two nights later, after news of the absolute failure of Brown's enterprise—and news as well of the papers found at the Kennedy farmhouse—Howe was far less calm and also less cryptic. Visibly shaken, the normally stalwart Howe confessed to Julia at least something of his involvement and assured her, as she recalled, that "Brown's plan had not been so impossible of realization as it appeared to have been after its failure." Then in the last stage of a difficult pregnancy, Julia was further discomforted to watch her husband succumb to a nervous agitation the like of which she'd never seen him suffer before. "Men may be coming," he said, suddenly getting up from his chair and throwing on his riding coat. "They must not find me." With that he went briskly out the door. Then Julia heard him on his horse, galloping away from the house. For a brief moment the night was punctuated by a fast tattoo of frantic, quickly fading whip slaps and hoof beats.[5]

Filled, as Mary Stearns would remember, "with a dread that threatened to overwhelm his reason," Howe showed up at the door of the Stearnses' mansion late Wednesday evening.[6] Howe raged about what he called "the great tragedy" and told Stearns they must both leave the country. In fact, he insisted that he would go insane if they did not depart immediately. The more prudent Stearns suggested that they first consult John Andrew.[7] By the time they saw Andrew the next morning, the lawyer had thoroughly examined the question of the Six's legal culpability and drafted an opinion as to the definition of treason—the act of levying war on one's own country—and the jurisdictions under which one might be put on trial for said offense.

"In order to constitute the offense of 'levying war,' " wrote Andrew, "there must be more than a mere *conspiracy* to do it: some *overt act of war* must be committed. In order to constitute guilt (in any given person) of the overt act, he must be present at its commission. But, he may be *constructively* present, though *actually* absent; that is to say, he may be remote from the principal scene of action, but performing some auxialliary [*sic*] or ancillary act, —such as keeping watch for the immediate actors, guarding them against surprise, having at hand for them means of escape, or the like; thus performing a part in that which constituted the overt act, or was immediately ancillary thereto."

Andrew crisply told Howe and Stearns that Brown's Northern supporters—guilty fools that they were—were nevertheless safe from prosecution. "A man cannot be held guilty of an overt act of levying war who was not present at the overt act of war; who participated in none of the transactions of the principal actors at the scene and did not, in any manner, render assistance, or attempt to do it, or put himself in a position where he might do so, if occasion offered at the time. . . . Still, if one joins in a conspiracy to levy war, and war is, afterward, in fact levied, and he performs any act, which in the case of a felony, would render one an accessory, he thereby renders himself a principal to the treason, since, in treason all who are guilty at all are principals. Thus—if he gives arms, ammunition, horses or what not, to aid the war, pursuant to the conspiracy, such acts, when the war has been actually levied, will doubtless be deemed *overt acts* of treason, in themselves; but the party committing them can only be tried in the District where they were committed. A man who gave a cannon in Maine to the service of the cause of treason could not be tried for it in Texas, merely because it was in Texas that other men, afterward, fired it."[8]

The law seemed clear. "I see no possible way in which any one can have done anything in Massachusetts for which he can be carried *to any other state*. I know nothing for which you could be tried even *here*," wrote Andrew to Stearns.[9] Hearing Andrew's good news, Stearns and Howe were relaxed and confident. Emerson wrote Sanborn in Canada to tell him it was safe to come home. Reassured, Sanborn returned to Concord on or about October 26.[10]

Feeling insulated from prosecution, Howe became reemboldened and set out to provide for Brown's defense. He wrote Amos Lawrence, asking for a contribution for Brown. "No stone must be left unturned to save his life and the country the disgrace of his execution," wrote Howe to Lawrence.[11] Through John Andrew, Howe wrote to the Missouri Republican Montgomery Blair, who had served as attorney for Dred Scott and would later be appointed postmaster general in the Lincoln administration, in the vain hope that Blair would consent to serve as counsel for Brown. In the midst of these queries, Howe dispatched an emissary of "pluck & discretion" to follow the developments in Virginia. This was George Sennott, a criminal defense attorney of dubious distinction whom Howe instructed to observe and report, but not to go outside legal means to aid the prisoner. "Beyond those I ask no man to follow me however far I may be disposed to go myself," wrote Howe suggestively.[12] According to Sanborn, George Sennott was believed by Howe to be the illegitimate son of an old friend from the Greek War, Col. J. P. Miller of Rutland, Vermont. Sennott was, remembered Sanborn, "an educated man, a lawyer, and rather celebrated for his defence of criminals. He was a low type, and much given to liquor."[13] Another lawyer, twenty-one-year-old George H. Hoyt of Athol, Massachusetts, was sent to Charles Town by John W. LeBarnes, a friend of Higginson's and an active abolitionist.

☆

The wheels of Virginian justice spun fast. Brown was indicted on October 25, along with Copeland, Edwin Coppoc, Shields Green, and the nearly dead Aaron Stevens. Stevens had to be propped up by two bailiffs in order to stand as the charges against him were read. The defendants were each to be tried separately. John Brown's trial for treason and murder, which began just two days later on October 27, was to end with a conviction on October 30.

Howe's man Sennott was almost immediately brushed to the side in favor of counsel appointed by the State of Virginia. Brown's court-appointed attorneys were to be Thomas C. Green, mayor of Charles Town, and a local lawyer by the name of Lawson Botts. These two men were joined by Hoyt in their brief representation of Brown. But the trial had barely been in session a day when two suave, high-priced attorneys in the persons of Samuel Chilton (of Washington) and Hiram Griswold (of Cleveland) arrived to take the defense. The expensive new lawyers were financed with money from Brown's Boston friends. Chilton and Griswold were both recruited by Montgomery Blair, who, after refusing the request from Howe and Andrew that he undertake the defense, acted as their agent in recruiting Chilton and Griswold for the sizable fee of $1,300.[14] "I understood through Mr. Blair, I think, and Mr. Andrew, that the money was raised by those whom he denominated the relatives and friends of Brown," remembered Chilton. "He [Andrew] said there was a small number of them, and that he stood responsible for the fee that was contracted to be paid me and for the expenses of the suit."[15] A large share of the money came from Stearns; the balance was whatever Howe, Higginson, and a few others were able to raise among Amos Lawrence, John Murray Forbes, and other wealthy supporters. Gerrit Smith, as we shall see, was not at this point a likely donor.

Brown's case was put before a jury of twelve Harpers Ferry locals. Through most of his brief trial, Brown lay on a cot in the courtroom listening silently to the testimony against him. When his first panel of attorneys tried to enter a plea of insanity, Brown rose in the court to denounce the plea and say he took complete responsibility for his actions. Chilton and Griswold opted for a more sophisticated yet equally inadequate defense. Their argument was that Brown, not being a citizen of Virginia, could therefore technically not be guilty of treason against that state. But all defense, even the ablest, was in this case mere shadowboxing. Brown's guilt was undeniable, and neither the authorities nor the citizens of Virginia were likely to have patience with technicalities. He was quickly found guilty of treason, murder, and inciting slaves to insurrection. Any one of these charges constituted a capital offense. Therefore on November 2, three days after the verdict, Brown was sentenced to die on the gallows in exactly one month's time.

No defendant but Brown was represented by Chilton and Griswold. There was no Boston money available for the defense of Brown's soldiers, although there would be some cash set aside for their burials. Hoyt represented Edwin Coppoc, while the blacks Shields Green and John Copeland had to make do with the often inebriated legal maneuverings of George Sennott. John Cook—who after his initial escape from Harpers Ferry was arrested with Albert Hazlett in Pennsylvania on October 26—received the benefit of slightly better counsel through the efforts of his influential family. Cook's three attorneys counted in their number his own brother-in-law, A. P. Willard, the governor of Indiana. But once again, high-powered attorneys failed in the face of incontestable guilt. All four men—Coppoc, Copeland, Green, and Cook—were, one after the other, convicted and condemned. They each received firm dates with the noose exactly two weeks after that of Brown. Brown would swing on December 2; and his four men would follow on December 16. The two remaining raiders—Aaron Stevens and Albert Hazlett—were not to be put on trial until February 1860.

☆

Barclay Coppoc, one of the few of Brown's raiders who escaped, wrote Sanborn on January 13, 1860, of how "but five of our little band [are] now away and safe, namely Owen [Brown], [Charles Plummer] Tidd, [Francis] Meriam, O. P. Anderson, or as we used to call him Chatham Anderson, and myself. . . . We were together eight days before [John Cook and Albert Hazlett were] captured, which was near Chambersburg, and the next night Meriam left us and went to Shippensburg, and there took the cars for Philadelphia. After that there were but three of us left, and we kept together, until we got to Centre County, Pa., where we bought a box and packed up all heavy luggage, such as rifles, blankets, etc., and after being together three or four weeks we separated and I went on through with the box to Ohio on the cars. Owen and Tidd went on foot towards the north-western part of Penn."[16] Anderson, Barclay Coppoc, and Meriam—traveling separately—all wound up in the area of St. Catharines, in Canada.[17] Owen Brown and Charles Tidd lurked in the neighborhood of Crawford County, Pennsylvania, under assumed names and got jobs working on an oil well.[18] All of them had been glad to get rid of the crazy Meriam. Tidd told Higginson that when he returned to the Kennedy farmhouse during the raid he found Meriam "down in despair." Hiking through the woods, the sulking Meriam was a burden for his fellow fugitives. "He had no endurance. [He would hike] for a mile & rest. Took them twice as long," recorded Higginson.[19]

In Boston, immediately after the raid, there was concern about the safety of the fugitives. Within days of the raid, Howe telegraphed John Brown, Jr., in Ohio, to see if he knew their whereabouts and asking him to come to Boston, to consult on finding them. Brown, who was himself a wanted man, was hiding out in the office of the *Ashtabula* (Ohio) *Sentinel.* He responded by post on November 11. "I have just learned from Mr. [Joshua] Giddings, that, in all probability, one motive in wishing my attendance in Boston was to aid in rendering, if possible, some assistance to our *poor wandering friends,*" he wrote. "The thought that, if I had gone *immediately to Boston, I might* have been in any way instrumental in aiding them, —but that such a possibility to me is perhaps at this date rendered less, almost makes me mad. If you know, or can think of any way by which I *can yet* help them, do, for God's sake, let me know it. Let me know of a *bare probability* and I will meet any hardship or danger in an effort to render assistance and protection to those noble spirits, among whom is my own brother. I very much regret that I did not go on immediately in on the receipt of what has since proved a telegram from you. My friends here were apprehensive that a letter which I had sent but a day or two before might have been intercepted and, if so, would have furnished such information as would enable enemies to have laid a trap for taking me to Virginia. If, in consequence of listening to their advice, I delayed in such a way as to lose a good opportunity of aiding in any feasible enterprise of that kind, I could never forgive myself. If it is *possible* in your judgment for me *yet to find them,* please give me by return mail any information or suggestion you may think it prudent to communicate."[20]

Young Brown was never to receive a response from Howe. By the time Brown's note arrived in Boston during the third week of November, Howe had vanished and become a fugitive himself.

19

FANTASIES OF ESCAPE

O N NOVEMBER 2, the day that John Brown was sentenced, a printed circular was distributed about Boston soliciting funds for his legal defense. "You are invited and urged to contribute and obtain contributions to aid in the defense of Capt. Brown and his companions, on trial for their lives in Virginia," read the brief announcement signed by Higginson, Howe, Samuel Sewall, and Ralph Waldo Emerson. "Every moment is precious, and whatever is done must be done now. The following gentlemen (with others who may be hereafter announced in the papers) will act as a Committee to receive money and appropriate it to this purpose only." Brown's trial was over, but the imposing bill from Chilton and Griswold still lingered, and then Sennott and Hoyt needed to be lodged and fed while they represented Brown's men. "An expense of about $1000 is already incurred for counsel," Higginson scrawled across the bottom of one circular. "Mrs. Brown must also be aided to join her husband, & her two widowed daughters-in-law, aged 20 & *16,* need help greatly."[1]

Higginson was at North Elba with Brown's family on the day of Brown's sentencing. In the afternoon, Brown's daughter Ruth

Thompson matter-of-factly showed Higginson the spot, beside a large boulder in a field nearby the house, where the younger boys had begun digging graves for their father and brothers. Higginson was impressed by the Browns' stoicism and their unshakable faith in the ultimate good that lay in what was happening to their family.

Prior to coming to know the Browns, wrote Higginson in a newspaper account of his visit to North Elba, "it had been my privilege to live in the best society . . . namely, that of abolitionists and fugitive slaves. I had seen the most eminent persons of the age: several men on whose heads tens of thousands of dollars had been set. . . . I had known these, and such as these; but I had not known the Browns. Nothing short of knowing them can be called a liberal education." They were content in the grief they had already borne, and ready for the grief that was yet to come. "To the Browns, killing means simply dying—nothing more; one gate into Heaven, and that one a good deal frequented by their family; that is all." As Higginson would remember, he was "the first person who had penetrated their solitude from the outer world since the thunderbolt had fallen. . . . They asked but one question after I had told them how little hope there was. . . . 'Does it seem as if freedom were to gain or lose by this?' That was all." Sitting on a brow of hill overlooking the farm, Higginson had a long talk with Salmon Brown. "He looked up in a quiet, manly way," remembered Higginson, "which I shall never forget, and said briefly, 'I sometimes think that is what we came into the world for—to make sacrifices.' . . . And it seemed to me that any one must be very unworthy the society I had been permitted to enter who did not come forth from it a wiser and better man."

When Higginson left North Elba the next day, he took with him Brown's wife, Mary—a "simple, kindly, slow, sensible creature." After a brief stay in Boston, Mary was to continue on to see her husband in Virginia.[2] "Mrs. Brown will reach the American House, Boston, at 8 P.M.," telegraphed Higginson to Sanborn from Burlington, Vermont, on Thursday, November 3. "I have telegraphed Howe to call on her there tonight, and to ask Stearns to go to Philadelphia with her—as I have been away for four days, and she is not good at traveling. She is a

noble woman, and the whole family are in the finest state of mind. . . .
I shall go to Worcester tonight, and Boston tomorrow A.M. to see about
her. She should go on tomorrow with somebody. Can't you come to
Boston tomorrow?"[3]

Julia Ward Howe wrote to her sister Annie of encountering Mary
Brown in Boston a few days later. "I have just been to church and heard
[James Freeman] Clarke preach about John Brown, whom God bless, and
will bless! I am much too dull to write anything good about him, but shall
say something at the end of my book on Cuba, whereof I am at present
correcting the proof-sheets. I went to see his poor wife, who passed
through here some days since. We shed tears together and embraced at
parting, poor soul. . . . [Brown's] attempt I must judge insane but the
spirit heroic. I should be glad to be as sure of heaven as that old man may
be, following right in the spirit and footsteps of the old martyrs, girding
on his sword for the weak and oppressed. His death will be holy and glorious—the gallows cannot dishonor him—he will hallow it."[4] Julia was
paraphrasing Emerson, who, in a lecture titled "Courage" delivered in
Boston on November 8, called Brown "that new saint than whom none
purer or more brave was ever led by love of men into conflict and death,
—the new saint awaiting his martyrdom, and who, if he shall suffer
[execution], will make the gallows glorious like the cross."[5]

On November 8, Mrs. Brown—whom Julia Ward Howe described as
"a strong, earnest woman, plain in manners and in speech"[6]—continued
on to the Philadelphia home of Stearns's friend J. Miller McKim. On
November 9, Sam Howe sent a note to Higginson. "A letter has just
arrived from Charles Town in Brown's handwriting directed to you and
to me which I have opened and read," reported Howe. The letter, Howe
told Higginson, was a request from Brown that all possible be done to
deter Brown's wife from visiting him at his prison. "If my wife were to
come here just now it would *only tend* to distract *her mind ten fold,*" wrote
Brown, "& would only add to my affliction. . . . *Do persuade* her to
remain at home for a time (at least) till she can learn further from me.
She will receive a thousand times the consolation at home that she can
possibly find elsewhere."[7] Brown would refuse to see his wife all through

November, although he would not say why beyond the reasons enumerated in his letter to Howe and Higginson. "I know nothing about Mr. Brown's motives for refusing to see Mrs. B.," wrote Hoyt to Higginson.[8] "I am sorry Mrs. Brown is not to see her husband," wrote Sanborn to Higginson, "and don't exactly see why she should not."[9] (In fact, Mary Brown would manage to see Brown for several hours on December 1, the day before his execution. Leaving him after dinner, she would remove to Harpers Ferry, accompanied by McKim, there to await the corpses of her husband and sons.)

As Howe well knew, Mary Brown's journey to her husband was part of an elaborate attempt by Higginson to plan and carry out a rescue of Brown and his men. Mary Brown's role in Higginson's plans was to go to the fatalistic Brown and convince him that his destiny lay not in martyrdom, but rather as a commander in glorious battles yet to be won against slavery. "Talking of rescue," wrote Sanborn to Higginson on November 19, "have you gone any farther in that matter? And can anything be done?"[10]

So far, Brown had refused to entertain the notion of escape. He made it plain to several visitors that he did not wish any rescue attempt to be made. Brown said he was content with the sentence of the court and was more than willing to die for the righteous cause of abolition. He would be more valuable dead than in any other capacity, he told one visitor— showing clearer foresight than at any other time in his career. In death, his symbol would serve as an inspiration for more and better acts of resistance. ("Let them hang me," Brown told Hoyt, who, against Brown's wishes, filed an appeal of his case on the grounds that he was a lunatic and therefore not responsible for his actions. "I am worth inconceivably more to hang than for any other purpose," he wrote from his jail cell.[11])

There were two schemes for the rescue of Brown and his men. Each was clearly a mere embryo of a notion when Sanborn wrote Higginson on the nineteenth. Both would be aborted almost as soon as they were begun, after what can only be called halfhearted attempts at their gestation. No more than nine days after Sanborn's mention of vague possibilities on November 19, he would be writing Higginson once more to mournfully declare the abandonment of hope.

The first of the plans—dubbed the German Project—took its name from German veterans of the Revolution of 1848, living in New York, who agreed to take part in the rescue. The Germans were to be joined by volunteers from Boston (including a somewhat hesitant James Redpath) and a contingent from the Ohio hometown of John Brown, Jr. The scheme, developed by Higginson with the support of the younger Brown, called for a band of men armed with revolvers, daggers, and bombs to go to Charles Town on the day of Brown's scheduled execution. After Brown had been marched out from within the walls of the prison, the guerrillas would make their attack on the estimated fifteen hundred federal troops assigned to guard him. "I have just come from Boston and go to Concord tonight," wrote Sanborn in a note that he dropped off at Higginson's Worcester home on November 24. "Redpath *must go* to Ohio. That is our *only* chance of rescuing Brown, and I have written him to do so, not being able to see him today in Boston."[12] We do not know the exact details of why the German Project failed to materialize, but it appears that the number of Ohio recruits did not turn out to be as large as expected. "Hoyt brings word that nothing is doing in Ohio," wrote Sanborn to Higginson in a businesslike note on November 28, wrapping things up. "Redpath did not go on—perhaps it is as well he did not."[13] Higginson must not have been surprised at Redpath's canceled journey to Ohio, for Redpath—busy finishing a biography of Brown that was to be published as soon after the execution as possible—had written Higginson on November 13 to say, "I have not the faintest hope of [Brown's] escape from martyrdom; have you?"[14]

The second blueprint for rescuing Brown, this one drawn by Lysander Spooner with the tacit backing of Higginson, was called the Richmond Plan. This adventure involved going to Richmond, Virginia, and there kidnapping Gov. Henry A. Wise, who would be held hostage for the safety of Brown. A small armed group of mercenaries would travel by steamboat, at night. We have "found a man, who will undertake to find the men, & pilot, and a boat, for the Richmond expedition if the necessary money can be had," wrote Spooner to Higginson from New York in an unsigned note dated November 20. "Will you not come

down at once, and help to move men here to furnish the money? . . .
Please burn this. We can do nothing without you. Do not fail to come."[15]
On November 22, John W. LeBarnes wrote Higginson from New York
quoting prices for renting a boat for the operation. He wrote again on
the twenty-seventh: "The men are ready and determined. . . . They are
confident, strange as it may seem to us, of success, but they want money.
. . . It is for you in Boston to say 'go' or 'stay.'"[16]

The Richmond Plan failed for want of cash, and it seems the lack
of cash was caused by Higginson's lack of faith in mercenaries.
George Stearns or John Murray Forbes could still have been turned
to, but Higginson refused. "It is an absurdity to suppose that we can
induce by money the worst men in the country to do a desperate act,"
wrote Higginson to Spooner, "when any one of them can make twice
as much money by betraying it." Higginson signed his name in full to
the bottom of the note. Below that he wrote, "There is no need of
burning this." He had signed so many letters with code names over
the course of the past year. He had concluded so many notes with the
sentence: "Please burn this." But now all plans were off. Everything
was finished. The need for subterfuge was over.[17] "LeBarnes is in
N.Y.," wrote Sanborn to Higginson, "and I have telegraphed him to
return, that nothing can be done. So I suppose we must give up all
hope of saving our old friend."[18]

Chimerical dreams of escape would continue to the end. In between
doing sketches of Brown, the sculptor Edwin Brackett, who was one of
Brown's last visitors, sketched the prison, the cell, the hall—carefully
noting the placement of windows, stairs, doors, and guards.[19] (Brackett
had been commissioned by George and Mary Stearns to execute a portrait bust of Brown. "At first the old Puritan [Brown] objected to having
the measurements taken," recalled Frank Stearns, "but when Mr. Brackett informed him whence he came, John Brown said: 'Anything Mr. and
Mrs. Stearns desire I am well pleased to agree to.'"[20]) When Judge Russell and his wife visited Brown, the judge noted a man-sized chimney
opening into the jail and declared: "Two good Yankees could get these
men out and away so easily!"[21]

☆

While Higginson and others busied themselves with rescues that would never happen, John Brown sat in his prison cell, a calm eye in the center of a hurricane of activity and debate, writing letters meant to define him and his mission for posterity. "You know that Christ once armed Peter," Brown wrote in response to a letter from a Quaker woman in Iowa. "So also in my case I think he put a sword into my hand, and there continued it so long as he saw best, and then kindly took it from me."[22] Brown also wrote Mary Stearns. She had written him a touching note of farewell, and now he responded in a letter that, as usual, he highlighted with long, dark underlinings. "No letter I have received since my imprisonment here," wrote Brown, "has given me more satisfaction, & comfort, than yours of the 8th inst. . . . may God forever reward you & *all yours. My love to All* who love their neighbors. I have asked to be *spared* from having any *mock; or hypocritical prayers made over me,* when I am publicly *murdered:* & that my *only religious attendants* be poor *little, dirty, ragged, bare headed, & barefooted, Slave Boys, & Girls,* led by some old gray headed, Slave Mother. Farewell. Farewell."[23] Similar eloquent notes went out in response to letters from Lucretia Mott, Horace Greeley, and others.

One letter Brown did not answer was from Mahala Doyle, whose husband and two sons he'd executed along the Pottawatomie several years before. "Although vengeance is not mine," wrote Mrs. Doyle, "I confess that I do feel gratified to hear that you were stopped in your fiendish career at Harpers Ferry with the loss of your two sons. You can now appreciate my distress in Kansas when you then and there entered my house at midnight and arrested my husband and two boys, and took them out in the yard, and in cold blood [killed] them dead in my hearing." All the letter drew from Brown was silence. No pardon was asked. No remorse was registered. While he carefully preserved the hundreds of adulatory letters he received, Doyle's note landed in the trash box with other critical missives only to be preserved by a guard.[24]

While Brown wrote the letters meant to set his place in history, James Redpath wrote the book chartered with the same purpose. In the somewhat apologetic letters that Redpath wrote to Higginson and others requesting information about Brown, he tried to assuage the crass opportunism his project smacked of by mentioning again and again that an unspecified portion of the royalties would go to aid Brown's family. "I want all his letters recently written or that are illustrative of his character," wrote Redpath to Higginson on November 13. To everyone whom he asked to cooperate in the project, Redpath made it clear that the book was to be an exercise in heroic mythmaking. Redpath wrote Higginson that he would "quietly repudiate" the notion that the loss of Brown's son in Kansas "had any influence on his recent movements; for . . . such a notion degrades him from the position of a Puritan warrior of the Lord to a guerilla chief of vindictive character."[25] What Redpath would paint instead was a glowing portrait of Brown as the saintly, "predestined leader of the second and the holier American Revolution."[26] (Twenty years later, sensing another opportunity for a best-seller, the wily Redpath would befriend an aged Jefferson Davis and help him write his *Short History of the Confederate States,* Davis's hotly argued defense of virtually everything John Brown despised.[27])

THE NOT SO SECRET SIX

ETTERS FROM GERRIT Smith, Samuel Gridley Howe, and Franklin Sanborn, found among Brown's papers at the Kennedy farmhouse, showed up in the press during the last week of October. THE EXPOSURE OF THE NIGGER-WORSHIPING INSURRECTIONISTS ran a headline in the copperhead *New York Herald*. The *Herald* gained and printed texts of the letters found in Brown's possession, as well as several letters purchased from the still-annoying and dangerous Hugh Forbes. All of the Six save for Parker were named and implicated just as, somewhat erroneously, was Wendell Phillips, several letters from whom were found in Brown's bags. "This is no list of low-born, ignorant, and despised traitors to the Union and its States," ranted the *Herald*. "It is no concoction of local disaffection. It shows that the treason had infested all classes."[1] In an editorial several days later, the *Herald* continued in the same vein. "So accustomed have thousands of our citizens become to sit under and follow the 'higher law' . . . that many have forgotten their paramount duty to their country."[2]

The *Herald* sent a reporter to find Gerrit Smith and interview him. On his way to Peterboro, the reporter stopped at a tavern in nearby

Oneida. Smith, the tavern keeper told the reporter, was seriously disturbed—losing his mind. The innkeeper, who doubled as a telegraph operator, had seen a great deal of Smith recently. "He is telegraphing from here all the while," said the innkeeper.

When the correspondent arrived at Peterboro, he found the whole village much excited. The general expectation was that Smith was about to be kidnapped and transported south for trial with Brown. Men of the community were taking turns guarding Smith's mansion. Smith seemed in terrible shape. The agitation "has not only impaired his health, but is likely to seriously affect his excitable and illy-balanced mind," wrote the *Herald* reporter. "He is a very different man from what he was twelve months since. His calm, dignified, impressive bearing has given way to a hasty, nervous agitation, as though some great fear was constantly before his imagination. His eye is bloodshot and restless as that of a startled horse. He has lost flesh, and his face looks as red and rough as though he had just returned from one of old Brown's Kansas raids." When the reporter asked Smith about Harpers Ferry, Smith flew into a frenzy. "I am going to be indicted, sir, indicted!" he ranted. "You must not talk to me about it. If any man in the Union is taken, it will be me."

The *Herald*'s reporter closed his narrative with his own indictment: "I sum up my experience at Gerrit Smith's home thus: He is in evident alarm and agitation, inconsistent with the idea that his complicity with the plot is simply to the extent already made public. I believe that Brown's visit to his house last spring was intimately connected with the insurrection, and that it is the knowledge that at any moment, either by the discovery of papers or the confession of accomplices, his connection with the affair may become exposed, that keeps Mr. Smith in constant excitement and fear."[3]

Always unstable, Smith's mind gave way—or at least he gave the very strong impression that his mind had given way—within two weeks of Harpers Ferry. But interestingly, in the midst of his mental collapse, he managed a few key sane and sensible acts. He sent his brother-in-law to Boston and Ohio to find and destroy letters that might further incriminate him. He sent Edwin Morton, who knew so much of Smith's involvement with Brown, overseas to tutor a Smith son who was away at Cambridge.⁴ And then, with all the housekeeping of self-preservation completed, he suffered a breakdown. Smith "went down under a troop of hallucinations," reports his biographer Frothingham. "He [thought he] was an outcast; reduced to poverty . . . hunted for his life." He believed that certain unnamed people "meant to carry him about the country in a cage and submit him to horrible tortures." He spent long hours brooding in silence, "gentle as usual, but melancholy," and spoke repeatedly of having to go to Virginia to be with Brown. Smith, reported the *Herald,* was "haunted with the idea that he was culpably responsible for all the lives that have been and will be sacrificed" on account of the affair at Harpers Ferry.

On November 7, Smith was committed to an asylum for the insane in Utica, New York. A report in the *Herald* of November 12 stated that Smith had been coaxed to the asylum by being given the impression he was actually going to join Brown in Charles Town. This account is substantiated by Caleb Calkins, Smith's clerk, who wrote in a memoir that Smith "became wild—was determined to go to Virginia and be with John Brown in Charlestown—left his home for that purpose—talked repeatedly . . . about it—determined to suffer if necessary, with Brown—Went off with the undoubting expectation of going to Virginia." Smith's case, reported the *Herald,* was "one of decided lunacy" and his mind was "considerably disordered." The article quoted a letter from Smith's physician stating that Smith was "quite deranged, intellectually as well as morally; and he is also feeble physically."⁵

Two months after Brown's execution, the dying Theodore Parker sent a letter to Gerrit Smith from Rome: "It is with great pain that I have heard of the illness which the recent distressing events have brought on your much-enduring frame. When I saw you last I did not think that my next letter would be from such a place or for such a purpose. But such is the uncertainty of all mortal things." Parker wrote that he felt "great anxiety about the immediate future of America. . . . We must see much darker hours before it is daylight—darker and also bloody, I think."⁶

☆

Higginson sent Sanborn several taunting notes in early November, daring him to answer whether he could be relied upon not to abscond to Canada yet again now that Brown had been convicted and sentenced. There was another trial pending for several of Brown's men. And a formal Senate investigation of the event at Harpers Ferry was likely. Higginson demanded to know whether Sanborn would stand or retreat.

"Yours of yesterday and of Monday have been received," replied Sanborn with restraint, "and in answer to the last I would say, that I have no intention of going to Canada to avoid arrest as a criminal, nor for any cause, if I felt reasonably sure of being protected here. If I am summoned as a witness, I shall refuse to attend. If . . . I am likely to be taken out of the State as a witness, I shall disappear rather than go, for I fear Massachusetts would not protect you or me taken for such an object as that. . . . But . . . I shall not elope at present nor ever without sufficient cause."[7]

Sanborn's note to Higginson was written on November 10, when all of the Massachusetts members of the Six were still feeling relatively safe, trusting in Andrew's opinion that it was highly unlikely any of their number would or could be extradited to Virginia. "Of course all the stories about the Northern Abolitionists are the merest stuff," a confident Julia Ward Howe lied cheerfully in a letter to her sister on November 6. "No one knew of Brown's intentions but Brown himself and his handful of men."[8]

It was a thunderbolt to the Howes and to the other members of the Six when John Andrew changed his opinion about the likelihood of their extradition. During the second week of November, the lawyer discovered an old and problematical statute that he'd not previously been aware of. "I had a talk with Andrew last night who showed me the statute about witnesses," wrote Sanborn to Higginson on November 13. "It appears that by a law of August 8th, 1846, a witness whose evidence is decreed material by any U.S. judge, may be arrested by a warrant from a judge, without any previous summons and taken before that judge. . . . This leaves no room for a writ of *Habeas Corpus,* unless the state judges are willing to take the ground that the statute is unconstitutional, [or that the warrant is only binding within the assigning judge's] district or circuit. And Andrew does not think that our [Massachusetts] judges are ready to take either ground. Therefore, if arrested, a witness can only be released by a tumult." That being the case, there should be, said Sanborn, "a sane decision come to" about "some concert of action" between those likely to be arrested. A vigilance committee had been formed in Worcester to protect Higginson. "Would your Worcester people go down to Boston to take Dr. Howe or W. Phillips out of the Marshal's hands?" asked Sanborn.[9]

Howe and Stearns were advised of Andrew's new opinion a day after Sanborn. Suddenly feeling quite unsafe, the two departed together for Canada by train in mid-November, to remain there until after Brown's execution on December 2.[10] They stopped in Worcester, where it was Howe's intention to contact Higginson, educate him to the 1846 statute, and coax him to join in the flight. Stearns and Howe had not sent word to Higginson before their arrival. Consequently, the busy Higginson was not at home when they knocked at the door of his house on Harvard Street. Anxious to be on their way, Stearns and Howe left an unsigned note for Higginson apprising him of their plan, and the reasons behind it. Back at the Worcester train station, Howe occupied himself while waiting for the train that would connect to Montreal by writing a letter to the editor of the *New York Tribune* in which he distanced himself from Brown.[11]

"Several grave questions are coming up soon," wrote Sanborn to Parker on November 14. "One relates to the arrest of witnesses. There is a statute of 1846, by which any United States judge can order the arrest of any witness whose evidence he deems material; and have him brought before him, to give bonds to appear and testify; thus giving Virginia means to get Dr. Howe and others in her power. Many think the attempt will be made; and to prevent the possibility of this, Dr. Howe and Mr. Stearns of Medford have gone to Canada for a week or two."

Higginson despised the idea of Howe and Stearns "deserting" to Canada. He thought the action reprehensible in one respect, and unfortunate in another. First, on the face of it, it seemed to Higginson that the "fugitive behavior" of Howe and Stearns was simply dishonorable when the man they had put into greater danger had no option of retreat. Secondly, the Canadian sojourn looked to be a strategic error. Better to stay in Massachusetts, ignore federal or Virginia subpoenas, and in that way force Massachusetts to take a stand, argued Higginson. "[The retreat of Howe and Stearns to Canada] is censured by Higginson," wrote Sanborn to Parker, "who wants all to stay and try the question, and, if possible, raise a conflict between Massachusetts and the United States."[12]

Higginson was further infuriated a few days later, on November 16, when he saw Samuel Gridley Howe's published denial of John Brown in the *New York Tribune*. Paraphrasing the letter to the editor Howe had composed at the train station a few blocks from Higginson's house, the *New York Tribune* reported that the events at Harpers Ferry were "unforeseen and unexpected by him [Howe]. He bears testimony to the heroism of Brown, and says if his testimony to Brown's high qualities can be of any service to him or his, it shall be forthcoming at the fitting time and place." The doctor's letter concluded with a justification for retreating to Canada while at the same time denying any guilt. "I am told by high legal authority that Massachusetts is so tramelled by the bonds of the Union that, as matters now stand, she cannot, or dare not, protect her citizens from . . . forcible extradition; and that each one must protect himself as he best may. Upon that hint I shall act, preferring to forego anything rather than the right to free thought and free speech."[13]

After reading Howe's statement, Higginson immediately wrote a note to the doctor to which he attached a clipping of the article. "I write to you under a sadness very rare for me," wrote Higginson to Howe. "Soon after the affair at Harpers Ferry I said to you . . . in allusion to some rumors about you in the papers—that I thought it would be the extreme of baseness in as to *deny* complicity with Capt. Brown's general scheme—while we were not, of course, called upon to say anything to *criminate* ourselves. . . . What am I, that I should judge you? But Gerrit Smith's insanity—& your letter—are to me the all too sad results of the whole affair. I know how skillfully that letter is written. Since language was first invented 'to conceal thought' there has been no more skillful combination of words. But the [illegible] interpretation of all intelligent readers, not previously enlightened, *must* be—that you disclaim all knowledge not merely of the precise time & place & opening of John Brown's great drama—but of *the Enterprise itself.* That you should deliberately go out of your way to cause this impression to be created is the realization of my worst fears as expressed at your rooms on the day referenced to. Would to God, my friend, that I could see the case differently now from what I did then. Do not receive this in anger—it is not written so."[14]

Howe would not respond directly to Higginson for nearly three months. He instead tried to justify himself to Theodore Parker. "I am very sorry . . . that my 'card' seems to have conveyed an impression stronger than I meant it to do—that of a total disclaimer," wrote Howe to Parker.[15]

Sanborn disagreed with Higginson's wholesale indictment of Howe. "How differently people look at things!" wrote Sanborn to Higginson on November 17. "Yesterday, my brother[-in-law] Walker wrote me that Dr. Howe's letter was 'the height of impudence.' Today you call it 'the extreme of baseness.' I don't think it either, though I am a little sorry that it was written. I do not think the time has yet come for declaiming the whole truth about Brown; better the members, the names and the plans of his accomplices should be unknown, so that they can work in the same way hereafter, if they choose. I can't see why it is any worse to conceal the facts now than before the outbreak, provided that Brown and his men do not suffer by such concealment. What has been prudence is prudence still and may be for years to come."

If any person—Higginson, for instance—wished to come out and declare himself in Brown's plot, he would have a right to do so, yet no right at all to implicate others, said Sanborn. "To do that now, would not only be an abuse of confidence," said Sanborn, "but so far as a well meaning man can be base, would be the 'Extreme of baseness.' . . . Dr. Howe has not acted in all ways as I should have done. Neither have you, but so long as each person acts for himself we must allow such diversities. If however the Dr. or yourself should act so as to compromise others, I should have a *much sharper feeling bout that.*"[16] Sanborn was obviously alarmed at the prospect that Higginson might, out of guilt over the position Brown found himself in, go public in confirming published reports speculating on the names of Brown's associates. He'd gotten this distinct impression from the latest of Higginson's letters to him. Now Higginson responded that Sanborn of course had no need to fear; Higginson would reveal no names besides his own when the time came.

On the nineteenth, Sanborn wrote back a letter containing what was almost an audible sigh of relief: "I have destroyed your letter as I do all letters which might be used against anyone, but my impression certainly was that . . . you meant to introduce the names of others besides yourself. . . . I am much relieved to find that you did not mean this, and perhaps your language did not justify my conclusion. As to Dr. Howe, I cannot see the matter as you do, though I regret the letter. My own position is stated in my last, to which I would now add that I shall pursue my usual occupations, or any that I may take up, whatever command or other process may be issued; that I shall resist arrest by force; shall refuse to sue a writ of *Habeas Corpus* but if arrested shall consent to be rescued only by force. It is possible, the anxiety of friends may induce me to modify this course, but I think not."[17]

$$\left(\begin{array}{c} 21 \end{array}\right)$$

THE DIRGE OF THE
CATARACT

ONCORD HELD A public service on Friday, December 2, 1859, the day of Brown's execution. "Sanborn has written a dirge, which will be sung," reported Bronson Alcott in his diary.[1] Sanborn told a friend he felt "terribly impotent, completely without power" as he listened to his poem being sung and realized that at that same moment his friend Brown was walking "the last steps." Sanborn commented that he was a "very useful and very valuable" friend to have whenever one needed a dirge composed, but that he was not very good at helping friends "avoid that need."[2]

Henry Thoreau participated in the service, as did Emerson, Alcott, Hoar, and other Concord worthies. "Some eighteen hundred years ago Christ was crucified," said Thoreau. "This morning, perchance, Captain Brown was hung. These are the two ends of a chain which is not without its links. He is not Old Brown any longer; he is an angel of light."[3] Sanborn, in turn, read a letter regarding Brown that Theodore Parker had recently sent from Rome. "I don't think it quite just to impute Capt. Brown's conduct to a desire to take vengeance for the murder of his son," wrote Parker, referring to Frederick Brown, who had been killed in Kansas three years earlier. "If that were the motive he would have sought a cheap and easy revenge in . . . Missouri. But if I am rightly informed he has cherished this scheme of liberating the slaves in Virginia for more than 30 years, & laid his plans when he was a land surveyor in that very neighborhood where his gallows (I suppose) has since grown. This is in accordance with his whole character and life."[4] Not far away, Henry Wadsworth Longfellow told another group of listeners to be of good cheer, for "this will be a great day in our history." It was a day, said Longfellow, that would mark "the date of a new Revolution, quite as much needed as the old one." When Virginia killed Brown she would be "sowing the wind to reap the whirlwind, which will come soon."

As if to compound Sanborn's depression and distraction, the fugitive Francis Meriam came to Concord from Canada and looked up Sanborn the day after Brown's execution. (Two weeks earlier, Meriam had dropped in on a surprised and horrified Howe in Montreal at the St. Lawrence Hotel and applied to him for aid. Howe sent Meriam away with nothing, and checked out of his hotel the same day lest the madman return. Meriam, recalled Howe, was in a "wild state. . . . I saw that he was in a state of painful excitement, and declined talking to him."[5] Stearns likewise denied aid to Meriam.)[6] Meriam, of course, was a wanted man. The astonished Sanborn wondered aloud whether or not Meriam's return was triggered by a "wish for suicide." In the evening, Sanborn arranged for Henry Thoreau to drive Meriam, disguised as a "Mr. Lockwood," to the South Acton train station in a horse and carriage borrowed from Emerson.[7] Thoreau did not know the details of who his passenger was, but he guessed enough not to inquire too closely into things. Meriam went by train from Acton to Boston, where he hid at his grandfather's home for several days.

While Francis Meriam remained shuttered inside Francis Jackson's house on Hollis Street immediately after John Brown's execution, a dazed and bewildered Jackson consulted with friends as to what the boy should do. Higginson proposed that Meriam come and stay at his Worcester home, where the same vigilance committee that guarded

Higginson's safety would also guard Meriam. Jackson declined Higginson's offer and decided instead to send his grandson back to Canada. Meriam, wrote Jackson to Higginson on December 6, was "wrought-up & overexcited about the scenes of Harpers Ferry; among friends, he dwells upon it continually, & with increasing ardor. We therefore advise him to go out of the country for the present, into a quiet atmosphere where there would be little or no inducement to discuss that matter."[8] After Meriam's second removal from the country, Hoyt wrote to Sanborn that "Meriam . . . was

The grave of Theodore Parker in Florence, Italy. Photo courtesy Boston Public Library.

chagrinned at your lack of confidence in his judgment. I think him clearly insane."[9] Meriam was still at Chatham, Canada West, ten months later, at which time he was sighted by another Harpers Ferry fugitive, O. P. Anderson.[10]

At Rome, Theodore Parker spent the day of John Brown's execution in quiet seclusion, contemplation, and prayer. His only visitor was one of his doctors. In Parker's darkened bedroom, the physician—an Englishman of noble birth whose patients included most of the British diplomatic community in Rome—mentioned that Brown had been compared to Garibaldi in a recent *London Times* article. The doctor wondered aloud what Brown might think of the analogy. "I could not say," replied Parker, gasping amid one of the prolonged bouts of coughing that every attempt at speech now triggered. Recovering after about a minute, he continued briefly: "I shall be seeing Brown soon. We two have an appointment; my old friend and I are booked on separate trains to the same distant place. I shall ask him when I see him there. Hold a séance and I shall let you know his answer." Now more coughing, more blood in the white napkin, going on for several minutes this time—five, six, seven. Then, settling down again, and smiling dolefully, Parker concluded, "Yes, good doctor. Hold a séance as old Garrison will most assuredly do, and—should I get through, should I even be a thing that would know to want to get through—I'll give you that and oh, so many other answers."[11]

At the time of the execution (approximately 11:30 A.M.), while Concord sang Sanborn's dirge, a glum George Luther Stearns sat on the Canadian side of Niagara Falls with Samuel Gridley Howe, listening to what Stearns later called "the dirge of the cataract." Howe, energetic as ever, had earlier taken his usual morning ride, whipping his horse harshly to an ever greater gallop, charging violently and recklessly over fences and across streams. Stearns did nothing more active than read his mail, which likely included the daily missive from Higginson calling both Stearns and Howe cowards for retreating to safety. In the late morning, the two sat and pondered the constant, crashing flood of Niagara as, hundreds of miles away, John Brown silently rode in the back of an open wagon that carried him to his fate.

Brown sat on his black walnut coffin, which was enclosed in an outer box of poplar that lay on the wagon bed. He wore the same clothes he'd been arrested and put on trial in—a black frock coat, black pantaloons, black vest, a blue shirt, and a black slouch hat. The coat and pantaloons were still bloodstained despite the recent efforts of a friend at cleaning them. He looked as much like a preacher as he ever had, save for a pair of bright red prison slippers. When, at last, the slow-moving wagon finished traveling the long, heavily guarded road to the outskirts of Charles Town where Brown's gallows, as Parker put it, had "grown," Brown climbed down out of the wagon unaided and ascended the scaffold. One witness—Prof. Thomas J. (later known as "Stonewall") Jackson of the

Virginia Military Institute—wrote admiringly of Brown's "apparent cheerfulness" and "unflinching firmness" as he mounted the steps. Another witness, John Wilkes Booth, who borrowed a uniform and posed as a member of a Richmond militia in order to attend the hanging, considered Brown with more disgust than admiration. Booth congratulated himself in his diary on having had the honor to attend Brown's demise. Booth wrote of the "unlimited, undeniable contempt" with which he viewed "the traitor and terrorizor."

"The sheriff placed the rope around his neck, then threw a white cap over his head, and asked him if he wished a signal when all should be ready," recalled Jackson. "He replied that it made no difference, provided he was not kept waiting too long. In this condition he stood for about ten minutes on the trap door, which was supported on one side by hinges and on the other side (the south side) by a rope. Colonel L. Smith then announced to the sheriff 'all ready'—which apparently was not comprehended by him, and the colonel had to repeat the order, when the rope was cut by a single blow, and Brown fell through . . . his knees falling on a level with the position occupied by his feet before the rope was cut. With the fall his arms, below the elbows, flew up horizontally, his hands clenched; and his arms gradually fell, but by spasmodic motions. There was very little motion of his person for several moments, and soon the wind blew his lifeless body to and fro."[12] As Brown swung in the autumn breeze, Col. J. T. L. Preston of the Virginia Military Institute was heard to shout, "So perish all such enemies of Virginia! All such enemies of the Union! All such foes of the human race!"[13]

The scene would be painted and written of again and again over generations, building John Brown's legend larger with each repetition. Whitman, citing Brown's execution as the beginning of what he characterized as a "Year of Meteors," imagined himself as a witness at the hanging: "I would now sing how an old man, tall, with white hair, mounted the scaffold in Virginia / (I was at hand, silent I stood with teeth shut closed, I watched / I stood very near you old man when cool and indifferent, / but trembling with age and your unheal'd wounds / you mounted the scaffold.)"[14] Herman Melville wrote of Brown "hanging from the beam . . . slowly swaying" while "hidden in the cap is the anguish none can draw."[15] Writing a week before the execution, young William Dean Howells envisioned Brown on the gallows as an "Old Lion, tangled in the net. . . . A captive but a lion yet."[16]

Gerrit Smith, at his Utica lunatic asylum, spent day one in Whitman's year of meteors glumly silent and refusing nourishment. Smith's nurses and guards had instructions not to give him any word of Brown, no matter how much he prodded them. Still, he well knew this to be the day of Brown's hanging. The date had been widely published a week before Smith was committed and cut off from all news. On the morning of the execution, when the lock on the door of his sparse room clicked, and a silent, muscular orderly brought in a breakfast he would not eat, Smith neither expected nor needed confirmation of his fear. "The great and the good go to the noose," he wrote in a note that, while communicating his emotions, could never be used to explicitly link him with Brown. "Only the mean and the treacherous avoid it. Do those serve also who helped prepare the martyr to shed his righteous, cleansing blood? Do those serve also who now stand aside, who hide and are silent? Are they guilty of abandonment who, like him, are bound and fettered? I make this a day of fasting, meditation, and prayer—all I can do within the bars that hold me. The one who dies has nothing to fear. God will gather the beloved, his fierce defender, to him. It is we, the rest of us, who need ask mercy. We who will be left—it is we whose blood will flood tomorrow to follow today's rivulet."[17]

At Concord, on the evening of the execution, a copperhead mob burned Brown in effigy in reaction to the public mourning ceremony earlier in the day.

THE COMMITTEE

GEORGE LUTHER STEARNS was ostracized by many circles in Massachusetts because of his now-public relationship with John Brown. "Mr. Stearns was now a marked man," recalled his son Robert Preston Stearns. "Old merchants whom he had known from boyhood passed him on State Street without recognition; and he sometimes heard himself cursed by others of the meaner sort who had nothing to hope or fear from him. He even found it necessary to keep his accounts with a bank which had an abolitionist for a cashier."[1]

In the aftermath of Harpers Ferry, anti-abolitionist sentiment grew throughout the Northeast, particularly among the working class and the Hunker businessmen and politicos. During that time of general upheaval after Harpers Ferry and before the start of the Civil War, Boston, remembered Franklin Sanborn, "came under the dominion of mobs, and for months was the scene of ongoing attempts to put down antislavery free speech by the uproar and threats of repeated mobs, —led not by the outlaws and refuse of your slums, but by merchants and bankers and distillers. Your Mayor was then on the side of the mobs, and our Governors were averse to calling out the troops and restoring order."[2] Higginson joined a new vigilance squad impaneled to stand guard at antislavery meetings in Boston after the proslavery mayor refused to assign police officers to protect Wendell Phillips and others.[3] George Luther Stearns carried a revolver with him at all times. And he consulted regularly with the equally ostracized Howe. The two men shared their chagrin, consternation, and anger when they learned that there was to be an official Senate investigation into the events at Harpers Ferry.

Three days after Brown's execution, Sen. James Mason of Virginia—author of the fugitive slave law—moved for the appointment of a committee to study and report on Brown's raid. When the committee was formed and charged on December 14, Mason was appointed chairman. Jefferson Davis of Mississippi, anxious to uncover and prosecute the chief conspirators in what he was sure was an intricate plot by Northern abolitionists to wreak havoc throughout the slaveholding South, was made the committee's chief inquisitor. Graham N. Fitch of Indiana rounded out the proslavery majority of three. Wisconsin's James R. Doolittle and Jacob Collamer of Vermont constituted the antislavery minority. And the Secret Six, by default, were appointed the committee's prime targets. Brown, after all, was already dead. His men were all either dead, doomed, or in hiding. Tellingly, a key clause of the Mason Committee's charter stipulated that it must ascertain whether the invasion and seizure of the federal arsenal was made "under color of any organizations intended to subvert the government of any of the States of the Union; . . . the character and extent of such organization; and whether any citizens of the United States not present were implicated therein, or accessory thereto, by contributions of money, arms, munitions, or otherwise."[4]

One participant was to remember the tension within the committee room was "palpable," as was the tension throughout Congress. "The members on both sides are mostly armed with deadly weapons," one senator wrote his wife, "and it is said that the friends of each are armed in the galleries." Thaddeus Stevens, from Pennsylvania, was attacked with a bowie knife by a Mississippi congressman during a heated debate on the floor of the House of Representatives. Congress, now as always, mirrored the country. And the country was a war waiting to happen. "Washington, as it is today, is the meanest hole in creation, and Congress the meanest part of Washington," wrote Stearns to Howe on February 27, shortly after he finally, after months of delay, agreed to give testimony before Mason. "The members of both parties are split up into petty cliques, each intent on grinding its own little axe and trying to prevent all the others from using the grindstone. If they are our *representatives,* we are indeed of a low type. If I had my way I would put a hundred barrels of powder under the Capitol, and if Congress did not clear *out,* blow *them* and *it* sky high. At any rate, if they go on as they do now a few years more, we shall have to abolish the govt. and let the states take care of themselves."⁵

Late December of 1859 found the members of the Six mapping out policies on exactly how to deal with the threat of subpoena to appear before Mason. "On Saturday and Sunday I had conferences with Dr. H. and Mr. S. [Stearns] and with [Wendell] Phillips and [John] Andrew," wrote Sanborn somewhat cryptically in an unsigned letter to Higginson on December 20. "It was resolved by G.S. and myself that we would not go to Washington to testify but would do so in Mass. [and have written the committee to say so]. . . . I, an avowed abolitionist, and friend of Brown, cannot be safe in a city so near Virginia. . . . Howe will probably return to Canada."⁶ Howe made a decision—destined to be repealed within two months—to refuse to render testimony for the committee in Massachusetts or anyplace else; he said he would quit the country for good before doing so.

"In Canada, if you should go there," wrote Sanborn to Howe on December 19, "there is a matter to be looked after at St. Catharines—the condition of the fugitives. . . . If I am in Canada again, I shall go and look into it." Perhaps remembering Howe's penchant for writing letters to the newspapers, Sanborn added his opinion that "until we get some response from Washington I should not think it advisable to appear in *print* with our determination [not to go to Washington], but I declare it to all persons with whom I talk and speak it so. Mr. Emerson suggests that Banks [Nathaniel P. Banks, Governor of Massachusetts] should be notified of our purpose and be allowed to endorse our determination not to go to Washington, if he will do so. I think the plan is a good one, and that we shall have the support of public sentiment here."[7] Howe, for his part, was intending to stay as far away from the fugitives, and anyone else associated with Brown, as possible. He would not in fact return to Canada until mid-January; and during that short visit he would not go anywhere near St. Catharines.

Confused and worried, the indecisive Sanborn changed his mind within a week after deciding definitely not to go to Washington, then almost as quickly changed it once again. "You are not allowed to withhold evidence which criminates yourself in your examination before the Senate Committee," wrote Sanborn to Higginson on Christmas Day from his family farm near Hampton Falls, New Hampshire. "This is an important fact; before I knew it, I determined to go to Washington. Now I shall not if I can help it. You are liable to a year's imprisonment and a fine of $1000 if you refuse to answer any question this committee sees fit to put. I don't believe it is wise for those who know anything of consequence to go before the committee, especially if Realf appears there. Did you see he has brought you out in his statement, and Mr. Parker too? [I therefore] go to Canada tomorrow." After the signature Sanborn wrote: "I hope you burn all my letters about these things."[8]

Richard Realf, whom no one of the Six had heard from in more than a year since he'd asked them to pay for his trip to England and then defrauded them, surfaced in Austin, Texas. Realf sold his story—all he knew of Brown and the Virginia experiment—to several newspapers. He initially named Higginson and Parker as active participants in the plot and would eventually name Howe, Smith, and Sanborn as well. The threat Realf posed was formidable, for he did know a great deal of the truth, and his story was bound to be corroborated by many of the documents, signed by Sanborn and others, found by investigators among Brown's effects at the Kennedy farmhouse after the raid. The members of the Six viewed the certain prospect of Realf's testimony with foreboding.

It is unclear whether Sanborn actually went to Canada after Christmas, as he told Higginson he would, or simply returned directly to

Concord. In any event, he was back at Concord by January 2. "I am still firm . . . not to go to W. [Washington], not seeing any good that will result from it, and a chance of Evil," he wrote Higginson, who must have wondered how firm Sanborn had been previously. "There are a thousand better ways of spending a year in warfare against slavery than by being in a Washington prison. If I were you, I would decline to go." Howe, reported Sanborn, was thinking of going back on his pledge not to cooperate with the committee. "Howe thinks he may go; Stearns will not."[9] Sanborn wrote Parker on the same day to say, "It is probable that Dr. Howe, Higginson, myself and others will be summoned to Washington in the course of two weeks. The summons cannot well reach here till Saturday next, and may be much longer deferred. I do not mean to go, but to avoid the arrest may retire for awhile. Howe may go, but I think will not; Higginson inclines to go."[10] No summons had yet been issued for any of them. The summonses for Sanborn, Howe, and Gerrit Smith were drafted on January 11, and one for George Stearns a few days later.

On January 16, Sanborn wrote to Higginson with an invitation to stay at his house the following week, when Higginson was scheduled to be lecturing at Concord. "Mrs. Emerson also invites you, and if any chance should take me from home at that time, (which I do not anticipate) you would find hers the pleasanter place. Perhaps you would at any rate, so please make your own choice. There is more reason here, more beauty there. Mr. E. will not be at home, being in the West, for which he started this morning." Sanborn commented to Higginson that he had heard nothing from him of late with regard to the Mason Committee. "They told me in Boston Saturday that you had not decided whether to go to W. [Washington] or not. I shall *not,* nor do I think I shall be arrested. If I am annoyed sufficiently to injure my schoolkeeping I shall go abroad in March, I think, —or perhaps in February and join Morton in England and Mr. Parker in Rome. . . . G.L.S. [has] gone to N. Elba. Dr. H. I know not where. I hope neither you nor W. Phillips will go to W. [Washington]. Redpath will not."[11] Sanborn was not aware that a summons drafted January 11, calling for his appearance in Washington on January 26, was already on its way to him, and that similar documents were on their way to Howe and Smith. Higginson—for all the discussion by himself as well as others on the question of whether or not he would cooperate with the committee—was not to be summoned at all.

Higginson wound up staying at the Emerson home during his visit to Concord, for by the time he got there his would-be host Sanborn had, in the spirit of Howe, embarked on yet another panic-driven flight. "I had just mailed my last letter to you a fortnight ago, when I was summoned [personally served the summons of the committee] by Marshal Freeman," wrote Sanborn to Higginson from Montreal on January 29. "I had warning of this the day before, but did not care to avoid it. I had made arrangements to remain in Massachusetts, but my own family and so many of my friends urged me to go away, that I decided to do so, having first sent on a paper to Mason refusing to appear in W. [Washington] and alleging apprehension of personal danger, and asking to be examined in Mass."

Sanborn said he'd had no formal response from the committee and had not, as yet, been harassed by any officer of the Senate. Sanborn then implored Higginson, should he wind up testifying, not to volunteer the names of his coconspirators. "No notice seems to have been taken of this as yet, but I suppose when two or three others have refused, the matter will be brought before the Senate, and some action had about it. I left home last Monday and arrived here [Montreal] the next day, not letting my place of retreat be known generally. I shall remain here a week more, by which time I can see how things are going and whether or not I can go back to my school. If not, I shall perhaps remain here, but more likely go abroad. Should I stay in Canada I shall go down among the fugitives and explore their condition, with a view to some better organization among them. I was sorry to miss meeting and entertaining you at Concord."[12]

Higginson had several suppers with the Thoreau family during his brief stay in Concord. "Henry told me," wrote Higginson to a close friend, "that he did not at all understand FBS [Sanborn]. Henry said civil disobedience, in the pure form, required staying in place, [it required] a certain willingness to suffer the consequence—whatever that might be—of refusing to participate in an immoral act, statute, or investigation."[13] This, wrote Higginson, was entirely his point of view. He would

remain accessible to senatorial summons and would refuse to retreat to
any jurisdiction outside that of the U.S. Senate.

☆

"G.L.S. gone to N. Elba," Sanborn had written. The mid-January trip
of George Luther Stearns and his wife to North Elba was inspired by
two things: Stearns's personal desire to be close to the Canadian border
when a summons to appear before Mason was due to arrive at any day,
and his and his wife's wish to visit and bring comfort to Brown's widow
and family. "We shall be most happy to see you at our house any time
that you think best," wrote Mary Brown to Stearns on December 27, in
response to an inquiry from Stearns as to whether he might pay his
respects at the grave of Brown.[14]

Ruth Thompson, in a letter written to Mary Stearns the day after
Christmas, voiced some similar words of welcome. "Although personally
unacquainted with you," wrote Ruth, "yet I do not feel that I am a
stranger, for I have so often heard my dear Father speak of you and Mr.
Stearns as being his very dear friends, that helped him so much while he
was in Kansas, and since he came from there, also having had the pleasure of reading the letters from you & Mr. S. to my Mother, I have felt a
desire to write you, that I might become better acquainted with you. I was
much interested in your excellent letters too so full of heart-felt sympathy
for Mother, and respect for my dear lost Father. I copied his last letter to
you, and every time I read it, I feel assured that in you & your husband we
shall find warm friends. You wrote that you wanted to come to North
Elba and see his family. *We all want you to come.* . . . Nothing would give
us more pleasure than to have Father's friends come and make us a visit.
It would comfort us much to see you & Mr. Stearns, for we feel *very lonely
now.* Oh, I know you do sympathize with us, and realize to a great extent
what a *loss is ours.* I can never think of my dear Father without feeling
that his happy spirit is watching over me. But my dear Brothers & Brothers in-law, I cannot realize that they are dead. It seems as though they
should soon come, but alas they too are gone. . . . Were it not for the

thought that my noble Father & Brothers died in a *righteous cause* I could hardly endure it. It is very comforting to know that 'God reigns.'"[15]

On the same December day that Ruth Thompson wrote her letter to Mary Stearns, George Luther Stearns was at work closing the book on some of Brown's men, who, ten days after their deaths, he was still trying to do right by. "On the 14th of this month," he wrote to the Reverend Samuel May, "I addressed a letter to J. Miller McKim of Philadelphia, requesting that peaceful measures might be taken to procure the bodies of Copeland and Green and have them properly interred in Pennsylvania, and also requesting him to [rely] on me for the necessary finances. I enclose his reply which please place on file in the Anti-Slavery Office for reference should we at any time be charged with neglect in this matter."[16] The attached note from McKim stated that he had been refused access to the corpses of the two black men.[17]

At North Elba, Stearns and his wife spent several hours in the cold, standing beside the grave beneath the foot of the boulder—the dirt still freshly turned—where Brown lay. Stearns paid a local mason to carve Brown's name and dates on the face of the rock. He also gave Mary Brown a sum of money, approximately $100, for current expenses. And he offered to send a stenographer from his Boston office to spend a week at the farm, there to help the largely illiterate Mary respond to the close to one thousand pieces of mail she'd received in the past several weeks. (The harried postmaster in nearby Elizabethtown was holding the mail. It was stacked in a veritable mountain of sacks by his back office, awaiting Henry Thompson's horse and wagon to cart it away.) Stearns told Mary he thought all letters born of goodwill and sincere sympathy should be answered; while the many critical and insulting notes should be ignored. When Henry finally went to get the letters, and Mary gradually opened them, she found more than $300 in checks and cash from Brown's admirers, and an equal amount of scathing indignation from his detractors. "We are coming there [to North Elba] to dig him up," wrote one critic from Kansas. "Our ambition isn't to mistreat the corpse—but only to make sure he's dead."[18]

Stearns spent time not only with the Browns, but also with the few black families who remained at Timbucto. Lyman Epps, titular head of the shrinking community, remembered Stearns as "the saddest of men." The eloquent Epps told an interviewer a few years later that Stearns "was very solemn. He said that a great crime had been done, a great sin transacted, in what had happened to our mutual friend John Brown. He said he was not sure that the country was not done for. He in fact thought it must be. He said he no longer believed that the United States could be redeemed—that he thought the 'American experiment in liberty,' as he called it, was completed and that it had proved something distinctly negative." The ideal of liberty, Stearns told Epps bluntly, was buried in the ground beneath a boulder in the Adirondacks that bore the name of John Brown.[19] Stearns's pessimism would prove short-lived; he would soon begin to see Harpers Ferry and the martyrdom of Brown as a beginning, rather than an end. "I believe John Brown to be the representative man of this century, as Washington was of the last," an unapologetic Stearns would say two months later. "The Harpers Ferry affair, and the capacity shown by the Italians for self-government, [are] the great events of this age. One will free Europe and the other America."[20]

When a summons to appear before Mason was left at his house on January 23, Sam Howe's reflex action was to flee once more to Canada. This he did despite his intimations of late that he might well agree to testify. Thus Howe failed to appear before the committee on the appointed date of January 26. Then he thought better of his action and realized he had committed a blunder. He returned to Boston after only a few days in Canada, and concocted a story for the press. "There was an error in our statement with regard to the summons to Dr. S. G. Howe to testify before the Senate Investigating Committee, which we desire to correct, having obtained reliable information," reported the *New York Tribune* on February 2. "Dr. Howe has been at home for the last five or six weeks attending to his usual business. He had been preparing for an exhibition of his pupils in Canada, and was about to leave town when the summons from the Investigating Committee at Washington reached him. This was last Monday evening. The time fixed for his appearance was the next day. Of course, it was impossible to conform. He telegraphed, however, immediately to inquire whether he should await a new summons, assigning a future day for his appearance, or whether he should go on immediately. He has had no official reply, but is ready to go and testify if required."[21]

Howe, ever vain, did not want his fellow conspirators to think he had panicked. He wrote Parker to tell him his quick skip to Canada was a carefully thought-out maneuver to insure his safety in Washington. He told Parker he did not mind the prospect of testifying before Mason so much as he minded the idea of traveling so near to the Virginia border when the threat of abduction to give testimony—or worse, stand trial— in the slave state seemed very real. Brown's confederates Aaron Stevens and Albert Hazlett were scheduled to go on trial in the Virginia state court on February 1. "When that trial has really been had," wrote Howe to Parker, " and the men are condemned or acquitted, *that* trap will have been sprung, and Northern men may, if they choose, obey the summons of the inquisitorial Committee and go to Washington, without fear of being carried over the Ferry into Virginia, [nominally] as witnesses, but really as victims for the maw of the slavery mob."[22] When arrested on the Polish/German border, Howe remembered, he'd not been charged with anything but rather detained as a witness. It seemed all too probable, he told Parker, that history might repeat itself. In addition to this, he told at least one correspondent he had forebodings about the committee itself and was not absolutely sure he would surrender himself to it. "An extra judicial investigating committee may be better than a Virginia District Court," Howe wrote Senator Wilson on January 23, "but it is not American in its origin or character. Akin to the Inquisition, its Chairman may well take a leaf out of the books of a Prussian Minister of Police. If I should be summoned by the Inquisitional Committee, I shall consider whether I am bound by those principles which ought to guide good citizens . . . and shall act accordingly."[23]

Evidently, what convinced Howe to go to Washington and cooperate with Mason was the very clear evidence, as printed each day in the newspaper accounts of the testimony given, that the committee's investigation was blundering, inept, and off the point. Therefore it was also undangerous. "Realf's testimony has not been so important as the committee hoped," Sanborn wrote to Higginson on February 3, "and an impression is quite strong that the investigation will develop little farther. Acting partly under this, and partly from other motives, Dr. Howe has gone to Washington." Other motives: Julia had given birth to a boy, Samuel Gridley Howe, Jr., on Christmas day. The prospect of long-term Canadian exile was made harder for Howe to accept when it embraced separation from his young namesake. One of Howe's further motives was certainly to vouchsafe the innocence of his friend Sen. Henry Wilson, who had been partially implicated in the Brown affair by the otherwise benign and disorganized testimony rendered by Richard Realf on January 21. "I suspect one reason [for Howe's testifying] is a desire on Wilson's part to have Howe corroborate him," wrote Sanborn to Higginson. "If this be so, it is great generosity in Dr. Howe."

After his first failure to appear on January 26, Sanborn received a civil letter from Senator Mason assuring him that he would be protected from any violence, which would be an affront to the Senate, and allowing him more time to obey the summons. "I intend to answer, declining to appear at all . . . ," wrote Sanborn to Higginson, "and to test the question of contempt in Massachusetts, if possible. For this purpose I shall return to Concord." It was the first week of February and Sanborn was writing from Vergennes, Vermont, where he was stopping on his way from Montreal to North Elba. "I am here tonight on my way to North Elba, where I mean to spend Sunday with Mrs. Brown. If for any reason it seems best, after my return, still to avoid an arrest by the Marshal, I may [return to Canada], and may even embark for England, though this is not probable."[24]

Sanborn spent February 5 at North Elba and reached Concord on February 7. He was followed to Concord by two daughters of John Brown, Anne and Sarah, whom he had invited to be enrolled as students in his school. Their tuition was paid by several subscribers, the largest contributor being the wealthy Rebecca B. Spring of Perth Amboy, New Jersey, an abolitionist and jailhouse correspondent of John Brown's.[25] The Brown daughters spent a night with the Emersons before going to live at a local boardinghouse where George Stearns paid their expenses.[26]

Meanwhile, Redpath's hastily written *The Public Life of Captain John Brown,* which was out for only about a month, had already sold forty thousand copies. "It is expected that the sale will reach 100,000," Redpath wrote delightedly to the condemned Aaron Stevens, who with Hazlett had been convicted after a brief trial conducted the first week of February. (Stevens and Hazlett were defended by George Sennott, promptly convicted, and sentenced to die. They were to be executed on the gallows March 16.) "The profits to the family will amount to $5000. That is my contribution to the cause. There is no doubt that all the families will be provided for—Brown's, I think, will be made rich," Redpath told Stevens, who might not have shared the author's excitement. "I intend to write another Book in which I propose to sketch your career in Kansas; & that of Cook, Kagi, Hazlett, & as many of the Men as are dead. . . . Can you not furnish me with a lot of facts about the boys—as many biographical items as you recollect? I want particularly to know about the families left destitute by the blow made at Harpers Ferry. Are you married? Can you give me the addresses of the boys where their families can be reached?"[27]

☆

Higginson's position with regard to the Mason committee must have been confusing to other members of the Six. Initially, at the time of Brown's trial, he had cooperated in the raising of a Worcester vigilance committee formed to guard him from being taken either to give testimony against Brown or to stand trial with him. Then, at the start of the Mason investigation, Higginson openly said that he would not retreat to Canada, and that if summoned, he would go to Washington and speak the whole truth bravely. At times in the preceding weeks, when others of the Six had shown signs of weakness, he had urged them to take the same stand. But now, when Howe and Stearns agreed to testify, Higginson thought to berate them for it. Perhaps, strange as it may seem, a tinge of jealousy was at work here. Men such as Realf and Redpath, whom Higginson viewed as far less central to Brown's scheme than himself, were summoned as witnesses. But Higginson was not. Bruised and apparently confused by this odd slight, Higginson flirted with the idea of urging his colleagues not to bear witness.

"I do not pretend to understand your position or Howe's," wrote Higginson to Sanborn on February 3, 1860 (the same day Sanborn left Montreal and Howe testified at Washington) in a letter that he never sent. In the note, Higginson ignored the fact that he'd previously expressed willingness to give testimony for Mason. "My greatest objection to testifying was always the unwillingness to say anything that might implicate you two & if I had ever thought of [testifying] I should have consulted you first. . . . What Howe means by going to Washington after twice fleeing to Canada, I do not know. What you mean by offering to testify in Boston, I cannot conceive . . . [the committee is] afraid of the effect on the country of witnesses who shall defend John Brown. And I am more and more inclined to think that the reason why I have not been summoned is that I have always openly said that I should *not* go to Canada."[28] (Five years earlier, when confronted, briefly, with the possibility that he would not be charged in the Burns affair, he had postulated virtually the same reason for the judicial neglect: the prosecutors were afraid of him. "It is now rumored that there are to be no more arrests," he'd written his mother on June 1, 1854. "If so it is because they fear the effect of imprisoning me; for I know my participation in the affair is notorious."[29])

On the same day, Higginson wrote another letter to Sanborn. Again he did not send it. "There is no great use in my writing, differing as we do about the fundamentals of the present action," wrote Higginson. "As I understand, Howe is on his way to Washington, and you have offered to testify in Boston. Of course if they are shrewd they will take you at your word. Yet you (& I suppose Howe) think 'the keeping back of evidence too important to run any risks' & urge that on me!! To reconcile this contradiction is beyond me. Perhaps when Howe's testimony &

yours are reported I may understand better. Keyes tells me he thinks you are 'Exceedingly desirous to testify' anywhere but in Washington! But I do not think you will ever be called upon. . . . No one who leaves the country will be pursued, and no one who stands his ground indicted. . . . Mason does not want to have John Brown heartily defended before the Committee and before the country. . . . If his witnesses go to Canada or Europe, he is freed from all responsibility."[30]

Still, Higginson reiterated that he would testify if asked. And in his journal he made it quite plain that he was stung by not being called: "I think it was a disappointment to me not to be summoned to testify before the [Mason] Committee, nor do I know why I was passed over. . . . Certainly I should have told them all I knew—and whether that would have done good or harm, I cannot say."[31]

In testifying before the Mason Committee on February 3, Howe categorically denied his prior knowledge of the Harpers Ferry raid. "In all your conversation or communication with Brown," asked Senator Doolittle, "had you ever, at any time, from him any intimation of an organized attempt or effort, on his part to be made, to produce an insurrection among the slaves in the slave States of the South?"

"Never," replied Howe confidently.[32]

On February 24, Stearns did the same under questioning from Senator Collamer. "Did you," asked Collamer, "at any time before the transaction at Harpers Ferry, in any way, directly or indirectly, understand that there was any purpose on the part of Brown to make any inroad upon the subject of slavery in any of the States?"

Stearns shook his head. "No, sir; not except that Brown was opposed to slavery, and as he had in Kansas he would work again. I did not suppose that he had any organized plan."

After a few minutes more of questioning around the subject, Collamer once again assayed the topic directly: "Had you any idea that these arms were to be used for any such purpose as making an inroad into any State?"

Stearns thought for a moment, then said, "I think I do not understand you."

Collamer, exasperated, pounded his fist down on the table of papers before him. "John Brown has made an inroad into Virginia," exclaimed Collamer loudly, "with force and arms to relieve slaves; *you understand that?*"

Stearns nodded. "Yes, sir."

Collamer stood and looked down at Stearns in his chair before delivering the final question. "Now," demanded Collamer, "did you ever, before that took place, have any intimation of what was contemplated to be done, intended to be done, by him?"

Stearns shook his head once more. "No, sir; I never supposed that he contemplated anything like what occurred at Harpers Ferry."

Under questioning from chief inquisitor Jefferson Davis of Mississippi and Virginia's James Mason, Stearns answered shrewdly when asked whether or not he approved of Brown's actions at Harpers Ferry. Carefully threading his way through the gray area between complicity and sympathy, Stearns confidently endorsed actions he had already denied prior knowledge of in his perjured testimony, finding a safe way to praise Brown's enterprise while maintaining his own innocence and insulating himself from prosecution. "I should have disapproved of it [the Harpers Ferry invasion] if I had known of it," said Stearns, "but I have since changed my opinion."[33]

When Stearns's testimony was done and all had left the committee room, Stearns found himself alone with an informal, off-the-record Mason. "He handed me a bright Sharp's Rifle and asked with a smile if I had ever seen it." When Stearns said no, Mason asked, "Doesn't your conscience trouble you for sending these rifles to Kansas to shoot our innocent people?" Stearns answered that it was a matter of self-defense, that the Southerners had begun the game: "You sent Buford and his company with arms before we sent any from Massachusetts." Mason took the rifle from Stearns, an expression of impatience and displeasure on his face. "I think," said Mason, "when you go to that lower place, the old fellow will question you pretty hard about this matter, and you will have to take it." "Before that time comes," countered Stearns, "I think he will have about two hundred years of slavery to investigate, and before he gets through with that will say 'We have had enough of this business, better let the rest go.'" With that, Mason laughed and left the room, leaving Stearns alone in the empty, echoing chamber.[34]

23

MACHINES

I T TOOK SAMUEL Gridley Howe three full months to answer
the scathing letter that Higginson had written on November
16 in response to Howe's missive published in the newspaper.
Finally, after two retreats to Canada and giving testimony for the
Mason Committee, Howe sat down and wrote a response to his friend
Higginson. This remarkable letter, like the earlier one that Higginson
had protested, was a masterpiece of the art of obfuscation.

"I have deferred, from time to time, in answering your letter as one
is apt to defer an unpleasant and painful task," wrote Howe to Higginson in mid-February. "The letter seemed to me, at the time, unkind
and hard, and gave me great pain. You remarked that the publication
of my card gave you more pain than anything else which had occurred
in connection with the great tragedy, except the insanity of Gerrit
Smith. . . . [My card was written] in consequence of an opinion
which I held, and hold, that every thing which could be honestly done
to show that John Brown was not the Agent, or even the ally of others,
but an individual acting upon his own responsibility, would increase
the chances of escape for him and his companions. I believed and I
believe, that manifestation at that time of public sympathy for him and

his acts lessened the chances of his escape, whether by rescue or otherwise. . . . You say that it was skillfully written; but you seem to imply that honorable men, who knew all the facts, would disapprove it. But my friend, it was *simply* written, and not intended to carry a false impression. . . . As it has turned out, the publication of the Card did no good; but I have the satisfaction of thinking it did no harm, except perhaps to me. As to my leaving the country, that seems *now* to have been a mistake: but it was made under the deliberate advice of the best legal counsel which I could get. It was done the more readily as my health was greatly deranged, and some change was needed. Besides, there were other considerations not necessary to mention. With regard to present action, I have to say, that I think every man not *actually engaged* in the 'Harpers Ferry' affair, who may be summoned before the Investigating Committee, ought to go testify. I think they can do so with perfect safety to themselves, and with advantage not merely to the Republican, but to the veritable anti-slavery party."[1]

Higginson, for his part, was feeling strangely guilty. He seemed to be getting away from this thing without the merest scratch of a wound and without the slightest hint of public humiliation. In a way, he envied Brown and his men their martyrdom just as he envied Howe and Stearns their squirming under senatorial inquisition. In January Higginson kept busy (and vainly tried to get noticed by Senator Mason) by loudly sponsoring a fund to raise a monument to Dangerfield Newby and the blacks who had fought and died with Brown.[2] In February, however, he grew weary of monument-making and decided it was time once again for action. Now Higginson decided he would attempt to rescue Stevens and Hazlett, who, convicted during the first week of February, were scheduled to die on March 16.

Higginson's plot for rescuing Stevens and Hazlett was every bit as suicidal as had been Brown's plan of attack at Harpers Ferry. A large band of armed men would hike from Harrisburg, Pennsylvania, to Charles Town.[3] This would involve walking for a week through mountainous country, traveling only by night, carrying arms, blankets, and provisions. After the exhausting journey, the squad would attack the heavily fortified Charles Town jail, with its fourteen-foot walls and sentinels without and within—the same jail that had already been surveyed and pronounced impenetrable when schemes for rescuing Brown were under discussion. And then all this would be followed by a retreat by daylight through the same mountains, this time possibly carrying wounded comrades and most assuredly with Virginia militia companies in hot pursuit.

In the midst of his planning of the raid, Higginson met with the fugitive Charles Plummer Tidd, who knew the region around Charles Town very well. "My plan is impossible at this season," wrote Higginson, recording Tidd's comments in his notes of their meeting. "Could not camp out in that ice."[4] But Higginson was not prepared to abandon the project on the strength of the opinion of one man—especially if that man was one whom Higginson was naturally disposed to distrust. (In Higginson's world of absolutes, a survivor of Brown's band at Harpers Ferry was at worst a traitor, at best a quitter or a coward, and in either case *suspect*.) If there was impracticality here, Higginson wanted verification of it from someone other than Tidd. Thus he sent to Kansas for James Montgomery—Montgomery, from whose ranks Brown had recruited Stevens and Hazlett in the first place.

Montgomery and seven of his men (whom he furtively called "machines" in letters and telegrams) rendezvoused with Higginson in Harrisburg on February 17. Higginson traveled under the name Charles P. Carter. He brought with him about a dozen men from Worcester and Boston, plus a few Germans from New York. Posing as cattle buyers, the group stayed at a Harrisburg hotel for several days while Higginson and an increasingly cynical Montgomery reviewed strategy for the improbable mission. The more Montgomery learned of the terrain and timing of the foray, the more concerned he became about its chance for success. Eventually, Montgomery insisted on going off for several days with one of his men to reconnoiter both the mountain route to be traversed and the situation at Charles Town.

Returning forlornly to Harrisburg, Montgomery mouthed a verdict that echoed that of Tidd: the mission was a logistical impossibility.

Heavy snowfalls were only part of the problem; the authorities and community of Charles Town were on alert—all well armed and expecting trouble. Furthermore, while in Charles Town, Montgomery's man had managed to speak with Stevens and Hazlett. Feigning intoxication, the man got himself thrown into jail for a night, during which Stevens and Hazlett told him that even they considered all attempts at rescue hopeless. Thus the thing was abandoned. Higginson and Montgomery would find themselves working together closely once again in the near future, when they both obtained colonelcies to command black troops in the Union Army.

Subsequently there was one more attempt to rescue Stevens and Hazlett—one that Higginson was not even aware of. The thing was engineered by Charles Lenhart, the Kansas guerrilla chieftain, who had come east with Montgomery. After Higginson and his cronies gave up on their rescue scheme and dispersed, Lenhart returned to Charles Town, where he somehow managed to enlist in the company of men guarding the jail. With a few coconspirators, Lenhart planned to cause a violent disturbance when Stevens and Hazlett were walked out the prison gates toward the gallows. We have no more details than this. Just why the thing did not come off is not known. But according to Richard Hinton, Lenhart was very nearly successful in engineering the escape.[5]

While Higginson's attempt did not free Stevens and Hazlett, it did manage to redeem Higginson's self-image, which, on at least one level, had been the real object of rescue all along. "I was worn and restless with inability to do anything for John Brown," Higginson remembered. ". . . The effort to rescue Stevens and Hazlett—undertaken on my sole responsibility—restored my self-respect. It did not fail like the Burns rescue through the timidity of others—but simply through the impracticability of the thing. I would not have accepted any one's assurance of that impracticability except Montgomery's." Higginson felt a need to point out his effort and exonerate himself to others, as well as to himself. "As I cannot see you in the body," he wrote Aaron Stevens in his prison cell, "I feel a strong wish to stretch out my hand to you once and say *God bless you.* You may not remember me, but I saw you in September, 1856, at Nebraska City when you were coming out of the Territory with Gen. Lane. . . . Death is only a step in life and there is no more reason why we should fear to go from one world into another than from one room to another. . . . The world where John Brown is cannot be a bad one to live in. . . . My wife would have been willing that I should risk my life to save yours had that been possible."[6] Higginson also made sure to let Mary Brown know that he had tried his best to help Stevens and Hazlett. "It gave me great satisfaction," she wrote him, "to think that there was some effort made to save the lives of those poor men."[7]

Gerrit Smith photographed at Matthew Brady's New York studio in the early 1860s, after emerging from the asylum and returning to public life. Photo courtesy Massachusetts Historical Society.

☆

Gerrit Smith—released from the asylum shortly before Christmas, 1859, after being there a little over a month—was judged too unwell to comply with the summons of the Mason Committee. Smith's dispensation came over the strenuous objections of Jefferson Davis, who believed the New York aristocrat was the key to unraveling a malignant, complex, criminal conspiracy to sponsor John Brown. All the members of the Six, Higginson included, must have breathed a sigh of relief when Smith was finally not required to appear. Smith and the committee would not have been a good combination. Smith knew as much about Brown's plans as anyone. On his best day, without undue pressure, he was loudly self-right-eous, hotheaded, unstable, and unpredictable. He could lose his demeanor quite easily. Cool heads, such as Howe and Stearns, would fare better and reveal less under the unimaginative questioning of the committee. Armed with what Smith might have given away, the committee's questions for Howe and Stearns might have been that much more targeted.

John Brown, Jr., hiding out in Ohio, was summoned and refused to appear. An arrest warrant was issued for him as well as for James Redpath and Thaddeus Hyatt, all of whom had ignored their summonses and were now in contempt of Congress. Of these, only Thaddeus Hyatt was arrested. Appearing in chains before the committee, Hyatt refused to render testi-mony and was committed to the jail of the District of Columbia. A sum-mons for Lewis Hayden was not served when it was realized Hayden was black.[8] Sanborn was reported to the Senate as a contumacious witness, and his arrest voted, on February 16, 1860. On the heels of that, Sanborn retired once more to Canada in the latter part of February, stopping at North Elba on his way. By late March, Ebenezer Rockwood Hoar, himself a peripheral supporter of Brown, wrote Sanborn to say he thought the thing was done with: that there would be no formal attempt at arrest. San-born decided to relax and return home to Concord, where he found Hoar was quite wrong: U.S. marshals came with a warrant for him on April 3.

At seven o'clock that evening, Sanborn and his sister Sarah went out to make calls. Sarah returned alone at nine o'clock. As she approached the house, running because it was cold, a man on the opposite side of the way followed her along, "but when I reached the gate he was not to be seen, and I thought no more about [it]," recalled Sarah. "Mr. Sanborn returned soon after, locked the door, and put out the entry light. In our absence a young man had come in and up stairs. He [had] wanted to see Mr. Sanborn, had a note for him which he declined to leave, and asked if he might wait. Julia [Julia Leary, the maid] was suspicious, —she offered to take the note, —but refused to let him wait, saying 'it is a pretty time of night for you to be waiting for the gentleman; you can come again in the morning.'" After Sanborn returned home, the maid went to bed in a distant part of the house. Sanborn put on his dressing gown and slippers and sat down to his evening work—writing—and Sarah went with a book to the opposite room. "I had scarcely read a page when some one knocked," wrote Sarah. "I did not think it prudent for Mr. S. to go open the door in the night time, but he did not share in my opinion. I took my lamp and went quickly to answer the knock, but when I came to the top of the stair Mr. Sanborn had already opened the door and was speaking. I listened and knew by the tone of his voice that he was in trouble. Carrying the lamp, I ran down stairs. Mr. Sanborn was standing near the open door, as in the act of showing his visitor in, between two men, one of whom held a paper in his hand. I couldn't tell whether he was trying to read from it or not. I don't know whether they held him or not. Mr. Sanborn said to me 'these men pretend to arrest me without showing any authority for it; go and' (hesitating a moment) 'call Col. Whiting.'"

Sarah started to do so, but met three more men waiting in front of the house, who tried to stop her. "Then I screamed 'murder' and ran into the street. One of the men said, with a sneer, 'that's enough,' and ran after me, apparently to stop me, but he only went to the gate and whistled, and a carriage which was standing a few rods off up the street started to come towards us. I went to the nearest house, found a woman, and told her that five men were arresting Mr. Sanborn and she must go to Col. Whiting's. Then I ran toward Mr. Bigelow's until they heard me scream 'murder' and opened their windows. I said 'five men are arresting Mr. Sanborn.' I then ran back to our house. All this must have taken three minutes."

When Sarah returned to the house, she saw that the carriage was at the gate. The driver stood by four horses. Four men were in the act of putting Sanborn into the carriage, two lifting his shoulders and two his legs. His slippers had fallen off and he was handcuffed. The side of the carriage was broken, as if there had been a previous unsuccessful attempt to put him into it. He was saying, in a voice frightfully loud, "Murder, these men are carrying me off without any authority whatever." Springing to her brother's aid, Sarah caught one of the arresting marshals by the beard. "He loosed his hold of Mr. S., who now came down upon his feet, and turned upon me but did not strike me," wrote Sarah. "As soon as my fingers were out of his beard, he turned back, and they again lifted up their prisoner. I took the whip from the carriage and struck the horses. They jumped forward taking the carriage out of the reach of the men. The driver got possession of the whip, and I then found a strip of wood lying on the ground, with which I struck the horses, and the second time they jumped forward leaving the men behind. This was their fifth attempt to put Mr. S. into the carriage."[9]

Soon the whole town of Concord was up and about. Church bells chimed a call to battle. The air was electric. It was as though the British were coming once more to challenge the patriots of Concord. A lawyer shouted to Sanborn to ask if he wished to petition for a writ of habeas corpus. Sanborn answered that he did. "In this manner a crowd quickly collected, including Mr. Sanborn's largest boys [students], who ran in a body to his rescue," remembered Frank Preston Stearns, who as a student at the Sanborn School witnessed the event. "One of them was a Southerner, named Mason, who had often cursed his master for an abolitionist, but was now foremost in his defence. The cause of the marshals seemed hopeless, but they still held on to their prisoner. In less than twenty minutes Emerson appeared, although he lived half a mile away; and immediately after Judge Hoar came holding up the promised writ of habeas corpus. Before the mandate of the law, the officers were compelled to give way. They took the bracelets off Mr. Sanborn's wrists, and left the town followed by the execration of the populace."[10]

A hearing was held in Boston on the following day, April 4, before Massachusetts State Supreme Court chief justice Lemuel Shaw. John Andrew and Samuel Sewall served as counsel for Sanborn, for whom the case was won on a technicality of irregular procedure."[11] That evening, in Concord, there was an enthusiastic celebration at the town hall. Higginson gave a vigorous speech in which he congratulated the citizens for their successful act of resistance. The brave Sarah Sanborn was presented with a revolver. Within days, the United States marshals were handed a state indictment for felonious assault.

☆

The majority report of the Mason Committee, authored by Mason himself, summarized and roundly condemned the support for Brown demonstrated by Northern sympathizers. "Dr. Howe," wrote Mason, "holds the highest professional and social position in the city of Boston. . . . Mr. Stearns is a merchant in the same city, of wealth and with all the influence usually attending it. With such elements at work, unchecked by law and not rebuked but encouraged by public opinion, with money freely contributed and placed in irresponsible hands, it may easily be seen how this expedition to excite servile war in one of the States of the Union was got up, and it may equally be seen how like expeditions may certainly be anticipated in future whenever desperadoes offer themselves to carry them into execution."

Mason also singled out Gerrit Smith's support for Brown. "This gentleman, Mr. Smith, is known to the country as a man of large wealth and a liberal contributor to this pretended 'cause.' By reason of his very infirm health he was not summoned as a witness before the committee; [but checks and letters from Smith to Brown serve as] persuasive proof of the utter insecurity of the peace and safety of some of the States of this Union, in the existing condition of the public mind and its purposes in the nonslaveholding States. It may not become the committee to suggest a duty in those States to provide by proper legislation against machinations by their citizens or within their borders destructive of the peace of their confederate republics; but it does become them fully to expose the consequences resulting from the present license there existing, because the peace and integrity of the Union is necessarily involved in its continuance."

Mason wrote further that "the committee cannot but remark on the feeble, and, as it resulted, the abortive effort of the chairman of the Massachusetts committee [Stearns] to prevent a murderous use of [the arms in Brown's possession]; certainly in striking contrast with the assurance given by Dr. Howe to Mr. Wilson, that prompt measures had been taken, and would be resolutely followed, to prevent such a 'monstrous perversion of the trust' connected with them. But a perusal of the testimony at large of Mr. Stearns may show that he had at best but vague and undefined opinions as to what would be a perversion of the trust spoken of by Dr. Howe." Mason also found damning the evidence that after the revelations of Forbes, and after Brown's "treasonable proceedings at

Chatham," Brown "went back to New England, traveled through its several villages, collecting money, which was freely contributed under the auspices both of Dr. Howe and Mr. Chairman Stearns and others, with a knowledge that he retained the large supply of arms of which they had failed to dispossess him."[12]

Writing the minority opinion, Jacob Collamer said, "There is no evidence that any other citizens than those there with Brown were accessory to this outbreak or invasion, by contributions thereto or otherwise, nor any proof that any others had any knowledge of the conspiracy or its purposes in the year 1859, though Realf, Forbes, and some very few may have understood it in 1858, when it failed of execution." Collamer continued, "Although some of the testimony tends to show that some abolitionists have at times contributed money to what is occasionally called practical abolitionism—that is, in aiding the escape of slaves—and may have placed too implicit confidence in John Brown, yet there is no evidence to show, or cause to believe, they had any complicity with this conspiracy, or any suspicion of its existence or design, before its explosion."[13]

The Mason Committee closed its investigation and issued its report on June 15, 1860. Just a month before this, far away in distant Florence, Theodore Parker died. Several months after Parker's death, Sam and Julia Ward Howe were among those present at the Massachusetts State House to watch John Andrew—now governor of the Commonwealth—present the state legislature with a gift bequeathed to it by the late minister: the British rifle Parker's grandfather had captured at the battle of Lexington. "After a brief but very appropriate address," remembered Julia Ward Howe, "the governor pressed the gun to his lips before giving it into the keeping of the official guardian of such treasures."[14] In the end, one of the most precious gifts Parker had to leave the people of his state was the relic of a man who, like John Brown, had insisted on exacting blood payment for liberty's absence.

The Howes had a stranger souvenir by which to remember Parker. For some reason that Dr. Howe couldn't quite fathom, the Florentine physicians who tended Parker at his death sent Howe his old friend's brain floating in a jar. Howe was horrified, as was his entire household.

The brain was placed on the top shelf of a back cupboard, after which the family did their best to forget that it was there.

☆

When the Civil War began in April 1861, it was accompanied by an immediate fear for the safety of the city of Washington. Higginson conceived a scheme for recalling Montgomery and his men from Kansas and going with them into the mountains of Virginia, there to engage in guerrilla activity to divert the attention of the Confederacy from the capital. Like the two would-be rescues of Brown and the one of Stevens and Hazlett, this dramatic effort by Higginson never got off the ground. Neither did a subsequent notion of Higginson's to equip a company of men for John Brown, Jr., to command on the Pennsylvania/Virginia border, including the region of Harpers Ferry. "I want at least to get the name of John Brown rumored on the border and then the whole party may come back and go to bed—they will frighten Virginia into fits all the same."

When Higginson traveled to Pennsylvania intending to propose the scheme to Governor Curtin, he carried with him a glowing letter of recommendation from Governor Andrew of Massachusetts. But Andrew wrote another letter to Curtin to follow up the one Higginson carried. In the second note, Andrew warned Curtin that Higginson was "a man capable of facing great perils, of gallant and ardent spirit, *and one whose plans I would not endorse in blank or in advance.*" After meeting with Higginson, Curtin wrote to Andrew that such a move as Higginson recommended would precipitate an immediate border war between Virginia and Pennsylvania, and that the time had not yet arrived for such a thing. Furthermore, should Higginson enter western Virginia with a force headed by John Brown, Jr., it would destroy whatever loyal sentiment still abided in that part of the state, and also influence people in Kentucky, Tennessee, and Missouri in a negative way.[15] Curtin vetoed the plot on his own authority just a few days before receiving urgent orders from Lincoln, who'd been apprised of Higginson's plan by a nervous Andrew, to do precisely that.

THE TRUE BELIEVER

FRANKLIN SANBORN'S OLD friend John Brown once told him he was too young to be married to a gravestone. In mid-1862, Sanborn finally conquered his longstanding grief over the death of Ariana Walker and married his cousin Louisa Augusta Leavitt, who would bear him three sons. At about the same time that he married Louisa, Sanborn shut down his school, the Civil War having reduced attendance dramatically by relegating older boys to the service and young southern students to schools within the Confederacy.

In 1863, Sanborn succeeded Moncure Daniel Conway as editor of the *Boston Commonwealth,* holding that post for seven months. He was to serve as resident editor of the *Springfield Republican* from 1868 through 1872, and would go on to author more than twenty influential nonfiction books. At the same time, he was very active in public life. In 1863, Governor Andrew appointed Sanborn Secretary of the Massachusetts State Board of Charities—the first office of its kind in the United States. Defining the position as he went, Sanborn instituted a system of inspection and report for state charities that has since been widely copied, made himself an expert on the care of the insane, and drafted many bills that were enacted into law. He retired as secretary in 1868 but remained on the board, serving as its chairman from 1874 to 1876. From 1879 to 1888 he was General State Inspector of Charities. He was also an officer of the American Social Science Association, the National Prison Association, the National Conference of Charities, the Clarke School for the Deaf, the Massachusetts Infant Asylum, and the National Conference of Charities and Corrections. And he lectured at Cornell University, Smith College, and Wellesley College while also founding, with William Torrey Harris and Bronson Alcott, the Concord School of Philosophy.

As the years accumulated, Sanborn became a venerable figure. Wealth, fame, and prestige were his. And he regularly used all three to promote the favorable memory of John Brown while at the same time providing for the general welfare of the Brown family.

In June of 1881, Franklin Sanborn wrote to John Brown's widow, Mary, in Santa Clara County, California, where she was living with her daughter Sarah. Sanborn said that some of John Brown's friends in the East thought of raising a fund, the interest to be applied for her benefit. He asked about her circumstances and whether such a fund would be appropriate or necessary. Sanborn's former student Sarah Brown answered for her mother, saying she was in no great financial distress, but that Mary was grateful for the gesture of Sanborn and his colleagues all the same.

In mid-July of 1882, Sanborn heard once more from Sarah. The daughter of John and Mary Brown wrote Sanborn of an article in the *San Francisco Bulletin* stating that a fund for Brown's family had in fact been gotten up, "the interest of which has been placed in the hands of trustees to be given to any of the family who in their judgement need it." If indeed the fund was established, wrote Sarah, then her mother and no one else should be the recipient even though her mother was not destitute. "As one of the family, I think there are none of them who need it but her. They are all able-bodied men or have husbands to take care of them, and as for me I have enough. The family have never supported mother and she has at times worked very hard and helped her children more than they could her. If now anything has been given for her comfort, I think it would be a shame to give it to any of them or for them to receive it. Mother lost her support by the death of her husband but most of the family were taking care of themselves at the time of their father's death and would not have received any further support from him if he had lived. I don't see any reason why they should not continue to take care of themselves." Although Mary Brown was not in any "distressing need," added Sarah, whatever was in the fund would certainly "add to her comfort."[1]

A small fund had indeed been started by Sanborn, Emerson, Higginson, John Russell, John Greenleaf Whittier, and several others; now Sanborn saw to it that Mary Brown was its beneficiary. "Mrs. Brown received the income of this fund while she lived," wrote Sanborn in 1885, "and at her death we sent $150 to her daughter to pay the expenses of her last illness." After Mary Brown's death, a cash account of more than a thousand dollars was left. Several hundred dollars was put into real estate investments. All of these funds were earmarked for the long-term benefit of Brown's children.

The money was not always well used. Like their father before them, neither Jason nor Salmon Brown were shrewd men of business. "What you say of your mother's legacy, and what became of it, is indeed a surprise," wrote Sanborn to Ruth Thompson in 1892. "It was a great pity the $600 had not come into your hands, rather than have it lost in Salmon's speculations. As to anything further from our small fund, I cannot say."[2] Jason Brown was no better. In the same year, a California friend of the Brown family wrote Sanborn explicitly warning him not to allow any money out of the fund to find its way to Jason Brown. "Jason sold over $4000 worth of land and water when he was here, and could and should have paid all his debts," wrote the friend. "Instead of that, he paid a little on each one, and then gave and frittered away the rest of the money. I like Jason Brown, but he is wholly incorrigible in money matters. If all his debts were paid today, he would be in just the same condition a year hence. I never saw his like outside of fiction, and very seldom in. When he was here he took money he should have used on his debts to go East to see his family. Now he is with them, and knows that his relatives here are anxious for him not to come here. He will never rest until he borrows enough to come here and burden them and shame us all by his borrowing; and in about a year he will be equally zealous to return or go somewhere else; and we shall have to take up a collection again to send him off. . . . I do not speak in any hardness. It is the simple truth, as I have learned to my cost, though he is not owing me. It is a real unkindness to loan him money or give him anything but cooked food."[3] Sanborn told Ruth Thompson that he was cutting off Jason altogether. "I am afraid we cannot be of much service to him [Jason] pecuniarily," wrote Sanborn, "for money placed in his hands does not answer any very useful purpose, as we see by the past."[4]

☆

Thirty-five years after John Brown's execution, the old man continued to make headlines in Virginia. And the Secret Six remained less secret than they would have cared to be. A three-column article in the *Richmond Dispatch* for Tuesday, August 7, 1894, was headed: "John Brown's Raid: The Atrocious Proposition to Erect a Monument to the Outlaw." The monument was to be raised at Harpers Ferry: a granite shaft costing $10,000 to $12,000 built on land donated by the Baltimore and Ohio Railroad Company. The writer for the *Richmond Dispatch*, D. H. Panhill, would have none of it: "This we can only regard as an atrocious proposition, against which we owe it to ourselves, to the memory of our fathers, to the gallant Confederate soldiers, living and dead, to protest in a manner that cannot be mistaken."

"A friend of mine," wrote Sanborn to Panhill shortly after publication of the article, "has sent me your interesting journal for August 7, (for I seldom see it), containing a long and angry protest, mingled with many historical errors, against the proposed monument to my noble old friend, John Brown, at Harpers Ferry. I have taken no part in the movement for such a monument, believing that, of all men I have ever known, the fearless emancipator of negro slaves, of whom several millions for whom he died were set free within four years after his martyrdom, least requires a monument to perpetuate his fame. Another correspondent of yours, in the same issue, proposes a monument to Governor Wise at Harpers Ferry, —a brave, passionate Virginian, whose name will be preserved from oblivion chiefly by his connection with the legal murder of John Brown."

Sanborn gave Panhill a compromise proposal for a monument "which ought to be welcomed by every Virginian, whether living in the old eastern portion, or in the new State of West Virginia, which contains the site of Brown's heroic, desperate, but triumphant deed, and the place of his execution." What Sanborn suggested was a statue of Virginia's favorite son Thomas Jefferson, author of the Declaration of Independence, holding in his hand a scroll inscribed with his prophetic words, written in 1781, in which he anticipated the coming struggle for the emancipation, by force, of the slave. Jefferson's exact words were: "I tremble for my country when I reflect that God is just; that his justice can not sleep forever. The Almighty has no attribute which can take side with us in such a contest. The way, I hope, is preparing for the total emancipation; and this is disposed to be with the consent of the masters, rather than by their extirpation."

"The prophecy of your far-seeing Virginian has been accomplished," wrote Sanborn to Panhill. "John Brown was a Jeffersonian, willing to give his life for its fulfillment, as he did. A monument to Jefferson, bearing this inscription, and nothing more, will be a better recognition of Brown's services than any that may recall his name; and I can hardly suppose that any Virginian will oppose such a tribute to your greatest political philosopher." Sanborn closed by saying that if Panhill's readers would go to Sanborn's *Life and Letters of John Brown* or his biography of Samuel Gridley Howe, they would "find the truth about Brown and his friends accurately stated, without fear, favor, or hope of reward."[5]

"I have heard nothing from the *Richmond Dispatch,* from which I infer that my letter was not published," wrote Sanborn to Samuel May, Jr., that September. "I will write to the editor and inquire. I should have supposed that a Virginian, in whose newspaper a gentleman and a stranger has been attacked, would allow him to say a word moderately on the issues raised; and perhaps it is merely inadvertence on the part of the Editor, in not sending me the paper, (as I requested, and as is customary). . . . I kept no copy of my letter, —but sent several to friends, — among others to John Brown, Jr., at Put-in-Bay, Ohio, —so that it may see the light in some Western newspaper. If you still have the copy I sent you, and will send it to me, I will perhaps publish it in the N.Y. *Sun,* which has a considerable Southern circulation, and the editor of which has lately asked me to write something for him."[6]

☆

Even after the turn of the century, Sanborn still felt compelled to take some measure of responsibility for the children and grandchildren of the man he'd helped put on the gallows. And the Brown family was, apparently, still quite willing to come to the remnants of the Secret Six for support. Salmon Brown ended up living in Oregon, where he was to commit suicide in 1919. In November of 1902, Sanborn briefly flirted with a plan to have Agnes and Nell Brown (daughters of Salmon), and one Grover (to whom Nell was engaged), go about "theatrically, and talk about their Grandfather, John Brown, and his work. They have all had experience in public performances. Nell, now about 24 years old, has been in the Salvation Army, and is a speaker and musician . . . ," wrote Sanborn to Higginson. "Agnes thinks it will pay, and wants a loan of money to begin with. Last summer they held meetings in a number of Oregon towns, and say they were very successful. Their plan is to come east as far as New York."[7] Sanborn failed to find backers for the project and the tour did not come off.

When Oswald Garrison Villard brought out his lucid and startlingly candid account of Brown's life in 1910, Sanborn condemned it. Among Villard's sins, in Sanborn's eyes, was his calling the Pottawatomie executions "murders." Sanborn—who for so long denied the very fact of the deaths along the Pottawatomie—now rationalized them as "an act of war." Sanborn also did not like Villard's portrayal of Brown as a restless, dissatisfied renegade who merely bumbled into being an icon of liberty.[8]

Franklin Sanborn in old age. Throughout his long life, Sanborn consistently defended Brown, the raid at Harpers Ferry, and the activities of the Secret Six. Photo courtesy Boston Public Library.

"I knew John Brown for a few years only," wrote Sanborn in 1916, less than a year before his death, "but I knew him intimately. From the first I honored him and the more I learned of his life the more I honored him. It is now 57 years since his death, and I have had no occasion to change my opinion. John Brown and Abraham Lincoln were the two most illustrious martyr-heroes of their time."[9] Sanborn attempted no apologies for Brown; he did not think he needed them. "[Brown] knew the inward cancer that was feeding on this republic," wrote Sanborn in 1897. "He pointed to the knife and the cautery that must extirpate it; he even had the force and nerve to make the first incision."[10]

After Sanborn's death on February 24, 1917, the House of Representatives of the Commonwealth of Massachusetts adopted a bill applauding him for his dedication to "the diseased, the unfortunate and the despised." The resolution gave special mention to Sanborn's role as "confidential adviser to John Brown of Harpers Ferry, for whose sake he was ostracized, maltreated and subjected to the indignity of false arrest, having been saved from deportation from Massachusetts only by mob violence."[11]

25

EPILOGUE

IN JANUARY OF 1863, George Luther Stearns held a quiet, dignified ceremony at his fine mansion in Medford. Sam and Julia Ward Howe were among the guests, as were Franklin Sanborn, Ralph Waldo Emerson, Wendell Phillips, and John Murray Forbes. Also in attendance was the sculptor Edwin Brackett, creator of the work about to be dedicated. Thomas Wentworth Higginson, now a colonel busy commanding a black regiment of Union soldiers near Beaufort, South Carolina, sent his regrets. (In his note to Stearns, who himself was a leader in the drive for black recruitment, Higginson told of how one of his infantry, in being asked insultingly, "What are you, anyhow?" answered "When God made me, I wasn't much, but I'm a *man* now.") Gerrit Smith did not respond to Stearns's fine, engraved invitation; nor did he show up.

Standing beside the black-shrouded work of art that all were anxious to see, Wendell Phillips made a brief speech. Then Julia Ward Howe recited her "Battle Hymn of the Republic" in what Stearns's son Frank recalled as a "weird, penetrating voice." And Ralph Waldo Emerson recited his abolitionist ballad "The Boston Hymn," inspired as it was by the Massachusetts rebellion against the fugitive slave law.

Then, when the speeches and readings were done, the black coverlet of the sculpture was pulled away to reveal a superb, heroic bust of John Brown. Light, dignified applause was aimed in the direction of the artist. The shy Brackett took his compliment graciously, modestly. He nodded his thanks, directed his eyes to the floor, and muttered something about how the greatness was in the man the work represented, rather than in the work.

At the end of the day, after the guests departed and the statue was left to gaze forlornly from a corner of Stearns's elaborate, Victorian foyer, the black caterer Stearns had engaged for the occasion refused to render a bill. This was a fugitive slave whom Stearns had set up in business several years before. The man insisted that he would donate his services. Only with great difficulty was he at last persuaded to accept a check for one hundred dollars, which Stearns wound up thrusting into the man's overcoat pocket as the caterer endeavored to drive away in his wagon.[1]

☆

Higginson's wife, Mary Channing Higginson, died of intestinal fever in September of 1877. Higginson—popularly called "Colonel Higginson" in honor of his Civil War exploits—married for the second time in February of 1879. His new bride, Mary Thacher, whom he met in Boston, came from a leading Harpers Ferry family. Not long after the marriage, Higginson made his first visit to Harpers Ferry in order to meet his bride's kindred. The welcome awarded him was decidedly different from that given his old friend John Brown twenty years earlier. Somewhat ironically, Higginson's reception included the loan of a black retainer to serve him for the duration of his stay. "Our arriving was an excitement to all Harpers Ferry," he recalled. "All knew that the bridal party was coming. In the evening came Jacob [the black servant]. He brought the largest round of beef I ever saw . . . also a basket of provisions and himself most important of all. He cooked, talked, waited at table in a Madras turban. . . ."

John Brown was not out of Higginson's mind, however. "We went to Charlestown, eight miles, a flourishing village with nice houses and buildings," he wrote. "Here we saw the jail yard where John Brown was confined, the field where he was executed, the new court house on the site where he was tried . . . the road we came was that over which they were brought, wounded, from Harpers Ferry. The only memorial of him at the latter place is the little building close by the railroad—the engine house which he held—which has 'John Brown's Fort' painted on it."[2]

☆

Through the years there were sporadic, hushed visits to John Brown's lonesome Adirondack grave. Higginson, Sanborn, and Stearns each went alone, without fanfare, more than once—although Howe and Smith did not. At first, the visits were ostensibly to the Brown family, the remnants of which lingered at the spot for a few short years before resuming that nomadism that had always been typical of Brown and his brood. Only after Mary departed for territories west did the visits become more blatantly a function of decades-long mourning. Only then did they become more clearly pilgrimages to a shrine.

After Mary was gone, the modest house became, for a time, an open, abandoned place. It was here that the amateur naturalist Higginson, characteristically combining his pilgrimage to the grave with his passion for ornithology and robust hikes, tossed the knapsack and binoculars he'd carried through the woods from the train station many miles distant. For Stearns, the house was a place where his carriage driver was instructed to wait while the master stood for an hour or more by the rock below which was Brown. And for Sanborn, during a long and strange night in the late 1870s, the house was a place where he slept alone and awoke after midnight to see the ghostly silhouette of his long-dead friend swinging from a noose.[3]

Who can say whether the house was—or is—haunted? Or the spot?

But we know that Higginson, Sanborn, and Stearns were haunted. And we know that even Smith, swimming in an ocean of denial, was equally haunted, if from a distance. We know less about Howe, who had an odd propensity for eschewing responsibility, kinship, friends. We do not know whether or not a white-bearded ghost stalked him as it did the others. We, in the end, doubt it. Howe was neither intimidated by nor in natural awe of larger-than-life heroes. He was considered by many a larger-than-life hero himself. He had, after all, been on a first-name basis with Paul Revere, Lafayette, and Dickens. While not unimpressed with John Brown, Howe was not likely to consider Brown unique among his legendary acquaintances.

Once, in the 1870s, Sanborn tried to interest an aging James Redpath in coming with him to Brown's grave. But Redpath was busy with the lecture agency he had recently taken over—the Boston Lyceum Bureau. Ironically, Redpath was also preoccupied with the cowriting of Jefferson Davis's unapologetic memoir, *A Short History of the Confederate States.* Thus he had no time to visit the bones of Brown, the martyr who had served as the subject for his first major success in publishing. But Sanborn visited the grave, as did Higginson and Stearns—again and again. After Stearns died, in the late 1860s, it was Sanborn and Higginson who, in individual annual visits, would kick up the leaves above the grave, stand silent, and meditate on who John Brown was, what his story meant, and how history would treat them all.

"We did what we did," an unreformed Higginson wrote a friend a few years before the close of his life. "In the end, we were trying to do right. And I believe, in the greatest measure, we *did* do right. The result of the attack at Harpers Ferry, the hastening of inevitable disunion and civil war, was good, healthy, positive. My one perennial wish, however, is that we would have achieved that end without the sacrifice of Brown. I persist in the belief that I, at least, could and should have realized the need to protect John Brown from himself. I should have recognized how incapable he was; I should have perceived the madness that dwelled within him, —the insanity that sat stealthily beside his great, selfless nobility. A counter-proposal to his Harpers Ferry scheme should have been made: something that would have both attracted and protected Brown. In retrospect, I think the bombing of a few fine southern buildings, or a few famous southern men, with notes crediting the blasts to some choice northern abolitionist groups, would have done the job. Such action would have brought disunion quickly, and without risk to any from our side. The Russian revolutionists, who were so efficient in making the tyrant Tsar Alexander II explode, have much to teach us about practical terror."[4]

In the end, Higginson was still the same romantic, impetuous seeker after justice he had always been. The elderly, voyeuristic revolutionary was simply more pragmatic now; and he was fascinated with the modern, strategic potential of combustibles for delivering remote, anonymous violence. Fifty years after Harpers Ferry he wrote that, given the same circumstances that confronted him in 1859, he would still take the law into his own hands and send violence into sovereign southern states. He would just do it through different means; and he would take it upon himself to protect an unbalanced, deluded friend from the risk of needless martyrdom.

In writing of "the insanity that sat stealthily beside [the] great, selfless nobility" of Brown, Higginson put his finger on the complex conundrum of the man who was at once a devout Christian, a devious business-person, a cold-blooded murderer, a terrorist, and a selfless martyr. Higginson's attitude toward Brown was paternalistic yet lionizing, condescending yet hero-worshipful. In short, it was confused. But this confusion was a necessary one, for Brown was confusion, chaos, and irrationality personified. The parts of him that were good, were very good. The parts of him that were bad, were very bad. Higginson once wrote that there were "few elements in the tale of Harpers Ferry that are strictly either black or white. Most elements of the story . . . are quite *gray*."[5] The grayest of things in this strange and vital story—for Higginson and the balance of the Secret Six, as well as for all of us—remains Brown himself: a unique and troubling blend of the martyr and the murderer, a puzzle to remain forever unsolved.

N o t e s

PROLOGUE: REUNION

1 Located in the state of Virginia before partitioning, Harpers Ferry is today in the state of West Virginia.

2 Nathan K. Sebastian, "Fifty Years After Harpers Ferry," New York-Tribune, 16 October 1909.

3 Louise Hall Tharp, Three Saints and a Sinner (Boston: Houghton Mifflin, 1956), 4.

4 Katherine Mayo went on to have a distinguished career as an author, with the best known of her many books being the classic Mother India.

5 Oswald Garrison Villard was the son of Henry Villard, Bavarian-born journalist and financier who died at the turn of the century after a career during which he enjoyed a close personal friendship with the Springfield attorney Abraham Lincoln, participated in the Pike's Peak gold rush (1859), married a daughter of William Lloyd Garrison (1869), wrote several books, acquired controlling interest in the Oregon and California railways (1870s), served as president of the Northern Pacific (1881–84), stood in as a founding partner of the Edison General Electric Company (1889), and acquired the New York Evening Post (1881). Oswald Garrison Villard served as editorial writer for the New York Evening Post (1897–1918), of which he was owner and president after the death of his father. Villard purchased the Nation in 1908 and served as editor until 1933. He authored several books in addition to the John Brown biography, including Fighting Years (1939), an autobiography. With Joel Springarn, W. E. B. Du Bois, and others, Villard was a founder of the NAACP.

6 Katherine Mayo, notes on meeting of 17 October 1909 with Franklin Sanborn, Thomas Wentworth Higginson, and Julia Ward Howe at Concord, Villard Papers, Columbia University.

7 Higginson to Mayo, Boston, 1 September 1909, Villard Papers, Columbia University.

8 Higginson, Letter to the Editor, Liberator, 28 May 1858.

9 Brown told Frederick Douglass in 1847 that armed rebellion would give black men "a sense of their manhood." He added that "no people could have self-respect, or be respected, who would not fight for their freedom." Stephen B. Oates, To Purge This Land with Blood (New York: Harper & Row, 1970), 63.

10 Sanborn to Higginson, Concord, 14 August 1909, Higginson Papers, Boston Public Library.

11 Higginson, Diary, Boston, 29 September 1909, Higginson Papers, Houghton Library, Harvard University.

12 Higginson to Gilder, Newport, 14 August 1907, Berg Collection, New York Public Library.

13 *Partial* letter from Higginson to Sanborn that is attached to a responding note from Sanborn to Higginson, Concord, 17 November 1859, Higginson Papers, Boston Public Library.

14 Higginson to Smith, Worcester, 7 July 1859, author's collection.

15 Franklin Sanborn, "Reminiscences of John Brown and His Friends, By One of Them: Remarks at the Meeting of the Mendon Historical Society Held in Bellingham, MA, June 22, 1911," typescript in Folder #4 in Sanborn's box of Brown-related material, Houghton Library, Harvard University.

16 Higginson to Oswald Garrison Villard, Boston, 12 November 1909, Villard Papers, Columbia University.

1. THE SECRET UNSPOKEN

1 Octavius Brooks Frothingham, *Gerrit Smith: A Biography* (Boston: Houghton Mifflin, 1878), 253–54.

2 Testimony of John Brown, Jr., taken at Sandusky, Ohio, 19 July 1867, Kansas State Historical Society.

3 Frederick Douglass, *Life and Times of Frederick Douglass* (Hartford: Park Publishing Co., 1881), 318.

4 Sanborn, narrative with typescript copy of letter from Sanborn to Gerrit Smith, Concord, 13 October 1872, in Folder #5 in Sanborn's box of Brown-related materials, Houghton Library, Harvard University.

5 Smith to Sanborn, Peterboro, 19 October 1872, typescript copy in Folder #5 in Sanborn's box of Brown-related materials, Houghton Library, Harvard University.

6 Sanborn, undated typescript narrative in Folder #5 in Sanborn's box of Brown-related materials, Houghton Library, Harvard University.

7 All general information regarding Gerrit Smith is from Octavius Brooks Frothingham's biography.

2. A DREAM OF MOUNTAINS

1 James Redpath, *The Public Life of Captain John Brown . . . with an Autobiography of His Childhood and Youth* (Boston: Thayer & Eldridge, 1860), 59.

2 Douglass, *Life and Times*, 277.

3 Franklin Sanborn, *The Life and Letters of John Brown, Liberator of Kansas and Martyr of Virginia* (Boston: Roberts Brothers, 1885), 33.

4 Gill to Richard Hinton, 7 July 1893. See also Gill's "Reminiscences." Hinton Papers, Kansas State Historical Society.

5 Douglass, *Life and Times*, 277–80.

6 Sanborn, *The Life and Letters of John Brown*, 57.

7 Oates, *To Purge This Land*, 62–63.

8   John Brown to Owen Brown, 10 January 1849, Brown Papers, Kansas State Historical Society.

9   Thomas Wentworth Higginson, *Contemporaries* (Boston: Houghton Mifflin, 1900), 219–44.

10 Richard Henry Dana, Jr., "How We Met John Brown," undated manuscript, Houghton Library, Harvard University.

11 Higginson, *Contemporaries,* 242.

12 Douglass, *Life and Times,* 280.

13 Brown to "Dear sons John, Jason, Frederick & Daughters," 4 December 1850, Brown Papers, Ohio Historical Society.

3. THE CHEVALIER

1   Higginson to Villard, 29 May 1910, Houghton Library, Harvard University.

2   Laura Richards & Maude Howe Elliott, *Julia Ward Howe, 1819–1910,* vol. 1. (Boston: Houghton Mifflin, 1916), 72.

3   Julia Ward Howe, *Reminiscences, 1819–1899* (Boston: Houghton Mifflin, 1900), 117–18.

4   Howe to Wilson, Boston, 23 January 1860, Howe Papers, Massachusetts Historical Society.

5   Franklin Sanborn, *Dr. S. G. Howe, the Philanthropist,* American Reformers Series (New York: Funk & Wagnalls, 1891), 22.

6   Richards & Elliott, *Julia Ward Howe,* 77–78.

7   Julia Ward Howe, Diary, 2 April 1880, Howe Papers, Houghton Library, Harvard University.

8   Parker to Howe, Boston, 31 December 1854, Parker Papers, Moorland-Springarn Research Center, Howard University.

9   Richards & Elliott, *Julia Ward Howe,* 169.

10 Higginson, *Thomas Wentworth Higginson,* 111.

11 Harold Schwartz, *Samuel Gridley Howe, Social Reformer* (Cambridge: Harvard University Press, 1956), 182–83.

12 Felton to Howe, Boston, 2 April 1851, Howe Papers, Houghton Library, Harvard University.

13 Richards & Elliott, *Julia Ward Howe,* 101.

14 Higginson, *Contemporaries,* 294–95.

4. ONE BRIGHT, CLEAR FLASH

1   Sanborn to Parker, Quebec, 22 October 1859, Sanborn's typed transcript in Folder #2 of Sanborn's box of Brown-related material, Houghton Library, Harvard University.

2   Oates, *To Purge This Land,* 319.

3   Sanborn to Parker, Concord, 14 November 1859, typescript copy in Folder #2 in Sanborn's box of Brown-related material, Houghton Library, Harvard University.

4   Howe, *Reminiscences,* 160.

5 Charles Capper, *Margaret Fuller: An American Romantic Life—The Private Years* (New York: Oxford University Press, 1992), 318–19.

6 Gay Wilson Allen, *Waldo Emerson* (New York: Viking Press, 1981), 600.

7 Sanborn, partial, undated typescript in Folder #5 of Sanborn's box of Brown-related material, Houghton Library, Harvard University.

8 Henry Steele Commager, ed., *Theodore Parker: An Anthology.* (Boston: Houghton Mifflin, 1956), 4.

9 Parker to Howe, Boston, 1 December 1851, Parker Papers, Moorland-Springarn Research Center, Howard University.

10 *Report of the Select Committee of the Senate Appointed to Inquire into the Late Invasion and Seizure of the Public Property at Harpers Ferry,* 167.

11 Howe, *Reminiscences,* 167.

12 Commager, *Theodore Parker,* 243.

13 Ibid., 166.

14 Garry Wills, *Lincoln at Gettysburg: The Words That Remade America* (New York: Simon & Schuster, 1992), 110. In this outstanding book, Wills eloquently argues that Parker (explicitly, his rhetoric citing slavery as an abomination against the principles stated in the Declaration of Independence) was the direct source of several key themes in Lincoln's Gettysburg Address.

15 Howe, *Reminiscences,* 243.

16 John White Chadwick, *Theodore Parker: Preacher and Reformer* (Boston: Houghton Mifflin, 1900), 240.

17 Julia Ward Howe, *A Trip to Cuba* (Boston: Hurd & Houghton, 1860), 234.

18 Social Circle of Concord, Editors, "Address of Thomas Wentworth Higginson," *The Emerson Centenary in Concord, 1903* (Boston: The Riverside Press, 1903), 66.

19 Howe, *Reminiscences,* 161.

20 Parker to Herndon, 17 April 1856, Parker Papers, Massachusetts Historical Society.

21 Thomas Wentworth Higginson, "Theodore Parker," *The Atlantic Monthly*, October 1860.

5. FUGITIVES

1 Theodore Parker, "Daniel Webster," in Henry Steele Commager, ed., *Theodore Parker: An Anthology,* 246–47.

2 Howe, *Reminiscences,* 164–65.

3 William Gilman, ed., *The Journals and Miscellaneous Notebooks of Ralph Waldo Emerson,* vol. 1 (Cambridge: Harvard University Press, 1960), 182.

4 Parker to Higginson, Boston, 27 July 1850. Higginson Papers, Boston Public Library.

5 Parker to Howe, Roxbury, 30 September 1846, Parker Papers,

Moorland-Springarn Research Center, Howard University.

6 Theodore Parker, *The Trial of Theodore Parker for the "Misdemeanor" of a Speech in Faneuil Hall against Kidnapping, Before the Circuit Court of the United States, at Boston, with the Defence* (hereafter referenced as *Defence*), Boston, 1855, 182.

7 Ibid., 187.

8 The Crafts were removed to Liverpool, England, by way of Halifax, Nova Scotia, in late October of 1850. They subsequently returned after the Civil War to establish a communal farm in their native Georgia. A receipt on deposit at the Boston Public Library itemizes $250 in expenses relating to the relocation of the Crafts to England, including $34 in spending money and $9 in railroad tickets for the couple "& a trusty friend with them as far as Portland," Maine. See Francis Jackson's "Account of expenses in sending Wm. & Ellen Craft to England by steam ship via Halifax," Boston. 11 November 1850, Jackson Papers, Boston Public Library.

9 Martin Duberman, *Charles Francis Adams, 1807–1886* (Boston: Houghton Mifflin, 1960), 170.

10 John L. Thomas, *The Liberator: William Lloyd Garrison* (Boston: Little, Brown, 1963), 378–79.

11 Higginson, *Thomas Wentworth Higginson,* 9.

12 Ibid., 85.

13 Ibid., 71–76.

14 Bradford Torrey, ed., *The Journal of Henry Thoreau,* vol. 6 (Boston: Houghton Mifflin, 1906), 358.

15 Howe to Forbes, New York, 5 February 1859, typescript copy in Folder #6 in Sanborn's box of Brown-related material, Houghton Library, Harvard University.

16 Sanborn to Higginson, Concord, 11 February 1858, Higginson Papers, Boston Public Library.

17 Higginson, *Thomas Wentworth Higginson,* 296.

18 Ibid., 87–97.

19 Ibid., 110.

6. RIOT

1 Frank Preston Stearns, *The Life and Public Services of George Luther Stearns* (Philadelphia: J. B. Lippincott, 1907), 84. The author must point out that both Franklin Sanborn and T. W. Higginson believed Frank Preston Stearns's book to be quite unreliable on the topics of John Brown and the Secret Six. Taking my lead from the misgivings of these two actual participants in the story, I here use Frank Stearns's book only as a general source and take no dates or other facts from it. See Sanborn's 21 April 1908 letter to Higginson at the Houghton Library, where Sanborn, in sending Higginson Stearns's book, writes, "That enfant terrible, Frank Stearns, has published the enclosed, which you

may not have seen. . . . I hardly think he has ever conferred with you, or read your collection of Ms. Letters. He is complicating a matter already sufficiently perplexed."

2   Stearns to Howe, Medford, 31 May 1859, Howe Papers, Houghton Library, Harvard University.

3   Higginson to the editors of the *Newburyport Evening News*, Boston, April 1851, Higginson Papers, Boston Public Library.

4   Parker to Howe, Boston, 16 February 1852, Parker Papers, Moorland-Springarn Research Center, Howard University.

5   Samuel J. May, *Some Recollections of Our Anti-Slavery Conflict* (Boston: Hurd & Houghton, 1869), 373–83.

6   John Brown to John Brown, Jr., 4 November 1850, Brown Papers, Ohio Historical Society.

7   Sanborn, *Life and Letters of John Brown,* 124–26.

8   William Wells Brown, *The Independent*, 10 March 1870.

9   Robert D. Richardson, Jr., *Henry David Thoreau: A Life of the Mind* (Berkeley: University of California Press, 1986), 370.

10 Higginson, Letter to the Editor, *Worcester Spy,* 24 May 1854.

11 Ralph Korngold, *Two Friends of Man: The Story of William Lloyd Garrison and Wendell Phillips and Their Relationship with Abraham Lincoln* (Boston: Little, Brown, 1950), 231.

12 Parker, *Defence,* 6.

13 Higginson, *Thomas Wentworth Higginson,* 144.

14 Korngold, *Two Friends of Man,* 229–32.

15 Thomas Wentworth Higginson, *Cheerful Yesterdays* (Boston: Houghton Mifflin, 1898), 152–53.

16 Chadwick, *Theodore Parker: Preacher and Reformer,* 426.

17 Higginson, *Cheerful Yesterdays,* 153–58.

7. REBELLION AGAINST TYRANTS IS OBEDIENCE TO GOD

1   Higginson to Mary Higginson, Boston, 27 May 1854, Higginson Papers, Boston Public Library.

2   Higginson to Louisa Storrow Higginson, Worcester, 29 May 1854, Higginson Papers, Boston Public Library.

3   Higginson to Louisa Storrow Higginson, Worcester, 31 May 1854, Higginson Papers, Boston Public Library.

4   Higginson, to George Luther Stearns, 7 April 1854, Stearns Papers, Boston Historical Society.

5   Higginson "Massachusetts in Mourning. A Sermon Preached in Worcester on Sunday, June 4, 1854." Pamphlet. (Boston: James Munroe & Company, 1854; a copy may be found in the Rare Books & Manuscripts Room, Boston Public Library.)

6 Higginson to Louisa Storrow Higginson, Worcester, 6 June 1854, Higginson Papers, Boston Public Library.

7 Higginson, telegram to Mary Higginson, Boston, 10 June 1854, Higginson Papers, Boston Public Library.

8 Higginson, telegram to F. G. Higginson, 10 June 1854, Higginson Papers, Boston Public Library.

9 Higginson to Louisa Storrow Higginson, Worcester, late June 1854, Higginson Papers, Boston Public Library.

10 Higginson, *Thomas Wentworth Higginson*, 149–50.

11 Parker, *Defence*, 203. The sermon was delivered at the Music Hall on Sunday, 28 May 1854.

12 Ibid., 6–7.

13 John Weiss, *Life and Correspondence of Theodore Parker*, vol. 2 (New York: D. Appleton, 1864), 140.

14 Parker to Howe, Boston, Thursday 1854 (probably a Thursday in December 1854), Parker Papers, Moorland-Springarn Research Center, Howard University. Parker's attorney was the same Hale whose daughter was, unhappily, to be engaged to John Wilkes Booth at the time of the Lincoln assassination.

15 Parker to Howe, Boston, 31 December 1854, Parker Papers, Moorland-Springarn Research Center, Howard University.

16 The attorneys were William L. Burt, H. F. Durant, and John A. Andrew.

17 Commager, *Theodore Parker*, 245.

18 Stearns, *George Luther Stearns*, 90.

8. SHARP'S RIGHTS OF THE PEOPLE

1 Parker to Howe, Boston, 17 April 1853, Parker Papers, Moorland-Springarn Research Center, Howard University.

2 Parker to Herndon, Boston, 2 January 1855, Herndon Papers, Illinois Historical Society.

3 Parker, sermon dated 29 January 1858, Parker Papers, Massachusetts Historical Society.

4 Sanborn, undated, untitled lecture typescript, Sanborn Papers (Boston Public Library).

5 Amos A. Lawrence, *Papers Relating to John Brown, Given to the Massachusetts Historical Society by Amos A. Lawrence, February 12, 1885*, 151. Maggie Moore to Amos A. Lawrence, Chattanooga, 26 May 1885, Lawrence Papers, Massachusetts Historical Society.

6 Charles Robinson, *The Kansas Conflict* (Boston: Hurd & Houghton, 1871), 93–94.

7 Redpath, *Public Life of Captain John Brown*, 51–52.

8 Salmon Brown, undated typescript dictated by Salmon shortly after Jason's death on 24 December 1912, Stutler Collection.

9 George B. Gill, MS interview with K. Mayo, 12 November 1908, Villard Collection, Columbia University.

10 John Brown to Ruth Thompson, 30 September 1854, Brown Papers, Western Reserve Historical Society.

11 John Brown, Jr., to John Brown, Brownsville, Kansas Territory, 24 May 1855, Dreer Collection.

12 John Brown, *A Brief History of John Brown,* Dreer Collection (Historical Society of Pennsylvania).

13 George Washington Brown, articles in the *Lawrence Herald of Freedom* for 15 December 1855 and 29 October 1859.

14 Sanborn, *Recollections of Seventy Years,* vol. 1 (Boston: Gorham Press, 1909), 129.

15 Oswald Garrison Villard, *John Brown: 1800–1859—a Biography Fifty Years After,* rev. ed. (New York: Knopf, 1943), 129.

16 John Brown, Jr., to "Friend Louisa." 29 March 1856, Stutler Collection.

17 Parker to Howe, Boston, 27 December 1855, Parker Papers, Moorland-Springarn Research Center, Howard University.

18 Frothingham, *Theodore Parker,* 439–40, 448.

19 Weiss, *Theodore Parker,* vol. 2, 160.

20 A large number of these same Sharp's rifles would be found in the armory at Harpers Ferry, and at a nearby schoolhouse Brown used for

provisioning, after the John Brown raid. These were the models of 1852 and 1853, with slanted breech and brass mountings, that are now known to contemporary gun collectors as the John Brown Sharp.

21 Frothingham, *Theodore Parker,* 437.

22 Lyman Abbott, *Henry Ward Beecher* (Boston: Houghton Mifflin, 1903), 211–12.

9. GIDEON

1 James Harris, Affidavit, 6 June 1856, "Howard Report," U.S. House Committee Reports, 1855–56, II, 1179–81.

2 Redpath, *Public Life of Captain John Brown,* 112–14.

3 Lawrence, *Papers Relating to John Brown,* note by Lawrence on first page, opposite a portrait of Brown. Lawrence Papers, Massachusetts Historical Society.

4 Ibid., clipping from the *Lawrence Weekly Journal* dated 12 May 1900, deposited in first few pages of the book.

5 Ibid., clipping from the *Lawrence Weekly Journal* dated 16 June 1900, deposited in first few pages of the book.

6 Ibid., 45. David N. Utter to Amos A. Lawrence, Chicago, 21 January 1885. Also see Utter's published account of the visit with Doyle, on pages 117–18.

7 Ibid., 151. Maggie Moore to Amos A. Lawrence, Chattanooga, 26 May 1885.

8 Ibid., 91. George W. Brown to Amos Lawrence, Rockford, Illinois, 18 December 1884.

9 Ibid., 104.

10 Henry Clay Pate, account of the Battle of Black Jack, *New York Tribune*, 17 June 1856. See also Pate's manuscript "John Brown," Kansas Collection, University of Kansas.

11 Higginson, *Thomas Wentworth Higginson*, 166–89.

12 Webb, *Life and Letters of Captain John Brown* (London: Chapman & Hall, 1861), 426.

10. TO SHAME INTO NOBLE-NESS UNMANLY YOUTH

1 Victor Channing Sanborn, *Memoir of Franklin Benjamin Sanborn, A.B.* A pamphlet reprinted from The New England Historical and Genealogical Register for October, 1917 (Boston: Stanhope Press/ F.H. Gilson Company, 1917; a copy is in the Sanborn family papers at the Boston Public Library).

2 Robertson and Wilky James attended Sanborn's school. Their famous older brothers Henry and William were never students of Sanborn's, and were barely aware of him. Wanting to verify details in his second volume of *Reminiscences*, Henry James would write from England to his friend Thomas Sergeant Perry in September of 1913 to ask, "Is it, e.g., right that *Sanborn*, of the Concord School, was *F.B.S.* by his initials?

Can you tell me *that?* and is he *living?*" See Leon Edel,. ed., *Henry James Letters*, Vol. IV, *1895–1916* (Cambridge, Mass.: Harvard University Press, 1984), 684.

3 Thoreau to Higginson, Concord, 1 February 1860, Higginson Papers, Boston Public Library.

4 Sanborn, "Personal Reminiscences of John Brown: Remarks at the Reunion of Anti-Slavery Men and Women, Boston, April 7, 1897," typescript in Folder #2 in Sanborn's box of Brown-related material, Houghton Library, Harvard University.

5 Stearns, *George Luther Stearns*, 130.

6 Most genealogists hold that Peter Browne of the *Mayflower* was not the founder of John Brown's family in America. Instead, they say, John Brown was descended from another Peter Browne who settled in Connecticut around 1650. Brown, however, probably believed he was telling Sanborn the truth.

7 Korngold, *Two Friends of Man*, 252–53.

8 Stearns's testimony in "Mason Report," *U.S. Senate Committee Reports, 1859–1860*, II, 227.

9 Stearns, *George Luther Stearns*, 129.

10 Mary Stearns to Hinton, undated, Hinton Papers, Kansas State Historical Society.

11 Katherine Mayo, *New York Evening Post*, 23 October 1909.

12 Howe, *Reminiscences*, 254.

13 James Redpath, ed., *Echoes of Harpers Ferry* (Boston: Thayer & Eldridge, 1860), 58.

14 Stearns, *George Luther Stearns*, 129.

15 Ibid., 130–34.

16 Stearns's testimony in "Mason Report," 227.

17 Sanborn to Higginson, Boston, 5 January 1857, Higginson Papers, Boston Public Library.

18 Higginson to Stearns, Worcester, 10 February 1857, Higginson Papers, Boston Public Library.

19 Sanborn, "Personal Reminiscences of John Brown."

20 Stearns, *George Luther Stearns*, 135.

21 Sanborn, "Personal Reminiscences of John Brown."

22 John Brown, Notes on Speeches Delivered at Concord and Elsewhere in New England and New York in the Winter of 1857, John Brown Papers, Kansas Historical Society.

23 Henry B. Hurd to John Brown, Chicago, 1 April 1857, Kansas State Historical Society.

24 Brown to Higginson, Boston, 1 April 1857, Higginson Papers, Boston Public Library.

25 Stearns to John Brown, copy, Boston, 15 April 1857, Howe Papers, Massachusetts Historical Society. See also Stearns's testimony in "Mason Report," 229.

26 Interview with Mrs. Thomas Russell, by Katherine Mayo, *New York Evening Post,* 23 October 1909.

27 John Brown, "Old Browns [*sic*] Farewell to the Plymouth Rocks, Bunker Hill Monuments, Charter Oaks, and Uncle Thoms Cabbins [*sic*]," John Brown Papers, Kansas State Historical Society.

28 Sanborn, *Life and Letters of John Brown,* 509–11.

29 Stearns's testimony in "Mason Report," 227–28.

30 Stearns, *George Luther Stearns*, 159.

31 Sanborn, "John Brown of Osawatomie," Concord, 27 April 1857, manuscript in Folder #2 in Sanborn's box of Brown-related material, Houghton Library, Harvard University.

11. ENTER HUGH FORBES

1 John Brown to wife and children, Chicago, 22 June 1857, Stutler Collection.

2 Frothingham, *Gerrit Smith*, 237.

3 Smith to Hyatt, Peterboro, 25 July 1857, Hyatt Papers, Kansas State Historical Society.

4 A photocopy of Brown's letter to Henry Stearns is in the Stutler Collection.

5 Stearns, *George Luther Stearns*, 144.

6 Stearns to Brown, Boston, 4 May 1857, copy in Folder #5 in Sanborn's box of Brown-related material, Houghton Library, Harvard University.

7 Stearns's testimony in "Mason Report," 228.

8 Sanborn, Ms letter to "My dear Sir," Peterboro, 3 August 1857, copy in Folder #5 in Sanborn's box of Brown-related material, Houghton Library, Harvard University.

9 Brown to Sanborn, Tabor, Iowa, 27 August 1857, Stutler Collection.

10 Sanborn to Brown, Concord, 19 October 1857, Sanborn Papers, Atlanta University.

11 Stearns's testimony in "Mason Report," 229–30.

12 Sanborn to Higginson, Concord, 11 September 1857, Higginson Papers, Kansas State Historical Society.

13 Testimony of George Luther Stearns, *Report of the Select Committee*, 243. Testifying a few weeks before Stearns at the Mason Committee hearings, Samuel Gridley Howe presented this letter from Stearns in evidence, deleting the name of the signer—Stearns. A copy of Stearns's letter transcribed for the committee in Howe's hand is in the Howe Papers, Massachusetts Historical Society. Also see testimony of Samuel Gridley Howe, *Report of the Select Committee*, 174. Assuming the copy of the letter in the Howe Papers at the Massachusetts Historical Society to be an original draft, Oates attributes this letter to Howe rather than to its proper author, Stearns. See Oates, *To Purge This Land with Blood*, 217.

14 Stearns to Whitman, Stearns Papers, Kansas State Historical Society.

15 Stearns, *George Luther Stearns*, 162.

12. TROUBLING ISRAEL

1 Testimony of Richard Realf, *Report of the Select Committee*, 90–92.

2 William S. McFeely, *Frederick Douglass* (New York: W. W. Norton, 1991), 192.

3 Sanborn, "Personal Reminiscences of John Brown."

4 George B. Gill to Richard Hinton, 7 July 1893, Hinton Papers, Kansas State Historical Society. See also Gill's "Reminiscences."

5 Sanborn to Brown, Concord, 12 January 1858, Sanborn Papers, Atlanta University.

6 Sanborn, *Life and Letters of John Brown*, 427–28.

7 Stearns, *George Luther Stearns*, 162. Stearns's letter was dated 4 February 1858. The original is in the Stutler Collection.

8 Testimony of Richard Realf, *Report of the Select Committee*, 93.

9 Sanborn to Higginson, Concord, 11 February 1858, Higginson Papers, Boston Public Library.

10 Higginson to Brown, Worcester, 7 February 1858, Higginson Papers, Boston Public Library.

11 Brown to Higginson, Rochester, 12 February 1858, Higginson Papers, Boston Public Library.

12 Stearns, *George Luther Stearns*, 163.

13 Sanborn, "Personal Reminiscences of John Brown."

14 John Brown to John Brown, Jr., Peterboro, 9 February 1858, in

Sanborn, *Life and Letters of John Brown,* 432–33.

15 Sanborn to Higginson, Concord, 19 February 1858, Higginson Papers, Boston Public Library.

16 Sanborn, "Personal Reminiscences of John Brown."

17 Sanborn, *Recollections of Seventy Years,* 146–47.

18 Brown to Sanborn, Peterboro, 24 February 1858, John Brown, Jr., Papers, Ohio Historical Society.

19 One-page fragment of typed manuscript from Sanborn with a long block quotation from Edwin Morton, undated, in Folder #3 of Sanborn's box of Brown-related papers, Houghton Library, Harvard University. Also note what appears to be Morton's original partial typescript for this anecdote, in Folder #5.

20 Sanborn, "Personal Reminiscences of John Brown."

21 Sanborn, Letter to the Editor of the *Outlook,* Concord, 15 December 1909, Norcross Papers, Massachusetts Historical Society.

22 Brown to Higginson, Boston, 4 March 1858, Higginson Papers, Boston Public Library.

23 Higginson, *Contemporaries,* 299.

24 Numerous historians, buying into the story told by George Stearns and Sam Howe during their testimony before the Mason Committee, have reported that Brown did not, during his March 1858 meetings or at any other time, divulge the location of his intended insur-

rection to the Secret Six. However, this seems unlikely since Brown was telling virtually everyone else he trusted, including his recruits and Frederick Douglass, that his principal target was Harpers Ferry. Why not then tell his lead supporters as well? Oates, within the scope of two paragraphs, tells the reader "Brown's friends still did not know the exact spot where he planned to 'raise the mill'" and at the same time states "Howe questioned how Brown would recross the Potomac in case of emergency." See Oates, *To Purge This Land,* 237–38.

25 Sanborn to Higginson, Concord, 8 March 1858, Higginson Papers, Boston Public Library.

26 Smith to Giddings, Peterboro, 25 March 1858, Giddings Papers, Ohio Historical Society.

27 Stearns to Higginson, Medford, 18 March 1858, Higginson Papers, Boston Public Library.

28 Sanborn to Higginson, Boston, 21 March 1858, Higginson Papers, Boston Public Library.

29 Stearns to Higginson, Medford, 1 April 1858, Higginson Papers, Boston Public Library.

30 Sanborn to Higginson, Concord, 20 April 1858, Higginson Papers, Boston Public Library.

13. AN EVIL HOUR

1 Sanborn to Higginson, Concord, 1 May 1858, Higginson Papers, Boston Public Library.

2 Sanborn to Higginson, Concord, 5

May 1858, Higginson Papers, Boston Public Library.

3 Sanborn to Higginson, Concord, 7 May 1858, Higginson Papers, Boston Public Library.

4 *Report of the Select Committee*, 160–61.

5 Higginson to Parker, Brattleboro, Vt., 9 May 1858, Parker Papers, Boston Public Library.

6 Parker to Higginson, Boston, 10 May 1858, Higginson Papers, Boston Public Library.

7 Sanborn to Higginson, Concord, 11 May 1858, Higginson Papers, Boston Public Library.

8 Sanborn, *Dr. S. G. Howe,* 259–60.

9 *Report of the Select Committee*, 48.

10 Brown to Higginson, Chatham, Canada, 14 May 1858, Higginson Papers, Boston Public Library.

11 *Report of the Select Committee*, 253–54.

12 Ibid., 140–43.

13 Ibid., 176.

14 Sanborn to Higginson, Concord, 18 May 1858, Higginson Papers, Boston Public Library.

15 Howe to Forbes, Boston, 10 May 1858, Howe Papers, Massachusetts Historical Society.

16 Testimony of Samuel Gridley Howe, *Report of the Select Committee,* 177.

17 Howe to Wilson, copy, Boston, 15 May 1858, Howe Papers, Massachusetts Historical Society.

18 Wood to Howe, Washington, 19 May 1858, Howe Papers, Massachusetts Historical Society.

19 Howe to Wood, copy, Boston, 26 May 1858, Howe Papers, Massachusetts Historical Society.

20 Testimony of Samuel Gridley Howe, *Report of the Select Committee*, 177.

21 Sanborn to Higginson, Concord, 7 May 1858, Higginson Papers, Boston Public Library.

22 Forbes to Higginson, Philadelphia, 6 June 1858, Higginson Papers, Boston Public Library.

23 Higginson to Parker, Worcester, 18 May 1858, Higginson Papers, Boston Public Library.

24 Higginson to Lysander Spooner, Worcester, 30 November 1858, Higginson Papers, Boston Public Library.

25 Higginson to Brown, Worcester, 18 May 1858, Higginson Papers, Boston Public Library.

26 Sanborn to Higginson, Concord, 18 May 1858, Higginson Papers, Boston Public Library.

27 Stearns to Higginson, New York, 21 May 1858, Higginson Papers, Boston Public Library.

14. THE REPUTED NEW ENGLAND HUMANITARIANS

1 Sanborn to Higginson, Boston, 24 May 1858, Higginson Papers, Boston Public Library.

2 Higginson's notes on June 1 meeting with John Brown, Worcester, 2 June 1858, Higginson Papers, Boston Public Library.

3 Sanborn to Higginson, Boston, 31 May 1858, Higginson Papers, Boston Public Library.

4 Higginson's notes on June 1 meeting with John Brown, Worcester, 2 June 1858, Higginson Papers, Boston Public Library.

5 Higginson, *Thomas Wentworth Higginson*, 192.

6 Howe to Conway, Newport, 30 May 1858, Howe Papers, Massachusetts Historical Society.

7 Forbes to Higginson, Philadelphia, 6 June 1858, Higginson Papers, Boston Public Library.

8 Realf to Stearns, Sanborn, Parker, & Others, Chatham, Canada West, 29 May 1858, Sanborn's typed copy in Folder #4 of Sanborn's box of Brown-related material, Houghton Library, Harvard University.

9 Testimony of Richard Realf, *Report of the Select Committee*, 105.

15. MANIFESTO

1 Sanborn to Higginson, Concord, 6 July 1858, Higginson Papers, Boston Public Library.

2 Brown to Sanborn, Lawrence, Kans., 28 June 1858 (this is a copy of Brown's letter, transcribed in Sanborn's hand), Sanborn Papers, Boston Public Library.

3 Brown to wife and children, Sugar Mound, Kans., 9 July 1858 (photocopy), Stutler Collection.

4 Brown to Sanborn, Missouri Line, Kans., 20 July & 6 August 1858 (completed and mailed on the later date), Sanborn Papers, Boston Public Library.

5 Brown to Sanborn, Lawrence, Kans., 10 & 13 September 1858, Higginson Papers, Boston Public Library.

6 Sanborn to Higginson, Concord, 13 October 1858, Higginson Papers, Boston Public Library.

7 One of the few existing copies of Spooner's broadside, "To the Non-Slaveholders of the South," is to be found in the Rare Books and Manuscripts Room at the Boston Public Library.

8 Higginson to Spooner, Worcester, 30 November 1858, Spooner Papers, Boston Public Library.

9 Parker to Spooner, Boston, 30 November 1858, Parker Papers, Boston Public Library.

10 Spooner to Octavius Brooks Frothingham, Boston, 26 February 1878, copy, Spooner Papers, Boston Public Library.

11 Spooner to Henry A. Wise, Boston, November 1859, copy (sent anonymously, signed by "The Author of the Circular"), Spooner Papers, Boston Public Library.

12 James Redpath, *The Roving Editor; or, Talks with Slaves in the Southern States* (New York: A. B. Burdick, 1859), iii–vii.

13 Frothingham, *Theodore Parker*, 481.

14 Weiss, *Theodore Parker,* vol. 2, 188.

15 Frothingham, *Theodore Parker,* 481–82.

16 Commager, *Theodore Parker,* 273. Parker wrote almost the same thing to Samuel May. See Sanborn's undated, partial typescript concerning Parker's death in File #5 in Sanborn's box of Brown-related material, Houghton Library, Harvard University.

17 Howe, *Reminiscences,* 168.

18 Ibid., 233–34.

19 Parker to Mr. Manley and the Standing Committee, Boston, 22 January 1859, Parker Papers, Boston Public Library.

20 Parker to Jackson, Santa Cruz, 21 March 1859, Jackson Papers, Boston Public Library.

16. THE STUFF OF WHICH MARTYRS ARE MADE

1 Ralph Volney Harlow, *Gerrit Smith: Philanthropist and Reformer* (New York: Henry Holt, 1939), 403. The letter was written on 10 January 1859.

2 Sanborn to Higginson, Concord, 19 January 1859, Higginson Papers, Boston Public Library.

3 Sanborn to Higginson, Concord, 4 March 1859, Higginson Papers, Boston Public Library.

4 Sanborn to Higginson, Concord, 6 April 1859, Higginson Papers, Boston Public Library.

5 Sanborn to Higginson, Concord, 19 April 1859, Higginson Papers, Boston Public Library.

6 John Brown, (signed "B") to John Henry Kagi, Westport, N.Y., 16 April 1859, *Report of the Select Committee,* 70–71.

7 Sanborn, untitled, undated, partial ms., Folder #5 in Sanborn's box of Brown-related material, Houghton Library, Harvard University.

8 John Brown, Jr. ("John Smith"), to John Henry Kagi ("Friend J. Henrie"), Syracuse, 11 August 1859, *Report of the Select Committee,* 68.

9 Edwin Morton to Sanborn, Peterboro, 13 April 1859, published in Sanborn's *Recollections,* 161–62, and in Harlow's *Gerrit Smith,* 403.

10 Sanborn to Higginson, Concord, 9 May 1859, Higginson Papers, Boston Public Library.

11 Howe to Forbes, New York, 5 February 1859, typescript copy in Folder #6 in Sanborn's box of Brown-related material, Houghton Library, Harvard University.

12 Anne Brown, short ms. entitled "Dr. Howe," undated, Folder #3 of the Sanborn box of Brown-related material, Houghton Library, Harvard University.

13 Sarah Forbes Hughes, ed., *Letters and Recollections of John Murray Forbes,* vol. 1 (Boston: Houghton Miffin, 1899), 238. The exact date of Howe's letter is 19 August 1861.

14 Howe, *Reminiscences,* 254.

15 Howe to Higginson, 8 May 1859, Higginson Papers, Boston Public Library.

16 Howe to Forbes, Boston, 9 May 1859, typescript copy in Folder #6

in Sanborn's box of Brown-related material, Houghton Library, Harvard University.

17 Hughes, *John Murray Forbes*, vol. 1, 179–82.

18 Forbes to Howe, Milton, Mass., 12 May 1859, Howe Papers, Massachusetts Historical Society.

19 Howe to Forbes, Boston, 25 May 1859, Howe Papers, Massachusetts Historical Society.

20 Sanborn, untitled and undated typescript memoir in Folder #6 in Sanborn's box of Brown-related material, Houghton Library, Harvard University.

21 Sanborn to Higginson, Boston, 30 May 1859, Higginson Papers, Boston Public Library.

22 Nathaniel Bowditch, "John Brown and His Execution at Harpers Ferry, in a Letter to the Massachusetts Historical Society," typescript, Boston, 9 June 1887, Massachusetts Historical Society.

23 Testimony of Samuel Gridley Howe, *Report of the Select Committee*, 167.

24 Sanborn to Higginson, Concord, 4 June 1859, Higginson Papers, Boston Public Library.

25 Harlow, *Gerrit Smith*, 405–6.

26 John Brown, Jr. ("John Smith"), to John Henry Kagi ("Friend J. Henrie"), Syracuse, 11 August 1859, *Report of the Select Committee*, 68.

27 Douglass, *Life and Times*, 317–20.

17. HARPERS FERRY

1 Sanborn to Higginson, Concord, 24 August 1859, Higginson Papers, Boston Public Library.

2 *Report of the Select Committee*, testimony of Samuel Gridley Howe, 165.

3 Ibid., appendix, 69

4 Ibid., testimony of George Luther Stearns, 235.

5 Ibid., appendix, 68.

6 Sanborn to Higginson, Concord, 4 September 1859, Higginson Papers, Boston Public Library.

7 Sanborn to Higginson, Concord, 14 September 1859, Higginson Papers, Boston Public Library.

8 Sanborn to Higginson, Concord, 14 September 1859, Higginson Papers, Boston Public Library.

9 Sanborn to Higginson, Concord, 6 October 1859, Higginson Papers, Boston Public Library.

10 Testimony of Samuel Gridley Howe, *Report of the Select Committee*, 169.

11 Lewis Hayden to Mary Stearns, 8 April 1878, copy in Villard Papers, Columbia University.

12 *Report of the Select Committee*, 66–67.

13 Oates suggests that the $600 Meriam delivered was his own. In fact, it was the result of fund-raising by the Six, as the letter of Sanborn's referenced below makes clear.

14 Sanborn to Higginson, Concord, 13 October 1859, Higginson Papers, Boston Public Library.

15 Jackson to Spooner, Boston, 3 December 1858, Spooner Papers, Boston Public Library.

16 Testimony of Lewis Washington, *Report of the Select Committee*, 29–36.

17 Villard, *John Brown*, 439.

18 Osborn P. Anderson, *A Voice from Harpers Ferry* (New York: Putnam, 1867), 36.

19 Higginson's notes on conversation with Charles Plummer Tidd, Worcester, 10 February 1860, Higginson Papers, Boston Public Library.

20 Villard, *John Brown*, 443. (See also Harry Hunter's testimony at John Brown's trial as reported in the *New York Herald*, 31 October 1859.)

21 Ibid., 448.

22 Testimony of Lewis Washington, *Report of the Select Committee*, 40.

18. THE STEEL TRAP

1 Edwin Morton, partial typescript of reminiscence of Brown, 1883, in Folder #5 in Sanborn's box of Brown-related material, Houghton Library, Harvard University.

2 *New York Herald*, 21 October 1859.

3 Deborah Pickman Clifford, *Mine Eyes Have Seen the Glory: A Biography of Julia Ward Howe* (Boston: Little, Brown & Co. 1979), 167.

4 Sanborn to Higginson, Portland, Me., 21 October 1859, Higginson Papers, Boston Public Library.

5 Howe, *Reminiscences,* 255

6 Undated statement of Mary Stearns, Hinton Papers, Kansas State Historical Society.

7 Howe to Higginson, Boston, 16 February 1860, Higginson Papers, Boston Public Library.

8 John Albion Andrew, *"Legal Opinion for Franklin Sanborn,"* 21 October 1859, Sanborn Papers, Boston Public Library.

9 Stearns, *George Luther Stearns*, 188.

10 The approximate date of return comes from Sanborn himself. See his note at the bottom of his typed copy of his 22 October 1859 letter to Parker, Houghton Library, Harvard University.

11 Howe to Lawrence, 10 October 1859, Lawrence Papers, Massachusetts Historical Society. (Howe often misdated letters. Since the raid at Harpers Ferry only happened on October 17, it is likely that the actual date of the letter is October 23 or thereabouts.)

12 Howe to Lawrence, 24 October 1859, Lawrence Papers, Massachusetts Historical Society.

13 Franklin Sanborn, one-page, untitled typescript fragment, Gardiner, Me., 16 May 1911, in Folder #1 in Sanborn's box of Brown-related material, Houghton Library, Harvard University.

14 Howe, *Reminiscences,* 262. Howe indicates that Andrew underwrote the bulk of the expenses himself, but in this she is either mistaken or is trying, as she always did in later years, to cover the trail of her husband's association with Brown.

15 Testimony of Samuel Chilton, *Report of the Select Committee*, 138–39. Oates makes the astonishing suggestion that Chilton and Griswold, two of the most well-known and highly compensated attorneys in the country, were simply appointed by the court; and in doing so he completely misses the important Boston connection that lay behind their involvement. See Oates, *To Purge This Land with Blood*, 325.

16 Coppoc to Sanborn, Springdale, Iowa, 13 January 1860. Sanborn's typescript copy of the letter is in Folder #4 of Sanborn's box of Brown-related material, Houghton Library, Harvard University.

17 James Redpath to Aaron Stevens, Boston, 21 December 1859, Stevens Family Papers, Massachusetts Historical Society.

18 Annie Brown to Higginson, North Elba, 21 December 1859, Higginson Papers, Boston Public Library.

19 Higginson, notes on conversation with Tidd, Worcester, 10 February 1860, Higginson Papers, Boston Public Library.

20 Brown to Howe, Jefferson, Ohio, 11 November 1859, original, with typescript copy, in the Howe Papers, Massachusetts Historical Society. Typescript copy in Folder #6 in Sanborn's box of Brown-related material, Houghton Library, Harvard University.

19. FANTASIES OF ESCAPE

1 Circular letter by Higginson, S. E. Sewall, S. G. Howe, and R. W. Emerson to raise funds for John Brown, Boston, 2 November 1859, Higginson Papers, Boston Public Library.

2 Higginson, *Contemporaries*, 219–44.

3 Sanborn, *Recollections of Seventy Years*, 198.

4 Richards and Elliott, *Julia Ward Howe,* 176–77.

5 Emerson's interpolation on Brown was deleted when he published the lecture in *Society and Solitude*.

6 Howe, *Reminiscences,* 257.

7 Howe to Higginson, Boston, 9 November 1859, Higginson Papers, Boston Public Library.

8 George H. Hoyt to Higginson, Boston, 7 November 1859, Higginson Papers, Boston Public Library.

9 Sanborn to Higginson, Concord, 10 November 1859, Higginson Papers, Boston Public Library.

10 Sanborn to Higginson, Concord, 19 November 1859, Higginson Papers, Houghton Library, Harvard University.

11 Brown to "Dear Brother" Jeremiah, Charles Town, 12 November 1859, reprinted in the *Lawrence* (Kans.) *Republican*, 8 December 1859.

12 Sanborn to Higginson, Worcester, 24 November 1859, Higginson Papers, Boston Public Library.

13 Sanborn to Higginson, Boston, 28 November 1859, Higginson Papers, Boston Public Library.

14 Redpath to Higginson, Malden, Mass., 13 November 1859, Higginson Papers, Boston Public Library.

15 Spooner to Higginson, Boston, 20 November 1859, Higginson Papers, Boston Public Library.

16 Higginson, *Thomas Wentworth Higginson*, 195–96.

17 Higginson to Spooner, Worcester, 28 November 1859, Spooner Papers, Boston Public Library.

18 Sanborn to Higginson, Boston, 28 November 1859, Higginson Papers, Boston Public Library.

19 Ms. of interview with Edwin Brackett by Katherine Mayo, 13 January 1908, Villard Papers, Columbia University. For details on the unveiling of Brackett's statue at the home of George Stearns in 1863, see Stearns, *George Luther Stearns*, 275.

20 Stearns, *George Luther Stearns*, 194.

21 Ms. of interview with Mrs. Russell by Katherine Mayo, 11 January 1908, Villard Papers, Columbia University.

22 Sanborn, *Life and Letters of John Brown*, 581.

23 Brown to Stearns, Charles Town, 29 November 1859, copy in the collection of the Moorland-Springarn Research Center, Howard University. Original in Stutler Collection. Oates incorrectly states that this letter was written from Brown to *George* Stearns. See Oates, *To Purge This Land with Blood*, 346.

24 A. A. Lawrence, *Papers Relating to John Brown Given to the Massachusetts Historical Society by Amos A. Lawrence, February 12, 1885*, 117.

25 Redpath to Higginson, Malden, Mass., 13 November 1859, Higginson Papers, Boston Public Library.

26 Redpath, *Public Life of Captain John Brown*, 114.

27 William C. Davis, *Jefferson Davis: The Man and His Hour* (New York: HarperCollins, 1991), 683.

20. THE NOT SO SECRET SIX

1 Sanborn, *Dr. S. G. Howe*, 266.

2 Editorial, *New York Herald*, 29 October 1859.

3 "Gerrit Smith and the Harpers Ferry Outbreak," *New York Herald*, 31 October 1859.

4 Morton stayed at the home of Higginson's cousin by marriage William Henry Channing at Montpellier Terrace, Upper Parliament Street, Liverpool. Morton's pupil, Gerrit Smith's son Green Smith, had just enrolled at Cambridge. See Sanborn's typed copy of his 2 January 1860 letter to Parker, Sanborn Papers, Houghton Library, Harvard University.

5 *New York Herald*, 12 November 1859.

6 Sanborn, *Recollections of Seventy Years*, 242.

7 Sanborn to Higginson, Concord, 10 November 1859, Higginson Papers, Boston Public Library.

8 Richards and Elliott, *Julia Ward Howe*, 176–77.

9 Sanborn to Higginson, Boston, 13 November 1859, Higginson Papers, Boston Public Library.

10 Oates says Stearns and Howe departed for Canada on October

25—but this seems improbable since the statute that triggered their flight was not discovered until early November. In fact, on October 25 the various members of the Six were resting comfortably on Andrew's opinion that they could not be extradited out of Massachusetts; and Sanborn, based upon this opinion, was hurriedly *returning* from Canada to Concord. The most likely date for the departure of Stearns and Howe is November 14 or 15. See Oates, *To Purge This Land with Blood*, 313.

11 Sanborn to Higginson, Concord, 17 November 1859, Higginson Papers, Boston Public Library. In this letter Sanborn places both Howe and Stearns in "Canada East."

12 Sanborn to Parker, Concord, 14 November 1859, from Sanborn's typed copy of the letter, Sanborn Papers, Houghton Library, Harvard University.

13 Clipping attached to letter from Higginson to Howe, Worcester, 15 November 1859, Higginson Papers, Boston Public Library.

14 Higginson to Howe, Worcester, 15 November 1859, Higginson Papers, Boston Public Library.

15 Richards, *Samuel Gridley Howe*, vol. 2, 443. The letter was written on January 22, 1860.

16 Sanborn to Higginson, Concord, 17 November 1859, Higginson Papers, Boston Public Library.

17 Sanborn to Higginson, 19 November 1859, Higginson Papers, Houghton Library, Harvard University.

21. THE DIRGE OF THE CATARACT

1 Sanborn, *Recollections of Seventy Years*, 202.

2 Sanborn to Richard Watson Gilder, Concord, May 5, 1902. Author's collection. What follows is the text of Sanborn's hymn, which was sung at services in Concord on December 2 and in Boston on December 4. It was written, like so many chants and songs that Sanborn composed through the years, to the tune of "Auld Lang Syne."

Today beside Potomac's wave,
    Beneath Virginia's sky,
They slay the man who loved the slave,
    And dared for him to die.

The Pilgrim Fathers' earnest creed,
    Virginia's ancient faith,
Inspired this hero's noblest deed,
    And his reward is—Death!

Great Washington's indignant shade
    Forever urged him on—
He heard from Monticello's glade
    The voice of Jefferson.

But chiefly on the Hebrew page
    He read Jehovah's law,
And this, from youth to hoary age
    Obeyed with love and awe.

No selfish purpose armed his hand,
    No passion aimed his blow;
How loyally he loved his land
    Impartial time shall show.

But now the faithful martyr dies,
His brave heart beats no more,
His soul ascends the equal skies,
His earthly course is o'er.

For this we mourn, but not for him,
Like him in God we trust;
And though our eyes with tears are dim,
We know that God is just.

(Source: Franklin Benjamin Sanborn, "Hymn to be sung at the Music Hall, Boston, December 4, 1859"; printed copy in Folder #4 of Sanborn's Papers, Boston Public Library.)

3 Henry Thoreau. "The Last Days of John Brown," Louis Ruchames, ed., *A John Brown Reader* (New York: 1959), 304.

4 Parker to Rebecca and Mathilda Goddard, Rome, 26 November 1859, Goddard Papers, Boston Public Library.

5 *Report of the Select Committee*, testimony of Samuel Gridley Howe, 169.

6 Ibid., testimony of George Luther Stearns, 235–36.

7 Franklin Sanborn, *Henry David Thoreau* (Boston: Houghton Mifflin & Co., 1917), 291–94. Sanborn suggests that the train Meriam boarded was bound for Canada rather than Boston, but he was incorrect. See note #8 below.

8 Jackson to Higginson, Boston, 6 December 1859, Higginson Papers, Boston Public Library.

9 Sanborn, *Recollections of Seventy Years*, 204.

10 O. P. Anderson to Richard Hinton, Chatham, 18 October 1860, Sanborn's typescript copy in Folder #4 of Sanborn's box of Brown-related material, Houghton Library, Harvard University.

11 Viscount John Humphrey, *Memoranda Book, 1859*, 104, Humphrey Papers, Cambridge University.

12 Thomas J. Jackson to his wife, Charles Town, Va., 2 December 1859, Stutler Collection. Virtually all the details of the execution that I present here are taken from Jackson's eloquent, detailed description of the event.

13 Elizabeth Preston Allan, *Life and Letters of Margaret Junkin Preston* (Boston: Houghton Mifflin & Co., 1903), 111–17.

14 Walt Whitman, "Year of Meteors (1859–60)," in *Leaves of Grass*, edited by his literary executors (New York: G. P. Putnam, 1891, Centenary Edition), 291–92.

15 Herman Melville, "The Portent, (1859)," F. O. Matthiessen, ed., in *The Oxford Book of American Verse* (New York: Oxford University Press, 1950), 396.

16 William Dean Howells, "Old Brown," in Ruchames, *A John Brown Reader*, 266–68.

17 Smith to Edwin Morton, Utica, N.Y., 2 December 1859, Gerrit Smith Papers, Syracuse University.

22. THE COMMITTEE

1 Stearns, *George Luther Stearns*, 200.

2 Franklin Sanborn, "John Brown Then and Now: An Address Given in Faneuil Hall, Boston, December 2, 1909," typescript in Folder #3 in Sanborn's box of Brown-related material, Houghton Library, Harvard University.

3 Higginson, *Thomas Wentworth Higginson*, 201.

4 *Report of the Select Committee*, 1.

5 Stearns to Howe, Philadelphia, 27 February 1860, Howe Papers, Massachusetts Historical Society.

6 Sanborn to Higginson. Concord, 20 December 1859, Higginson Papers, Boston Public Library.

7 Sanborn to Howe, Concord, 19 December 1859, Howe Papers, Boston Public Library.

8 Sanborn to Higginson, Hampton Falls, N.H., 25 December 1859, Higginson Papers, Boston Public Library.

9 Sanborn to Higginson, Concord, 2 January 1860, Higginson Papers, Boston Public Library.

10 Sanborn to Parker, Concord, 2 January 1860, typed copy, Sanborn Papers, Houghton Library, Harvard University.

11 Sanborn to Higginson, Concord, 16 January 1860, Higginson Papers, Boston Public Library.

12 Sanborn to Higginson, Montreal, 29 January 1860. See also Sarah Sanborn to Thomas Wentworth Higginson, Concord, 23 January

1860. Both in Higginson Papers, Boston Public Library.

13 Higginson to Henry James, Sr., Worcester, 1 February 1860, collection of the author.

14 Mary Brown to Mr. & Mrs. George Luther Stearns. North Elba, 27 December 1859, Stearns Papers, Boston Public Library.

15 Thompson to Mrs. Stearns, North Elba, 26 December 1859, Stearns Papers, Boston Public Library.

16 Stearns to Samuel May, Sr., Boston, 26 December 1859, May Papers, Boston Public Library.

17 James Miller McKim to Stearns, Philadelphia, 22 December 1859, Stearns Papers, Boston Public Library.

18 Unsigned, undated letter to Mary Brown, Higginson Papers, Boston Public Library.

19 Transcript of interview of Lyman Epps by James Redpath, 12 August 1862, Syracuse University.

20 Testimony of George Luther Stearns, *Report of the Select Committee*, 241–42.

21 Clipping attached to unsent letter from Higginson to Sanborn, Worcester, 3 February 1860, Higginson Papers, Boston Public Library.

22 Howe to Parker, Boston, 22 January 1860, Howe Papers, Massachusetts Historical Society.

23 Howe to the Honorable Henry Wilson, Boston, 23 January 1860, Howe Papers, Massachusetts Historical Society.

24 Sanborn to Higginson, Vergennes, Vt., 3 February 1860, copy in Folder #5 in Sanborn's box of Brown-related material, Houghton Library, Harvard University.

25 Rebecca B. Spring to Thomas Wentworth Higginson, Eagleswood School, Perth Amboy, N.J., 19 January 1860, Higginson Papers, Boston Public Library. (Located on Raritan Bay, Eagleswood was formerly a commune founded by Rebecca and Marcus Spring. When the commune failed, the boarding school was organized by Marcus Spring and operated by Theodore Weld and Angelina and Sarah Grimke. When Brown's soldiers Aaron Stevens and Albert Hazlett were executed in Virginia, Spring allowed their remains to be interred with honors in the Eagleswood Cemetery. The Eagleswood School was subsequently closed. The Springs removed to California, and the Eagleswood property was given over to industrial pursuits. The graves of John Brown's men were neglected. Their remains were moved to lie in the Adirondacks, beside those of Brown, at about the turn of the century. For details on Rebecca Spring's relationship with Aaron Stevens, and the story of the burial and exhumation of Stevens and Hazlett, see the small collection of Stevens family papers at the Massachusetts Historical Society.)

26 Sanborn to Higginson, Concord, 20 February 1860, Higginson Papers, Boston Public Library.

27 Redpath to Aaron Stevens. Malden, Ma. 21 December 1859. Stevens Family Papers, Massachusetts Historical Society.

28 Higginson to Sanborn, Worcester, 3 February 1860, Higginson Papers, Boston Public Library.

29 Higginson to Louisa Storrow Higginson, Worcester, 1 June 1854, Higginson Papers, Boston Public Library.

30 Higginson to Sanborn, Worcester, 3 February 1860. Higginson Papers, Boston Public Library.

31 Higginson, *Thomas Wentworth Higginson,* 199–200.

32 *Report of the Select Committee,* testimony of Samuel Gridley Howe, 172.

33 Ibid., testimony of Stearns, 241–42.

34 Stearns to Howe, Philadelphia, 27 February 1860, Howe Papers, Massachusetts Historical Society.

23. MACHINES

1 Howe to Higginson, Boston, 16 February 1860, Higginson Papers, Boston Public Library.

2 Mary Peabody Mann to Higginson, Concord, 16 January 1860, Higginson Papers, Boston Public Library.

3 Higginson, *Cheerful Yesterdays,* 231–34.

4 Higginson's notes on conversation with Tidd, Worcester, 10 February 1860, Higginson Papers, Boston Public Library.

5 Richard Hinton, *John Brown* (New York: G. P. Putnam, 1862), 396–97.

6 Higginson, *Thomas Wentworth Higginson,* 199.

7 Brown to Higginson, North Elba, 25 July 1860, Higginson Papers, Boston Public Library.

8 *Report of the Select Committee,* Journal of the Select Committee, 38.

9 Sarah Sanborn, three-page-fragment manuscript recounts events of 3 April 1860, undated, in Folder #3 of Sanborn's box of Brown-related materials, Houghton Library, Harvard University.

10 Stearns, *George Luther Stearns,* 217.

11 See transcript of court decision in Folder #2, Sanborn Papers, Boston Public Library.

12 *Report of the Select Committee,* Report, 12–18.

13 Ibid., Views of the Minority, 22–23.

14 Howe, *Reminiscences,* 263.

15 Higginson, *Thomas Wentworth Higginson,* 204.

24. THE TRUE BELIEVER

1 Brown to Sanborn, Saratoga, Calif., 18 July 1882, Sanborn Papers, Boston Public Library.

2 Sanborn to John D. Ling and William Chaflin, Concord, 25 February 1885. Sanborn to Jason Brown, Concord, 16 January 1892. Sanborn to Ruth Thompson, Concord, 7 September 1892. All in Folder #3 of Sanborn's box of Brown-related material, Sanborn Papers, Houghton Library, Harvard University.

3 M. C. Lord, to Sanborn, South Pasadena, 19 August 1892, Sanborn's typed copy of the letter in Folder #3 of Sanborn's box of Brown-related material, Sanborn Papers, Houghton Library, Harvard University.

4 Sanborn to John D. Ling and William Chaflin, Concord, 25 February 1885. Sanborn to Jason Brown, Concord, 16 January 1892, Sanborn to Ruth Thompson, Concord, 7 September 1892. All in Folder #3 of Sanborn's box of Brown-related material, Sanborn Papers, Houghton Library, Harvard University.

5 Sanborn to the editor of the *Dispatch*, Richmond, Va., Concord, 24 August 1894, Sanborn's carbon copy in Folder #3 of Sanborn's box of Brown-related material, Sanborn Papers, Houghton Library, Harvard University.

6 Sanborn to May, Concord, 21 September 1894, May Papers, Boston Public Library. See also Sanborn's copy of his 21 September 1894 letter to the editor of the *Richmond Dispatch*, written from Concord, Sanborn Papers, Boston Public Library.

7 Sanborn to Higginson, 21 November 1902, Sanborn's typed copy, Folder #2 in Sanborn's box of Brown-related material, Sanborn Papers, Houghton Library, Harvard University.

8 See Sanborn's extended typescript critique of Villard's book in Folder #5 in Sanborn's box of Brown-related material, Houghton Library, Harvard University.

9 Sanborn, partial manuscript expressing views about John Brown and Abraham Lincoln, Concord, 1916, Sanborn Papers, Boston Public Library.

10 Sanborn, "Personal Reminiscences of John Brown."

11 *Resolution of the House of Representatives of the Commonwealth of Massachusetts Honoring Franklin Benjamin Sanborn*, Boston, 26 February 1917, Sanborn Papers, Boston Public Library.

25. EPILOGUE

1 Stearns, *The Life and Public Ser-* vices of George Luther Stearns, 275–76.

2 Higginson, *Thomas Wentworth Higginson: The Story of His Life,* 292–94.

3 Franklin Sanborn to Francis Bachelor Sanborn, Concord, 10 November 1913, author's collection.

4 Higginson to Richard Watson Gilder, Cambridge, 7 July 1906, Huntington Library.

5 Higginson to Hamlin Garland, Boston, 1 September 1911, Huntington Library.

Bibliography

Boyer, Richard O. *The Legend of John Brown*. New York: Alfred A. Knopf, 1972.

Capper, Charles. *Margaret Fuller: An American Romantic Life—the Private Years*. New York: Oxford University Press, 1992.

Chadwick, John White. *Theodore Parker: Preacher and Reformer*. Boston: Houghton Mifflin, 1900.

Cobbe, Francis Power, ed. *The Collected Works of Theodore Parker*. London: Trubner, 1863.

Commager, Henry Steele. *Theodore Parker: Yankee Crusader*. Boston: Beacon Press, 1947.

Du Bois, W. E. Burghardt. *John Brown*. Philadelphia: George W. Jacobs, 1909.

Eddelstein, Tilden G. *Strange Enthusiasm, a Life of Thomas Wentworth Higginson*. New Haven: Yale University Press, 1968.

Frothingham, Octavius Brooks. *Gerrit Smith: A Biography*. Boston: Houghton Mifflin, 1878.

Harlow, Ralph Volney. *Gerrit Smith: Philanthropist and Reformer*. New York: Henry Holt, 1939.

Higginson, Mary Thacher. *Thomas Wentworth Higginson: The Story of His Life*. Boston: Houghton Mifflin, 1914.

Higginson, Mary Thacher, ed. *Letters and Journals of Thomas Wentworth Higginson*. Boston: Houghton Mifflin, 1921.

Higginson, Thomas Wentworth. *Army Life in a Black Regiment*. New York: Longmans, Green, 1896.

————. *Cheerful Yesterdays*. Boston: Houghton Mifflin, 1898.

————. *Contemporaries*. Boston: Houghton Mifflin, 1900.

————. "Nat Turner's Insurrection." *Atlantic Monthly,* August 1861.

————. *Travellers and Outlaws: Episodes in American History*. Boston: Lee and Shepard, 1889.

Howe, Julia Ward. *Memoir of Dr. Samuel Gridley Howe . . . with other memorial tributes*. Boston: Howe Memorial Committee, 1876.

————. *Reminiscences, 1819–1899*. Boston: Houghton Mifflin, 1900.

Hughes, Sarah Forbes, ed. *Letters and Recollections of John Murray Forbes*, 2 vols. Boston: Houghton Mifflin, 1899.

Kasner, David. *John Brown, Terrible Saint.* New York: Dodd, Mead, 1934.

Korngold, Ralph. *Two Friends of Man: The Story of William Lloyd Garrison and Wendell Phillips and Their Relationship with Abraham Lincoln.* Boston: Little, Brown, 1950.

May, Samuel J. *Some Recollections of Our Anti-Slavery Conflict.* Boston: Hurd & Houghton, 1869.

McFeely, William S. *Frederick Douglass.* New York: W.W. Norton, 1991.

Oates, Stephen B. *To Purge This Land with Blood.* New York: Harper & Row, 1970.

Parker, Theodore. *The Trial of Theodore Parker for the "Misdemeanor" of a Speech in Faneuil Hall against Kidnapping, Before the Circuit Court of the United States, at Boston, with the Defence.* Boston, 1855.

Redpath, James. *Echoes of Harpers Ferry.* Boston: Thayer & Eldridge, 1860.

―――. *The Public Life of Captain John Brown . . . with an Autobiography of His Childhood and Youth.* Boston: Thayer & Eldridge, 1860.

―――. *The Roving Editor; or, Talks with Slaves in the Southern States.* New York: A. B. Burdick, 1859.

Richards, Laura E. *Samuel Gridley Howe.* New York: D. Appleton-Century, 1935.

―――. *Two Noble Lives: Samuel Gridley Howe, Julia Ward Howe.* Boston: Dana Estes, 1911.

―――, ed. *Letters and Journals of Samuel Gridley Howe,* 2 vols. With notes and a preface by F. B. Sanborn. Boston: Dana Estes, 1906, 1909.

Richards, Laura E. and Maude Howe Elliott. *Julia Ward Howe, 1819–1910,* 2 vols. Boston: Houghton Mifflin, 1916.

Sanborn, Franklin Benjamin. *Dr. S. G. Howe, the Philanthropist.* American Reformers Series. New York: Funk & Wagnalls, 1891.

―――. *Henry David Thoreau.* Boston: Houghton Mifflin, 1917.

―――. *The Life and Letters of John Brown, Liberator of Kansas and Martyr of Virginia.* Boston: Roberts Brothers, 1885.

―――. *Recollections of Seventy Years.* Boston: The Gorham Press, 1909.

Sanborn, Victor Channing. *Memoir of Franklin Benjamin Sanborn, A.B.* A pamphlet reprinted from The New England Historical and Genealogical Register for October, 1917. Boston: Stanhope Press/F. H. Gilson Company, 1917.

Schwarz, Harold. *Samuel Gridley Howe, Social Reformer.* Cambridge: Harvard University Press, 1956.

Stearns, Frank Preston. *The Life and Public Services of George Luther Stearns.* Philadelphia: J. B. Lippincott, 1907.

Villard, Oswald Garrison. *John Brown: 1800–1859—a Biography Fifty Years After,* rev. ed. New York: Alfred A. Knopf, 1943.

Warren, Robert Penn. *John Brown: The Making of a Martyr.* New York: Payson & Clarke, 1929.

Weiss, John. *Life and Correspondence of Theodore Parker.* New York: D. Appleton, 1864. (Note: This work was composed during the Civil War, when many papers of Parker and his colleagues regarding John Brown were not available, and when candid testimony from virtually anyone connected with the Harpers Ferry affair was virtually nonexistent. Commager's biography is much stronger on Parker's role in the Secret Six.

Wells, Anna Mary. *Dear Perceptor: The Life and Times of Thomas Wentworth Higginson.* Boston: Houghton Mifflin, 1963.

Wills, Garry. *Lincoln at Gettysburg: The Words That Remade America.* New York: Simon & Schuster, 1992.

Index